E842.9 .F84 2006
Fuhrman, Mark.
A simple act of murder
 :
Northeast Lakeview Colleg
33784000111658

Northeast Lakeview College

33784 0001 1165 8

A SIMPLE ACT OF MURDER

ALSO BY MARK FUHRMAN

Murder in Brentwood

Murder in Spokane

Murder in Greenwich

Death and Justice

Silent Witness

A Simple Act of Murder

of Murder

NOVEMBER 22, 1963

MARK FUHRMAN

WILLIAM MORROW   *wm*   *An Imprint of HarperCollinsPublishers*

A SIMPLE ACT OF MURDER. Copyright © 2006 by Mark Fuhrman. All rights reserved. Printed in the United States of America. No part of this book may be used or reproduced in any manner whatsoever without written permission except in the case of brief quotations embodied in critical articles and reviews. For information address HarperCollins Publishers, 10 East 53rd Street, New York, NY 10022.

HarperCollins books may be purchased for educational, business, or sales promotional use. For information please write: Special Markets Department, HarperCollins Publishers, 10 East 53rd Street, New York, NY 10022.

FIRST EDITION

Printed on acid-free paper

Library of Congress Cataloging-in-Publication Data has been applied for.

ISBN-13: 978-0-06-072154-1
ISBN-10: 0-06-072154-5

06 07 08 09 10 ❖/RRD 10 9 8 7 6 5 4 3 2 1

To a nation, and a family,
who have suffered

Contents

CHAPTER 1

A National Tragedy

EVERYONE who is old enough remembers exactly where they were when they learned President Kennedy had been killed.

I was in Los Angeles, visiting Olvera Street on a field trip with my sixth-grade class. We lived in Los Angeles for a brief time. My mother was working as a waitress, but she managed to send me and my brother to military school for a year.

The streets were festive, with bright colors. Small shops selling candles and blankets and trinkets. It seems so fresh now, in my memory. I was standing next to a post from which were hanging brightly painted gourds. My friends crowded next to me; we were all laughing and horseplaying, trying to evade our teacher's watchful eye. We were eleven years old, and the world seemed like this shop, brightly colored and full of adventure.

Then our teacher waved her hand and told us to be quiet. The radio that had been playing music now announced that our president, John F. Kennedy, was dead.

A silence came down among us. I felt heavy and sick, angry and confused. The silence was broken by one of my classmates saying: "Good. My dad didn't like him anyway."

The teacher slapped him with the back of her hand. No hesitation, no warning.

"Don't you ever say that!" she yelled at the boy. The teacher never apologized for hitting him, and no one felt an apology was needed.

For the next few days, the afternoons I usually spent playing basketball or army were spent sitting on the floor in front of a black-and-white Zenith television. I had no understanding of politics. I had never read *PT-109* or *Profiles in Courage.* I didn't know anything about the Kennedy family and didn't even understand what they meant when they called him "rich." I thought everybody lived pretty much like we did. Even if I didn't know or understand anything about the man, he was my president, and I was pulled into the drama of his violent death.

One afternoon, sitting just a couple of feet from our television, I watched carefully as the assassin walked in front of the cameras. Looking back over my shoulder, I saw my mom ironing our uniforms for school the next day. Turning back toward the television, I saw Lee Harvey Oswald shot and killed by Jack Ruby.

I turned back toward my mom.

"We killed him," I said.

I had forgotten I said that, but talking with my mom just a couple years ago about the JFK assassination, she asked me if I remembered what I said when Ruby shot Oswald. I didn't remember, but when she described the moment in detail, so many memories and emotions came rushing back.

What exactly did I mean when I said, "We killed him"? Was I voicing suspicions that the government had murdered Oswald to shut him up? Did I think there was a conspiracy to assassinate President Kennedy? Maybe the seed of doubt was planted those first few days and grew in my mind somewhere.

Now that Oswald was dead, there would be no trial. The FBI was preparing a report on its massive investigation, and the Texas Attorney General's Office planned its own inquiry. Two separate congressional committees were being formed to look into the assassination. Just after Oswald's murder, some were already talking about a possible conspiracy. To quiet these suspicions and keep the separate inquiries from turning into a political nightmare, President Lyndon Baines Johnson appointed a seven-man panel to investigate the assassination, presided over by Chief Justice Earl Warren and

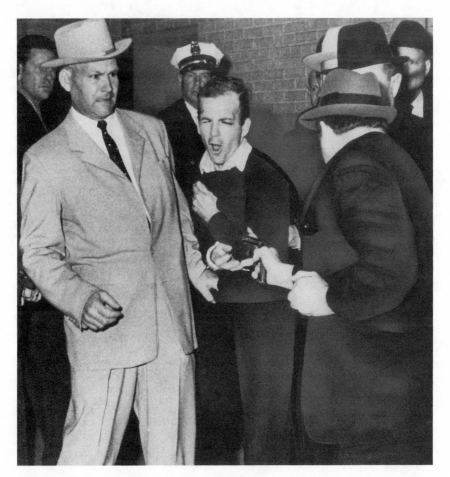

Jack Ruby shoots Lee Harvey Oswald. *Courtesy of National Archives.*

including senators Richard Russell and John Sherman Cooper, representatives Gerald Ford and Hale Boggs, former CIA director Allen Dulles, and John McCloy, former head of the World Bank.

Within days of its investiture, the Warren Commission was being urged by Assistant Attorney General Nicholas Katzenbach to issue a statement that Lee Harvey Oswald was the lone assassin. While they refused to make any public statement about the guilt or innocence of the only suspect, the commissioners apparently saw their task as presenting the evidence that Lee Harvey Oswald killed the President and dispelling rumors that Oswald might have been part of a larger conspiracy. Relying first on the investiga-

Warren Commissioners present the Warren Report to LBJ. *Photo by Cecil Stoughton/Courtesy of the Lyndon Baines Johnson Library and Museum.*

tive reports of the FBI, the Secret Service, and Texas law enforcement, the Warren Commission went on to conduct its own investigation. The Commissioners analyzed the information gathered by other agencies, called witnesses for hearings and depositions, and performed tests and reenactments to fill what they saw as holes in the evidentiary fabric.

The Warren Commission was a political body, created by politicians, made up of politicians, with the responsibility, in the view of its members, of resolving a political problem: fears that the President of the United States might have been assassinated through some conspiracy or even as part of a coup d'état.

But the commissioners were all busy men. Most of them attended only a small fraction of the hearings, and their participation in those hearings was minimal. Supporting the commissioners was a staff of fifteen lawyers, led by J. Lee Rankin, the former solicitor general. The legal staff was divided into two groups, senior counsel and assistant counsel. Since the senior lawyers were busy with their own private law practices, almost all of the work was done by the seven assistants, bright young lawyers who had graduated at the tops of their classes at prestigious law schools but had little or no experience in criminal investigations. They worked under intense pressure to gather all the necessary information and write it up into a publishable report before the presidential elections.

On September 24, 1964, the Commissioners presented Lyndon Johnson with the "Report of the President's Commission on the Assassination of President Kennedy," or the Warren Report. The first thing the President said was, "It's heavy." Then he gave it to one of his aides to read.

And that was just the 888-page report. Shortly afterwards, 26 volumes of hearings and exhibits were published. The Warren Commission had been established in order to squelch rumors about a possible conspiracy, yet the vast public record it created had the opposite effect.

Even before the Warren Report was published, several writers, mostly European, had speculated that Kennedy's assassination was the fruit of a conspiracy. Once the Commission's report and hearings were published, several American writers published books critical of its findings. Edward Jay Epstein's *Inquest,* Mark Lane's *Rush to Judgment,* Sylvia Meagher's *Accessories After the Fact,* and Josiah Thompson's *Six Seconds in Dallas* (to name only the earliest and most prominent criticisms) all raised troubling questions about the basic facts of the assassination.

Some of the questions had to do with evidence, such as the bullet found on a stretcher in Parkland Hospital that was alleged to have caused a series of wounds to both Kennedy and Texas governor John B. Connally, who was riding in front of Kennedy in the presidential limousine. This became known as the single bullet theory, and the bullet responsible was called the Magic Bullet. Others raised questions about the rifle linked to Oswald: it seemed inadequate to the task and impossible for him to have fired as quickly as the shots appeared in the amateur film of the assassination taken by Dallas dressmaker Abraham Zapruder. In addition to these, and other, questions about the evidence, there was talk of other gunmen and claims of a well-orchestrated cover-up to frame Oswald. The Warren Commission had made public all the testimony and evidence, but by keeping many records classified, it only fueled the suspicions.

The government could not ignore these accusations for long. Less than two years after the report was issued, the medical team from the President's autopsy at Bethesda Naval Hospital was asked by the Justice Department (under Attorney General Robert Kennedy) to authenticate the X-rays and photographs held at the National Archives. During the autopsy the doctors had seen the X-rays during a brief search for a bullet they believed was still lodged in the President's body, but they were denied access to this important evidence while writing their reports. Earl Warren had viewed the photographs and X-rays before deciding that his commission should not make use of them, for fear that they would then have to become part of the public record. During the Justice Department inquiry, the doctors concluded that the X-rays and photographs were authentic. Yet they still weren't released to the public.

On March 1, 1967, New Orleans district attorney Jim Garrison announced that he had solved the JFK assassination and arrested a prominent local citizen on charges of being part of the conspiracy. Garrison might have been something of a loose cannon, yet he seemed to be on to something. Lee Harvey Oswald had spent several months in 1963 in his native city of New Orleans, where he was engaged in pro-Castro political activities. There were several possible connections between Oswald and members of the anti-Castro movement, even the FBI and CIA. While Garrison made a long series of dramatic allegations in the press, the case he eventually presented in court was weaker than expected. After only forty-five minutes of deliberation, the jury acquitted the defendant, Clay Shaw. In later interviews, the jury members stated that they believed Garrison had made a compelling case for a conspiracy, even if he hadn't proved Shaw's involvement in the plot.

Meanwhile, questions concerning the medical evidence did not go away. In 1968 Attorney General Ramsey Clark (who had taken over the post when Bobby Kennedy decided to run for president) convened a panel of four doctors who had not participated in the autopsy or been connected to the Warren Commission to review the medical evidence. The Clark Panel examined photographs, X-ray films, documents, and other evidence to "evaluate their significance in relation to the medical conclusions recorded in the Autopsy Report." The panel confirmed the findings of the autopsy doctors and the Warren Commission and made an inventory and description of the evidence.

As the years passed the controversy over the JFK assassination continued. Growing up, I followed the case, listening to the criticism, reading the books, and asking some of the same questions myself. Was Oswald a good enough marksman to have made those shots with a cheap Italian army-surplus rifle? Could he have fired three shots so quickly? Why were the government investigations shrouded in so much secrecy? What were they afraid of? Were they trying to hide something?

The one question I kept coming back to was the single bullet theory and the "Magic Bullet," Commission exhibit 399. This 6.5-millimeter bullet, found on the stretcher used to transport Governor Connally into surgery, was supposed to have entered Kennedy's back, gone through his neck, entered Connally's back, shattered one of his ribs, entered his arm and shattered a wrist bone, then wounded his leg. Yet the bullet appeared undeformed.

I didn't buy it. And I wasn't alone. By the 1970s, there was no escaping speculation that there had been some kind of conspiracy. In fact, it became almost socially ignorant to believe otherwise. I was a patriot. I never doubted the draft or Vietnam. I enlisted in the Marines, just like Oswald. Yet I never connected JFK's assassination with larger motives, like war, politics, or crime. I never thought about who could be responsible—the CIA, the Mafia, Fidel Castro. I remained curious about the JFK assassination, not engaging in deep and serious study, like many of the independent researchers, but casually reading articles and books that crossed my path.

Then I saw the Zapruder film.

On March 6, 1975, Geraldo Rivera showed the Zapruder film on *Goodnight America,* a late-night talk show. Watching the film, I saw the assassination with my own eyes for the first time, and felt for a moment as I had twelve years before. Something was very wrong. All my instincts told me that someone other than Oswald had done the shooting. Maybe Oswald had been involved somehow, or maybe he was an innocent patsy, set up to take the fall.

At this moment I became convinced that the JFK assassination was the work of a conspiracy. I read the Warren Report and found mistakes in its investigation and holes in its arguments.

On August 4, 1975, I joined the Los Angeles Police Department and began my law enforcement career. I was twenty-three, incredibly naive, but also very stubborn and opinionated, particularly about two issues—patriotism and the JFK assassination. My colleagues shared these opinions. They were all patriots, yet they all believed there had been a conspiracy. This paradox of being deeply patriotic and convinced of a conspiracy in the assassination of our President was never resolved, because it was never really challenged. During my twenty years on the force, in countless conversations during stake-outs or over beers after work, I never once heard another cop say he believed Lee Harvey Oswald was the lone gunman.

In those dozen years following the JFK assassination, we lived through a long national nightmare. We saw Bobby Kennedy shot down, and Martin Luther King Jr. We experienced political, if not military, failure in Vietnam. First Vice President Spiro Agnew left office in the face of corruption charges, and then President Richard Nixon resigned as a result of the Watergate scandal. This led to an atmosphere of cynicism about our leaders and a corresponding loss of hope.

Former Warren Commissioner Gerald Ford had become president. In 1975 he appointed Vice President Nelson Rockefeller to head a commission charged with investigating the domestic activities of the CIA. As part of that investigation, the Rockefeller Commission appointed a medical panel to reexamine the JFK autopsy materials. The Rockefeller Panel confirmed the previous official findings.

More congressional investigations followed. Later in 1975 a Senate select committee chaired by Idaho senator Frank Church was convened to investigate the federal intelligence agencies. Church created a subcommittee, chaired by Senator Richard Schweiker, whose purpose was to investigate the performance of intelligence agencies in the investigation of the JFK assassination. The Schweiker subcommittee report, released in May 1976, documented the failure of the FBI, the Secret Service, and the CIA to examine the possibility of a conspiracy. Meanwhile, the Church Committee had uncovered several CIA plots to assassinate Fidel Castro. In some of these plots the Agency had been conspiring with high-ranking Mafia members to assassinate the Cuban leader.

Belief in a conspiracy reached an all-time high. By the time the House Select Committee on Assassinations (HSCA) was established in September 1976, a Gallup poll was reporting that 80 percent of the American people believed President Kennedy had been the victim of a conspiracy. The HSCA was charged with answering the questions about Lee Harvey Oswald's guilt and the possibility of a conspiracy. (The HSCA also investigated the possibility of a conspiracy in the assassination of Martin Luther King.)

After two years of investigation and hearings, the HSCA determined that "President John F. Kennedy was probably assassinated as a result of a conspiracy." While the Committee did not identify any conspirators, it suggested that the Mafia and/or anti-Castro Cubans had been involved. Because the HSCA's charter had run out, it recommended that the Justice Department continue the investigation.

The Justice Department conducted two scientific studies to evaluate the acoustic evidence that the HCSA used to come to its conclusion. In 1980 the FBI concluded that the HSCA's experts had neither proven that the sounds on the recording were gunshots nor shown that they originated in Dealey Plaza, where the assassination took place. Two years later a panel convened under the auspices of the National Academy of Sciences found that the Dictabelt had been recorded in another location minutes after the assassination. Later independent studies have both confirmed and contradicted the findings of the HSCA sound analysts, leaving the matter in dispute.*

Throughout the 1980s, the assassination controversy simmered, with no real breakthroughs on either side. At this point, assassination critics moved away from close examinations of the physical evidence and witness testimony to speculate about possible conspirators. Much of this speculation was fueled by the enormous amount of information generated by the previous government investigations and declassified documents. Robert Blakey, chief counsel of the HSCA, wrote a book stating what he could not get the Committee to agree upon—that President Kennedy had been killed by the Mafia. Several other books, including David Scheim's *Contract on America: The Mafia Murder of President Kennedy* and John Davis's *Mafia Kingfish: Carlos Marcello and the Assassination of John F. Kennedy,* made similar claims. Other authors blamed the CIA, anti-Castro Cubans, right-wing Texans, Corsican hit men, and the South Vietnamese.

The critics had much new material to work with. Not only had the HSCA generated volumes of hearings and findings, but a flood of documentation concerning the CIA, the FBI, the Warren Commission, the Kennedy family and JFK's presidency, the Mafia, the Vietnam War, the Cold War, and other highly charged subjects provided a great deal of information relating to the

---

*Another round of government-sponsored tests has been conducted on the acoustic evidence, yet the results were not released at press time.

assassination. Still, the one piece of evidence that would blow the case wide open (or close it shut) remained elusive.

In the early 1990s, two vastly different works showed that the JFK assassination remained a hotly contested issue, with no resolution in sight. Oliver Stone's film *JFK,* released in late 1991, portrayed the assassination as a coup d'état by the U.S. armed forces and the CIA, with Lyndon Johnson's complicity, to eliminate John F. Kennedy so that he would not pull American troops out of Vietnam. Many argued that the film was wildly inaccurate, and Stone himself admitted to taking a certain artistic license with the facts. Still, in numerous media appearances and interviews, Stone accused elements of the U.S. government of murdering the President and then covering up their crime.

Whether all of Stone's claims were accurate or not, his film reinvigorated the assassination controversy and introduced the basic questions of a possible conspiracy to a generation of Americans who were not even alive at the time. As a result of the renewed attention, and Stone's repeated demands that all the government records pertaining to the assassination be made public, in 1992 the federal government established the Assassinations Records Review Board (ARRB) to review the documents still sealed thirty years after the assassination. The ARRB decided to release nearly all the documents pertaining to the Warren Commission and also made a more comprehensive collection of documents from outside sources. Literally millions of pages of documents were made available, yet some still remained classified.

In 1993 a book was published that made the most comprehensive and, to the minds of some, convincing case for Lee Harvey Oswald as the lone assassin. Gerald Posner's *Case Closed: Lee Harvey Oswald and the Assassination of JFK* even made a strong argument for the single bullet theory. Posner's book was praised by defenders of the Warren Commission and attacked by its critics, just as Stone's movie had been praised by the critics and attacked by the defenders. These two polemics revealed how divided and antagonistic the debate over a conspiracy had become and how even the basic facts of the assassination were in question.

And so today we find ourselves lost in a fog of unresolved argument. A Gallup poll conducted in 2003 found that 75 percent of Americans still believe that President Kennedy was assassinated as the result of a conspiracy. Meanwhile, defenders of the Warren Commission continue to make a case for the guilt of Lee Harvey Oswald acting alone.

You might say that people believe what they want to believe, but that's taking the easy way out. We need to determine, beyond any reasonable doubt, who killed John F. Kennedy and how it happened. Although the questions provoked by his assassination and its subsequent investigations can still be debated, at some point we need to come to a conclusion. Otherwise, the nightmare continues, the wounds remain unhealed, and the controversy perpetuates itself, with no end in sight.

This book is an effort to try to clear away some of the fog that surrounds the JFK assassination so that we can see it for what it is—a simple act of murder.

At 12:30 P.M. on November 22, 1963, in Dallas, Texas, President John F. Kennedy was riding in a motorcade through Dealey Plaza when someone shot him, causing bodily trauma that resulted in his death. This is a fact. Whatever we might feel about the tragedy, there is only one series of events that led to it. Either Lee Harvey Oswald was responsible or he was not. If he was responsible, he either acted alone or was part of a larger conspiracy.

These are the questions this book tries to answer by examining the relevant evidence and arriving at logical conclusions. This is how murders are solved. And the JFK assassination, as traumatic as it has been, is like any other murder. A human being was killed intentionally and with malice. The suspect or suspects left clues that if gathered and analyzed correctly, will lead to their identity and establish a reasonably accurate hypothesis of how the murder occurred.

The JFK assassination presents a unique challenge to the investigator. Usually in a murder case there's not enough information. In this case, there is too much. Some 450 books have been written. Half a dozen government investigations have generated literally millions of pages—their final reports and published testimony alone number in the thousands of pages, and supporting documents are measured in cubic feet. Every year, as researchers write more books, papers, and Internet postings, the amount of information increases.

There is no way a single human can read, much less make sense of, all the available material. At first I worried about how I would ever be able to wrap my brain around it all. Then I began to see that for all the speculation, false leads, misinformation, and very interesting but irrelevant material, little of this information is actually evidence.

When you focus on the evidence, a great deal of the information on the JFK assassination becomes peripheral. Too many researchers have tried to solve this case backwards, by first identifying a suspect and then coming up with a scenario in which that person is responsible for the assassination. That's not the way murders are solved. Instead, a homicide detective starts at the crime scene and moves out from there, listening to the evidence and following where it leads him.

Although there are all sorts of issues over which we might never agree—like whether JFK was a great president or nothing more than a charming playboy—the question of who killed him can be answered, even at this late date. The murder of Lee Harvey Oswald deprived us of a trial that might have determined whether he had a role in the crime and/or any possible conspiracy. And all the subsequent controversy has made it difficult to sift through the available information and decide what is fact and what is fiction. Still, I believe it is possible and necessary to solve this case.

There are some mysteries in life that can never be solved. But murder is simple. Even this one.

CHAPTER 2

The Crime

PRESIDENT JOHN F. KENNEDY visited Dallas on November 22, 1963. The purpose of this trip was political—to raise funds for his reelection campaign and gain support in a state he needed to win in the 1964 presidential election.

White House advisers and Texas Democratic leaders had been planning the trip for months. President Kennedy had first mentioned the possibility of visiting Texas to Governor John B. Connally in the summer of 1962, and they spoke of it again a year later. In September 1963, White House aides told journalists that the President planned to visit Dallas as part of a four-city tour of Texas on November 21 and 22. The next month, Connally visited President Kennedy at the White House to work out details. One of the events would be a luncheon at the Dallas Trade Mart. Kennedy decided to travel in a motorcade through downtown Dallas on the way to the luncheon.

On November 1, Connally announced the President's itinerary in Texas. After extensive advance work involving the White House staff, the Secret Service, and local authorities, the motorcade route was decided upon on November 18 and published in the Dallas newspapers the next day.

On November 21, the President and Mrs. Kennedy, along with staffers

President and Mrs. Kennedy arrive at Dallas Love Field. *Courtesy of the John F. Kennedy Library and Museum.*

and Secret Service agents, flew on Air Force One to San Antonio, Texas, where they met Vice President Lyndon B. Johnson, who had traveled in a separate plane. Later that day the President and his entourage flew to Houston, and then to Fort Worth, where they spent the night. After a speech to the Fort Worth Chamber of Commerce the morning of November 22, they made the short flight to Dallas.

The morning had been rainy and cold, yet by the time Air Force One landed at Love Field the skies had cleared. It was sunny and sixty-eight degrees. Because of the weather, the President decided to have the plastic bubble-top removed from his limousine, so that the spectators along the motorcade route could see him and his wife. The bubble-top was not bullet-proof and served only as protection against the weather. Earlier, Kennedy had forbidden Secret Service agents from riding on the rear bumper or running boards of his limousine, as they blocked the public view.

The motorcade left Love Field at 11:50 A.M.

Dallas police motor officers led the way. Behind them was the pilot car, manned by Dallas police officers, who drove a quarter-mile ahead of the motorcade to alert police along the route that the President was coming and to "check for signs of trouble."

Another team of Dallas motor officers, used for crowd control, followed the five limousines. Following these cars were five cars for dignitaries, one press pool car, three convertibles for photographers, two buses for additional press, and a bus for White House staff. A Dallas police car and several motorcycles took up the rear.

A radio network linked the presidential limousine with other cars and fixed locations, including the Trade Mart, Love Field, and both presidential airplanes. The vice presidential car and follow-up communicated on a separate radio channel.

The motorcade began through the outskirts of Dallas, then made its way downtown. Despite fears that Dallas might not welcome the President, the crowds along the motorcade route were large and enthusiastic.

After traveling through the center of the Dallas commercial district along Main Street, the motorcade turned right onto Houston Street and into Dealey Plaza.

As the presidential limousine approached Elm Street, Nellie Connally

The motorcade departs from Love Field. *Courtesy of the Sixth Floor Museum at Dealey Plaza. Tom Dillard Collection, the* Dallas Morning News. *All rights reserved.*

The motorcade enters Dealey Plaza. *AP/WideWorld Photos.*

turned back toward Kennedy and said, "Mr. President, you can't say Dallas doesn't love you."

"That's obvious," he replied.

The limousine made a 120-degree turn onto Elm Street, passing by the Texas School Book Depository (TSBD). Here the crowd thinned out. Several members of the entourage began to feel relieved that the motorcade would soon end without incident. Once the limousine traveled a few hundred feet down Elm Street, it would enter the Stemmons Freeway and be able to pick up speed on the way to the Trade Mart. Looking ahead to the triple underpass, Jacqueline Kennedy, wearing a pink wool suit, thought it would be much cooler when they drove beneath the bridge.

It was 12:30 P.M.

A loud noise echoed across the Plaza. Many witnesses, including Secret Service agents, mistook it for a firecracker or the sound of a police motorcycle backfiring.

Governor Connally immediately recognized the sound as a rifle shot and feared an assassination attempt. He turned to his right, but could not see the President over his right shoulder. As he began turning to his left, Connally felt a bullet strike him in the back.

Seated beside her husband, Nellie Connally also heard the first sound, yet did not immediately realize it was a gunshot. She looked at President Kennedy, who was slumping to his left. His hands reached toward his throat. He had a dazed look on his face. Then Nellie Connally heard a second shot and saw her husband was hit. He screamed, "My God, they're going to kill us all!"

When she heard Connally scream, Jacqueline Kennedy turned toward her husband. He had a "quizzical" look on his face. His left hand was raised. She grabbed his left elbow and pulled him close.

At least one more shot rang out, and the President suffered a massive head wound.

"Let's get out of here fast," Roy Kellerman, head of the White House Secret Service detail, told William Greer, the agent driving the limo. Greer gunned the engine and the vehicle accelerated just as Secret Service agent Clint Hill, who had leapt from the follow-up car, was trying to climb onto the rear bumper. Hill lost his footing momentarily but was able to hang on to one of the handholds on the rear hood. Meanwhile, Jacqueline Kennedy was climbing onto the trunk. Hill pushed her back into the rear seat, where her husband was lying. Hill covered them both as the limousine raced to the nearest hospital.

The limousine races to Parkland Memorial Hospital. *Courtesy of the Sixth Floor Museum at Dealey Plaza. Photographer Al Volkland,* Dallas Times Herald *Collection. All rights reserved.*

CHAPTER 3

The Medical Evidence

THE PRESIDENTIAL LIMOUSINE arrived at the Parkland Memorial Hospital emergency area at 12:42 P.M. President Kennedy was taken immediately into trauma room 1. His color was cyanotic, an ashen blue, as a result of insufficient oxygen. His eyes were protuberant, which is common after a massive head injury, denoting increased intracranial pressure. His pupils were widely dilated, deviated laterally, and fixed to light. No reflexes or spontaneous movements were found. There was no blood pressure, but Dr. James Carrico, the first doctor to see the President, detected sounds that indicated his heart was still beating. His respiration was agonal—irregular, spasmodic, and not very effective. President Kennedy's overall condition appeared terminal, yet the Parkland Hospital doctors immediately began a series of resuscitative measures.

While they were trying to save the President's life, the trauma room doctors observed two wounds.

The largest and most apparent injury was a large avulsive (tearing) wound to the right side of the skull. Blood and brain tissue extruded from the wound. There was severe laceration to the underlying brain tissue and considerable loss of scalp and bone. Bleeding from this wound was profuse, and a significant amount of blood was already present on the patient, the stretcher, and the nearby floor. The skull was open enough that the doctors could look into the skull cavity itself and see a significant amount of brain tissue. (During the resuscitation efforts, Jacqueline Kennedy entered the trauma room and handed a piece of her husband's brain tissue to Dr. Marion T. Jenkins.)

There was also a small wound in the President's front neck, just below the larynx. The wound measured four to six millimeters in diameter. It was circular in shape with smooth edges and a minimal amount of disruption to the surrounding skin.

The two primary medical emergencies are airway and bleeding. Doctors must make sure the patient has an open airway, and then control any dangerous bleeding. Dr. Malcolm Perry saw dark blood oozing from the throat wound, an indication of insufficient oxygen. He attempted to aid the President's respiration by enlarging the throat wound into a tracheotomy, making a transverse incision straight through the bullet hole and the injured part of the trachea, since this would be the proper area in which to perform such a procedure. In fact, he had first asked whether that was an actual wound or whether Dr. Carrico had already begun a tracheotomy.

Perry inserted a tracheotomy tube and, seeing blood in the right mediastinum (the space in the middle of the chest between the two pleurae, or membranes that cover the lungs), requested a chest tube to drain the President's right lung area. Meanwhile, other doctors were infusing blood and fluids through intravenous cut-downs in the President's legs.

Dr. Carrico recalled that the President might have had an adrenal insufficiency known as Addison's disease. The doctors agreed that if Kennedy was Addisonian, as speculated during the 1960 presidential campaign and repeated in the local newspapers prior to his visit, he would require steroids immediately. A patient with adrenal insufficiency can go into shock or even die during a medical emergency of this type because his adrenal glands do not produce enough hormones. The President's personal physician, Rear Admiral George C. Burkley, entered the trauma room and asked if the President had been given steroids. Not hearing a reply, Burkley gave Dr. Carrico some vials, saying, "Give him these." Dr. Carrico added a cortisone-based steroid to the intravenous fluids going into the President's right ankle. Burkley did not discuss with the other doctors whether the President was Addisonian.

Cardiac arrest occurred while the doctors were still trying to maintain the President's respiration. The President had no blood pressure, and the pulse on the electrocardiogram had stopped. They administered external cardiac massage, yet soon noticed that with each cardiac compression, blood gushed from the President's head wound, indicating that there was severe vascular damage as well as brain tissue damage. Despite the apparent futility, cardiac massage continued for several minutes. Then Dr. William Kemp Clark stated, "Well, it's too late to get him back."

President John F. Kennedy was declared dead at approximately 1:00 P.M. Cause of death: gunshot wound to the head, causing irreparable damage to the centers of the brain controlling the heart and respiration. A Catholic priest gave him last rites. Jacqueline Kennedy had stayed in the trauma room until the very end, her clothes and gloves still covered with his blood. She took off her wedding ring and placed it on the finger of her dead husband.

At the time there was no federal law concerning assassination of a president. Therefore, Dallas had jurisdiction for the crime, yet the President's body was taken from Parkland Hospital by Secret Service agents and presidential staff. The body was loaded onto Air Force One and flown back to Washington. Aboard the plane, Lyndon B. Johnson took the oath of office and became the thirty-sixth President of the United States.

The Autopsy

En route to Washington, Jacqueline Kennedy was asked where she wanted her husband's autopsy performed. She decided that since he was a Navy veteran, it should be at Bethesda Naval Hospital. Air Force One landed at Andrews Air Force Base. The President's body, placed in a bronze casket at Parkland Hospital, was unloaded from the plane and put into a hearse that drove to Bethesda Naval Hospital, arriving at 7:35 p.m.

The autopsy began some twenty-five minutes later. The body was removed from the casket and placed on the autopsy table. A sheet covered the entire body. An additional wrapping, saturated in blood, covered the head. These wrappings had been placed on the President's body at Parkland Hospital, shortly after his death had been declared.

Performing the autopsy was Commander James J. Humes, senior pathologist at Bethesda. Humes was assisted by Commander J. Thornton Boswell, the hospital's chief of pathology. Neither doctor had ever conducted a medico-legal autopsy, nor did they have any experience examining gunshot wounds, so they called in Lieutenant Colonel Pierre A. Finck, chief of the military environmental pathology division and chief of the wounds ballistics pathology branch at Walter Reed Medical Center. Finck arrived at 8:30 P.M., when the autopsy was already in progress. Although not a forensic pathologist, Finck at least was accustomed to examining bullet wounds. Still, the autopsy team did not include an experienced forensic pathologist—a medical doctor trained to perform autopsies that might later become part of a criminal procedure. In 1963 forensic science was neither as advanced nor as widespread as it is today. However, there were several experienced forensic pathologists available, including Dr. Earl Rose, the Dallas County coroner, who would have performed the autopsy if President Kennedy's body had remained in that jurisdiction. The fact that no forensic pathologist took part in the autopsy would contribute to many subsequent controversies.

During the autopsy Jacqueline and Robert Kennedy waited on the seventeenth floor, along with members of the President's staff and Secret Service detail. Robert Kennedy and presidential aide Ken O'Donnell were in telephone contact with Dr. Burkley and Brigadier General Godfrey McHugh, the President's Air Force aide, who transmitted messages from the family to the autopsy doctors and expressed their concerns regarding the scope and duration of the autopsy. Prior to the commencement of the procedure, Dr. Burkley told Humes and Boswell that Jackie Kennedy had granted permission for a "partial autopsy" and that the family wanted it wrapped up as rapidly as possible.

The autopsy of President John F. Kennedy, perhaps the most important forensic examination in history, was conducted by doctors with very little experience in examining the wounds on gunshot victims for forensic purposes. There were some twenty unnecessary observers, and the victim's family and aides dictated the scope and duration of the procedure.

Viewing the President's body, the doctors first observed the trauma to the right side of his skull and a tracheotomy incision.

Turning the President over on his stomach, they observed a bullet wound in his upper back.

The wound itself measured approximately seven by four centimeters, with the long axis roughly parallel to the spinal column, indicating that the bullet had entered the President's body at a downward angle. Dr. Humes probed the wound with his index finger and estimated it to have gone in at a forty-five- to sixty-degree downward angle. The wound was small and elliptically round, with clean edges and an abrasion collar—obviously a wound of entrance. Yet they could find no corresponding exit. None of the autopsy doctors, and none of the observers, connected the tracheotomy incision with a possible exit wound. There was no communication between Parkland Hospital and Bethesda either before or during the autopsy.

Seeing an entrance wound on Kennedy's back with no obvious exit, the autopsy doctors hoped to find a missile still lodged inside the President's body. X-rays and photographs had been taken at the beginning of the autopsy. The X-rays were examined as soon as they were developed, for the purpose of locating any bullets or fragments. Once the X-rays were viewed and no bullets were found in the President's upper body, the X-rays and negatives, as well as the unexposed photographic film, were turned over to the Secret Service. The autopsy doctors were not able to use this vital evidence to assist them in writing the autopsy report. (Five photographs from the autopsy are printed in the center of this book.)

The doctors still hadn't found either the bullet that entered Kennedy's back or its exit wound. Burkley "questioned the feasibility for a complete autopsy to obtain the bullet," according to the FBI agents in attendance. After conferring with the FBI agents, Roy Kellerman told Burkley that "from an investigative and protective standpoint," the bullet should be located. Admiral Calvin B. Galloway, Bethesda's commanding officer, told Humes to perform a complete autopsy. Yet the neck tissue was never dissected. Although Humes had the authority to perform a thorough autopsy, he was obviously subject to the pressures and restraints exerted upon him by the Kennedy family and its representatives. Pierre Finck later testified that someone—he wasn't sure exactly who—ordered them not to dissect the missile track in President Kennedy's back and throat. Humes has stated, also under oath, that the decision not to dissect the neck tissue was his own.

After several attempts at probing the wound, the doctors decided they could not find an exit channel. Then the FBI agents were informed that a bullet had been found on a stretcher in Parkland Hospital. They notified the doctors, who then concluded that the bullet that had entered the President's upper back must have fallen out during cardiac massage. They did not know at the time that the bullet had apparently been recovered from Connally's stretcher, not Kennedy's.

The President's head wound was a large irregular defect of the scalp and skull measuring thirteen centimeters in its greatest diameter, located mostly in the parietal region of the skull, but also extending into the temporal and occipital regions.

The major portion of the President's right cerebral hemisphere was lacerated. Multiple fracture lines radiated from both the entry wound at the occiput and the larger exit wound toward the vertex. Three skull fragments were recovered from the crime scene. Even with these three fragments, the autopsy doctors were unable to completely reconstruct the President's skull. His scalp was already so damaged that the doctors did not have to saw the skull open in order to remove the brain, which was set aside and preserved in formalin (a solution used to solidify the soft brain tissue) for subsequent examination.

By the time the autopsy was terminated at approximately 11:00 P.M., the doctors had reached the following conclusions:

1. One bullet entered the rear of the President's skull and exited the front of his skull.
2. One bullet entered the President's back and was apparently dislodged during cardiac massage at Parkland Hospital.

The Autopsy Report

Once they had finished with the autopsy, Drs. Humes, Boswell, and Finck stayed with the body while four employees from Gawler's Funeral Home in Washington, D.C., prepared it for an open casket. The Kennedy family and the Secret Service remained at Bethesda until 3:56 a.m., when they returned to the White House with the President's embalmed body.

The next day Drs. Humes, Boswell, and Finck met to compare notes on the autopsy. Humes called Dr. Malcolm Perry at Parkland and discovered that Perry had performed the tracheotomy using an existing bullet wound. Humes realized that this throat wound must have been the exit of the bullet that entered Kennedy's back.

After meeting with his colleagues, Humes took a nap, and then began writing the autopsy protocol that evening. Fearing that his original notes and the draft of the autopsy report, which were covered with bloodstains from the late President, might "fall into the hands of some sensation seeker," Humes burned them in the fireplace of his recreation room.

Describing the head wound in the autopsy protocol, Humes wrote: "The complexity of these fractures and the fragments thus produced tax satisfactory verbal description and are better appreciated in photographs and roentgenograms [X-rays] which are prepared."

Yet neither Humes nor any of the doctors had access to the photographs or X-rays after they had examined them cursorily for bullets or fragments remaining in the President's body. Humes wrote the protocol without this vital evidence.

The autopsy protocol came to these general conclusions:

1. One bullet entered the rear of the President's skull and exited from the front. This was the fatal wound.
2. One bullet entered the President's back and exited from the front of his neck. The bullet apparently hit no bony structures along its path through the President's body. This wound would probably not have been fatal.

On the opposite page is the wound sketch drawn by Dr. Boswell. (Other wounds on the chest and leg are incisions performed by the Parkland Hospital doctors in order to place the chest tube and intravenous blood and fluid transfusions.)

"The deceased died as a result of two perforating gunshot wounds inflicted by high velocity projectiles fired by a person or persons unknown," the autopsy protocol concluded. "The projectiles were fired from a point behind and somewhat above the level of the deceased. The observations and available information do not permit a satisfactory estimate as to the sequence of the wounds."

Humes later testified to the Warren Commission that "scientifically...it is impossible for [the head shot] to have been fired from other than behind."

The defect in the rear skull was beveled on the inside, and fracture lines radiated outward from that wound, indicating an entrance wound. The defect

AUTOPSY DESCRIPTIVE SHEET　　　　　　　NMS PATH-8 (1-63)

AUTOPSY

NMS # A 63 # 272 DATE 11-22-63 HR. STARTED _____ HR. COMPLETED _____

NAME: _____ RANK/RATE _____

DATE/HOUR EXPIRED: _____ WARD _____ DIAGNOSIS _____

PHYSICAL DESCRIPTION: RACE: _____ Obtain following on babies only:

Color

Height _____ in. Weight _____ lb. Hair _____　Crown-rump _____ in.

Crown-heel _____ in.

Color eyes _____ Pupils:Rt _____ mm, Lb. _____ mm　Circumference:

Head _____ in. Chest _____ in.

WEIGHTS: (Grams, unless otherwise specified)　Abd. _____ in.

LUNG, RT. 320　　　　KIDNEY, RT. 135　　　ADRENALS, RT. _____

LUNG, LT. 290　　　　KIDNEY, LT. 140　　　ADRENALS, LT. _____

BRAIN _____　　LIVER 650　　　　　　PANCREAS _____

SPLEEN 90　　　　　　HEART 350　　　　　　THYROID _____

THYMUS _____　TESTIS _____　OVARY _____

HEART MEASUREMENTS: A 7.5 cm. P 7 cm. T 12 cm. M 10 dm.

LVM 1.5 cm. RVM .4 cm.

NOTES:

Autopsy wound sketch. *Courtesy of National Archives.*

on the front of the skull was beveled on the outside, indicating an exit wound. I describe this phenomenon in great detail in my illustration "Beveling on Exit Wound" in the center of this book.

Fragments visible in the X-rays showed a pattern of dispersion consistent with a bullet breaking into several pieces upon striking the skull and leaving tiny fragments as it traveled back to front through the brain. Trauma to the skull and brain indicated a projectile passing from the rear to the right front.

The autopsy report did not mention the President's adrenal glands, even though description of these organs is standard procedure. Admiral Galloway stated that the doctors examined the adrenal glands, but the results of this examination are not listed in the autopsy protocol or supplementary report. In his report on the autopsy, Dr. Finck stated that *"the organs of the neck were not removed: the President's family insisted to have only the head examined.* Later, the permission was extended to the *chest"* (emphasis in original).

Because of these lapses, Finck told Humes that he should not check the box "complete autopsy" on the autopsy report form. Humes checked the box over Finck's objections, arguing that the autopsy had accomplished its purposes as stated in determining the number of wounds, the direction of the projectiles, and the cause of death.

On December 6, 1963, the three autopsy doctors met again to examine the brain. They visually examined it but did not coronally section it in order to determine the exact wound channel. Even if the autopsy conclusions regarding the head wound were corroborated by the medical evidence available, it would have been helpful to section the President's brain (or at least still have it for future study) in order to determine precisely the wound path through the skull and recover any remaining bullet fragments.

The Second Victim

Brought into Parkland Hospital along with the President, John B. Connally was treated in trauma room 2, then wheeled in his stretcher up to operating room 5 on the second floor for surgery. The operation began at 1:00 p.m. and lasted nearly two and a half hours.

An entrance wound measuring eight by fifteen millimeters was present on the Governor's upper right back, between the shoulder blade and the armpit. The wound was roughly elliptical, shaped as if the bullet had entered at a slight declination, with the long diameter parallel to the vertical axis of the body.

The bullet passed through the latissimus dorsi muscle, just missing the shoulder blade. Striking the fifth rib in a tangential manner, the bullet channeled along the rib, following its line of inclination until it shattered approximately ten centimeters of the posterior and lateral aspect of the rib—from the midline at the armpit going to the front side of the chest. The bullet pushed the rib out, causing a secondary fracture some four centimeters from the spine (in the same way that a tree limb breaks from pressure exerted near its end). At this, the lateral portion of the rib, the bone is not particularly dense and is even spongy, offering very little resistance to pressure.

While Connally's right lung was not struck directly by the bullet, there was damage to the middle lobe owing to the "blast-like effect" of the bullet striking the fifth rib and turning pieces of it into secondary missiles. The middle lobe of the right lung was ripped into two segments, and there was a leak in the bronchus. The bottom two-thirds of the lower lobe of the right lung looked like "a bag of blood."

An exit wound of approximately five centimeters in its greatest dimension was present below the right nipple. It was irregular in shape and made a sucking sound with each attempted breath. When Governor Connally was in the limousine, he had been able to keep breathing by applying pressure to this sucking chest wound.

Another entrance wound was located on Connally's right arm just above the wrist on the dorsal (back) side. This wound was larger (two centimeters) and more ragged than the entrance wound in his back, indicating that the bullet was yawing or deformed upon entry. The radius suffered a comminuted fracture, which means the bone was broken into three or more pieces. Several small lead fragments and mohair cloth fibers matching fibers from Connally's suit jacket were removed from this wound. The bullet exited the volar (palm) side, causing a second two-centimeter ragged wound.

A superficial wound on Connally's left thigh was located five to six inches above the knee. The bullet caused a one-centimeter entrance wound and lodged, at least temporarily, in tissue some eight millimeters beneath the skin.

A small bullet fragment was left in Connally's leg because, while cloth threads may cause infection, small bullet fragments that are not close to arteries or organs usually pose less of a threat than attempts to excise them. Another small lead fragment was left in Connally's wrist. There were no fragments found in his chest, either during the operation or on X-rays.

At Parkland Hospital the doctors did not attempt to determine how many bullets caused the Governor's three separate wounds.

Best Evidence

The treatment of both President Kennedy and Governor Connally at Parkland Hospital and Kennedy's subsequent autopsy at Bethesda Naval Hospital were conducted under less than ideal conditions in terms of the preservation and recording of evidence. Even under the best conditions, the autopsy of a murdered president would be a difficult undertaking, yet JFK's autopsy was neither thorough nor precise in several important aspects. The channel of the back/throat wound should have been determined through dissection of the neck tissue. The channel of the head wound should have been determined by coronally sectioning the brain after fixing it in formalin. The autopsy doctors should not have been hindered or rushed during this very important procedure.

The President was dead. His body was the most important single piece of evidence in the investigation of his murder, anticipating the prosecution of a suspect. As evidence, it belonged to the government, not the Kennedy family. The efforts to keep hidden medical facts about the President cast a shadow of suspicion over the autopsy that has lasted until today. And the desire to get the autopsy over as quickly as possible, without committing to the record certain graphic images of the dead President, has made it much more difficult to solve his murder.

CHAPTER 4

The Ballistics Evidence

IMMEDIATELY FOLLOWING THE ASSASSINATION, several witnesses reported seeing a man with a rifle in a high window of the Texas School Book Depository or hearing the sound of gunfire coming from that building. Dallas police entered the Depository and began searching for the shooter and any evidence he might have left.

At 1:00 P.M., Deputy Sheriff Luke Mooney noticed a pile of cartons assembled in front of the southeast-corner window on the sixth floor. Moving behind these boxes, Mooney discovered an open window, with boxes stacked in front of it, indicating a sniper's nest. Nearby on the floor Mooney discovered three empty rifle cartridge cases. They were photographed before being recovered from the floor.

At 1:22 P.M., Deputy Sheriff Eugene Boone and Deputy Constable Seymour Weitzman discovered a bolt-action rifle with telescopic sight partially hidden between two rows of boxes in the northwest corner of the sixth floor.

The following photographs were taken during the collection of this evidence.

Shield of cartons discovered on the sixth floor of the Texas School Book Depository.
Courtesy of National Archives.

The sniper's nest. *Courtesy of National Archives.*

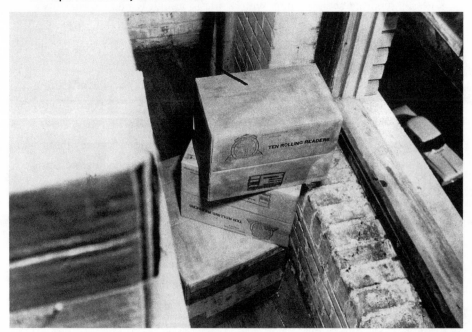

Cartridge cases as found on the floor. *Courtesy of National Archives.*

C2766 Mannlicher-Carcano as found in the northwest corner of the sixth floor of the Texas School Book Depository. *Courtesy of National Archives.*

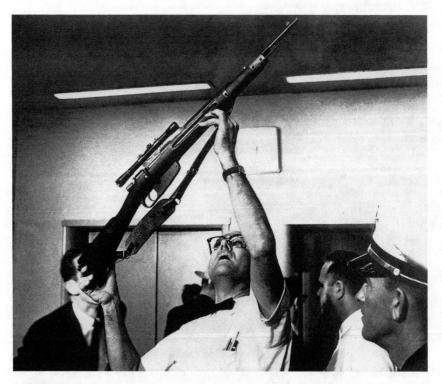

C2766 Mannlicher-Carcano in the possession of the Dallas police. *Courtesy of National Archives.*

The following evidence was recovered by the Dallas police and later given exhibit numbers by the Warren Commission:

Commission exhibit 139: Although initially assumed to be a 7.65-millimeter Mauser, the rifle was subsequently identified as a 6.5-millimeter Mannlicher-Carcano, model 91-38, serial number C2766—a bolt-action, clip-fed, six-shot, military-surplus rifle manufactured in Terni, Italy, in 1940. Mounted on the rifle was a four-power scope of Japanese manufacture. The rifle also had a homemade sling.

It is not surprising that the Dallas police mistook the Mannlicher-Carcano for a Mauser, since the rifle designs are similar. The Carcano has a Mauser action, and it was originally built for 7.65 ammunition prior to being rebarreled.

Once it was determined that the knob of the bolt and the rifle stock contained no fingerprints, Lieutenant J. C. Day and Captain J. W. Fritz opened the bolt and ejected a live round from the chamber.

6.5 mm. Mannlicher-Carcano cartridge from rifle
Commission Exhibit 141
FBI Exhibit C8

The unfired bullet
recovered from the C2766
Mannlicher-Carcano.
Courtesy of National Archives.

Commission exhibit 141: The unfired bullet ejected from the chamber of the C2766 Mannlicher-Carcano.

Commission exhibits 543, 544, and 545: Three expended 6.5-millimeter cartridge cases made by the Western Cartridge Company of East Alto, Illinois, found on the floor near the southeast-corner, sixth-floor window of the Texas School Book Depository. The placement of the cartridges was consistent with being ejected from the rifle while a shooter was kneeling behind the boxes near the window.

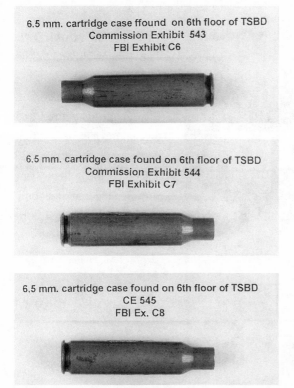

6.5 mm. cartridge case ffound on 6th floor of TSBD
Commission Exhibit 543
FBI Exhibit C6

6.5 mm. cartridge case found on 6th floor of TSBD
Commission Exhibit 544
FBI Exhibit C7

6.5 mm. cartridge case found on 6th floor of TSBD
CE 545
FBI Ex. C8

Commission Exhibits 543, 544, and 545. *Courtesy of National Archives.*

Rifle clip recovered from the C2766 Mannlicher-Carcano.
Courtesy of National Archives.

Commission exhibit 575: A brass magazine clip with six-cartridge capacity taken from the C2766 Mannlicher-Carcano.

At Parkland Hospital, the so-called Magic Bullet was recovered from a stretcher presumed to have been Governor Connally's.

The Magic Bullet.
Courtesy of National Archives.

Commission exhibit 399: The Magic Bullet. While often described as "pristine," this is inaccurate. Pristine means unfired, and this bullet has been fired. Although it is not severely deformed, the bullet is bent and flattened at one end, and lead has extruded from the base.

During the medical procedures at Parkland Hospital and Bethesda Naval Hospital, the following ballistic evidence was recovered:

Commission exhibit 842: Three lead bullet fragments recovered from Governor Connally's wrist wound. The largest fragment weighs 0.3 grains. The other two fragments are too small to weigh.

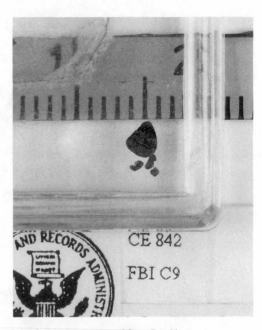

Lead fragments recovered from President Kennedy's brain. *Courtesy of National Archives.*

Commission exhibit 843: One large and two small lead fragments recovered from President Kennedy's brain during the autopsy at Bethesda Naval Hospital. The large fragment weighs 0.6 grains.

During the search of the presidential limousine in the White House garage, conducted by FBI and Secret Service agents between 2:00 and 4:00 A.M. on November 23, 1963, the following ballistic evidence was recovered:

Lead fragments recovered from Governor Connally's wrist.
Courtesy of National Archives.

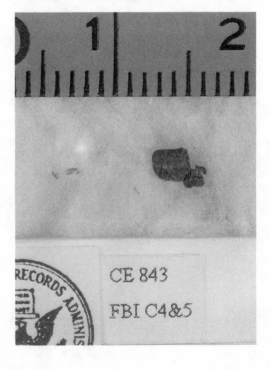

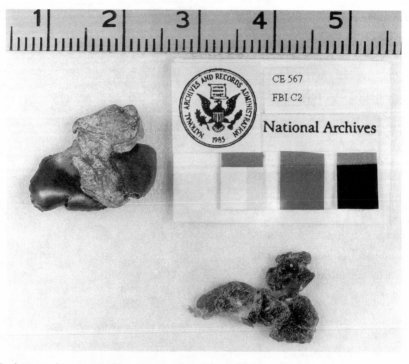

Bullet fragment (nose section) recovered from the limousine. *Courtesy of National Archives.*

Commission exhibit 567: A large lead and copper bullet fragment recovered from the right side of the front seat of the presidential limousine. This fragment weighs 44.6 grains and corresponds to the nose section of a Mannlicher-Carcano 6.5-millimeter bullet.

Commission exhibit 569: A large bullet fragment weighing 21 grains and corresponding

Bullet fragment (base section) recovered from the limousine. *Courtesy of National Archives.*

to the base of a Mannlicher-Carcano bullet, recovered from the floor of the presidential limousine, next to the right front seat.

Commission exhibit 840: Three small lead fragments recovered from the carpet beneath the left-hand jump seat of the presidential limousine, weighing 0.9, 0.7, and 0.7 grains. (One of these fragments is now missing from the National Archives.)

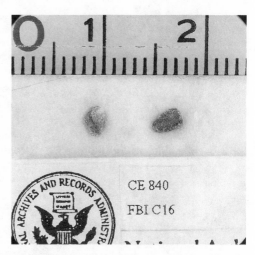

Lead fragments recovered from the limousine carpet. *Courtesy of National Archives.*

Commission exhibit 351: The windshield of the presidential limousine. The glass was broken by the impact of a projectile striking the inside.

Crack in the limousine windshield. *Courtesy of National Archives.*

Dent in the windshield trim. *Courtesy of National Archives.*

Commission exhibit 349: A small dent in the trim above the windshield, assumed to have been the result of a projectile.

Commission exhibit 841: Lead residue recovered from the inside surface of the windshield of the presidential limousine.

The Clothing Evidence

The evidence on both victims' clothing is an important link between the ballistic and medical evidence.

President Kennedy's Clothing

President Kennedy's suit jacket has a ragged oval hole, approximately fifteen millimeters long. Traces of copper were found in the margins of the hole. Cloth fibers around the margins are pushed inward, indicating that the hole was caused by a bullet entering the President's body.

The President's shirt has a ragged hole approximately nineteen millimeters long. Fibers around the hole are pushed inward, indicating that it was caused by a bullet entering the President's body. The holes on both the suit jacket and the shirt match up with each other and with the bullet wound on Kennedy's back.

On the front of Kennedy's shirt is a pair of linear holes fifteen millimeters long and located in the overlapping hems of the front of the shirt. One of the holes is below the collar button, and the other is below the collar buttonhole. Both holes are ragged, with the fibers pushed outwards. When the shirt is buttoned, both holes line up.

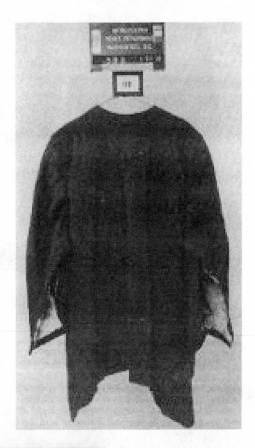

President Kennedy's suit jacket. *Courtesy of National Archives.*

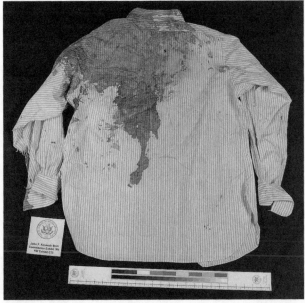

President Kennedy's shirt. *Courtesy of National Archives.*

President Kennedy's shirt collar. *Courtesy of National Archives.*

President Kennedy's necktie. *Courtesy of National Archives.*

At Parkland Hospital, medical personnel cut off President Kennedy's necktie, severing the loop immediately to the left of the knot, but leaving the knot intact. On the left side of the knot is a ragged tear approximately five millimeters in maximum diameter. The nick was created by a projectile that tore the fabric of the necktie by moving horizontally against it, but the fibers give no indication as to the projectile's direction or nature.

Governor Connally's Clothing

Governor Connally's clothing had been dry-cleaned before it was submitted to the FBI as evidence, so it was not possible to recover metallic fragments from the tears or examine the direction the fibers had been torn. His suit jacket was found in the closet of Representative Henry Gonzales in Washington. Gonzales had the jacket dry-cleaned, with the intention of donating it to the Texas state historical museum. Connally's shirt had been soaked in cold water by his wife. Even if these acts diminish the forensic value of the Governor's clothing, the location of the bullet holes still provides important evidence.

On the back of Connally's suit jacket is a hole measuring fifteen millimeters in length and six millimeters in height, forming a horizontal ovoid shape that indicates that the tear was made by a projectile moving horizontally downward into the Governor's back.

On the front side of Connally's suit jacket is a circular hole measuring one centimeter in diameter. A ragged hole measuring approximately fifteen millimeters in length and one centimeter in width is located near the end of the right sleeve.

The rear of Connally's shirt contains a ragged tear measuring fifteen by twelve

Governor Connally's shirt.
Courtesy of National Archives.

millimeters. This hole corresponds to the hole in the back of Connally's suit jacket.

On the front side of the Governor's shirt is a large, irregular, H-shaped tear, 3.8 centimeters high with the cross tear 2.5 centimeters wide. The French cuff of Connally's right shirt sleeve contains a ragged, irregularly shaped hole. On Connally's pants, a hole approximately six millimeters in diameter is located in the vicinity of the left knee.

Although the exact caliber of the bullet could not be determined from the clothing evidence, all the defects could have been caused by a 6.5-millimeter bullet.

Other Ballistic Evidence

Other ballistic evidence recovered from the crime scene included:

FBI exhibit C321: A piece of concrete curbing with a reported bullet mark on the curb of Main Street near Dealey Plaza, removed by the FBI in July 1964. FBI tests on the mark found it to contain lead and traces of antimony.

Section of curbing taken from Dealey Plaza with bullet mark. *Courtesy of National Archives.*

This indicates that a bullet fragment struck the curbing. If it had been an intact bullet, the mark would have contained copper from the bullet's jacket. This was probably the bullet fragment that went on to cause injury to bystander James Tague, who had been standing on Commerce Street near the triple underpass.

In addition, two bullet fragments were subsequently recovered from Dealey Plaza that do not seem to be connected to the Kennedy assassination. In 1967 a .30-caliber soft-point bullet was found on top of the Massey Roofing Building in the 1200 block of Elm Street, eight blocks away from the Texas School Book Depository. In 1974 a 6.5-millimeter soft- or hollow-point hunting bullet was found near the triple underpass. This bullet was found to have different land and groove marks than bullets fired from the C2766 Mannlicher-Carcano.

Examining the Evidence

Aside from these two bullet fragments, all the other ballistic evidence was connected to one or both of the victims, the limousine, and/or the rifle. Two forms of examinations were used to identify recovered bullets and fragments—traditional firearms identification and more sophisticated neutron activation analysis.

Traditional Firearms Identification

Certain unique characteristics are present in a firearm that allow investigators to determine whether a bullet was fired from, or simply loaded into, that weapon. These include marks made by the barrel's rifling, ejector, extractor, firing pin, bolt face, and magazine follower, and other machine marks unique to a specific weapon.

When the FBI and other crime labs make a positive match between a bullet and a weapon, that means the bullet was fired from that weapon to the exclusion of all other weapons. There is no such thing as an "apparent match" or "points of similarity." The bullet is either matched to the weapon or not.

The rifling on the inside bore of a barrel spins the bullet in a tight rotation that adds to the missile's gyroscopic stability in flight. The rifling also leaves marks called lands, grooves, and twist, which are unique to each weapon. The lands are the raised portions inside the bore. The grooves are the lower portions. The twist is the direction of rotation given to the bullet as it passes through the barrel. (Please refer to my illustration "6.5mm Mannlicher Carcano Bullet" in the center of this book.)

The C2766 Mannlicher-Carcano's barrel was rifled with four lands and four grooves, in a right twist. The bullet turns in the barrel beginning at one revolution in nineteen inches at the breech and increasing to one revolution in eight inches at the muzzle. This is called a "gain" twist. The spiral tightens as the bullet travels down the barrel, resulting in greater accuracy.

Commission exhibit 399, the bullet found on a Parkland Hospital stretcher, matched the unique identifying characteristics of test bullets fired through the C2766 Mannlicher-Carcano. Commission exhibit 567, the largest fragment found in the presidential limousine, had four lands and four grooves on its copper jacket, but experts were unable to determine the direction of the twist. However, correspondence with other identifying characteristics led the HSCA firearms panel to conclude that it was fired from the C2766 Mannlicher-Carcano. Commission exhibit 569, the other large bullet fragment recovered from the presidential limousine, had four lands and grooves and a right twist and was matched to the C2766 Mannlicher-Carcano.

The three empty cartridges recovered from the southeast-corner, sixth-floor window of the Texas School Book Depository were determined to have been fired from the C2766 Mannlicher-Carcano to the exclusion of all other weapons, owing to the unique characteristics of the weapon's firing pin and bolt face.

The magazine follower left characteristic markings on a bullet loaded into the bottom of this clip (the last bullet remaining or the first bullet loaded in a series into the clip). Marks found on Commission exhibit 141, the unfired bullet taken from the rifle's chamber, matched those made by the magazine follower, indicating that this bullet was loaded into the empty clip, probably as the first in a series of four bullets.

Neutron Activation Analysis

In 1977 Dr. Vincent P. Guinn performed neutron activation analysis tests for the House Select Committee on Assassinations on the recovered bullet and fragments, as well as on other Mannlicher-Carcano evidence. In neutron activation analysis, metallic samples are bombarded with neutrons so that they become radioactive. In this state, the radioactive decay of specific elements can be measured to a degree of precision where even the smallest variations can be detected. By comparing the lead, silver, and antimony content of a bullet fragment, neutron activation analysis can determine whether one fragment came from the same bullet as another fragment. It can also help scientists make more general conclusions regarding the source of small fragments, such as determining whether they came from similar bullets.

The FBI had performed both neutron activation analysis and emission spectography (which subjects samples to intense heat and is much less conclusive) for the Warren Commission. The FBI reported that its tests were "inconclusive." Guinn's later experiments, utilizing more sophisticated technology and greater understanding of the results, were far more determinative. He found that the Mannlicher-Carcano bullets had much lower levels of antimony (a metal compound used to harden lead) than most other bullets, so it was easy to identify the lead portion of the bullet fragments as being from Mannlicher-Carcano bullets. Also, owing to the lack of uniformity within each production run of Western Cartridge Mannlicher-Carcano 6.5-millimeter bullets, particularly in terms of antimony content, Guinn was able to differentiate between individual Mannlicher-Carcano bullets. Not only was Guinn able to match bullets as being close enough in metallic composition to be similar, but he could also distinguish between them.

Guinn determined that the "most likely origin" of the five largest bullet fragments recovered from the presidential limousine was a Mannlicher-Carcano bullet. He also concluded that these fragments were from the same bullet, but not Commission exhibit 399, the Magic Bullet. The only fragments matched to this bullet were the fragments recovered from Connally's wrist. These fragments were lead, which matched the antimony and silver content in the lead from the damaged base of the Magic Bullet so closely that Dr. Guinn "could not distinguish one from the other."

Guinn identified fragments as coming from only two bullets, both

Mannlicher-Carcano 6.5-millimeters fired from the C2766 rifle. He found no fragments that could have come from a third bullet.

He also determined that the FBI tests conducted in 1964 might have come to the same conclusions that he did if they had had a better knowledge and understanding of the unique characteristics of the Mannlicher-Carcano bullets. Analyzing the raw data generated by the FBI tests, Guinn found that the Bureau's results, if not the conclusions it drew from them, were similar to his own.

The Murder Weapon

Even if all of the identifiable ballistic evidence has been linked to the Mannlicher-Carcano, we still have to ask: was that rifle capable of firing the shots that killed President Kennedy and wounded Governor Connally?

The Mannlicher-Carcano was the military rifle for the Italian army from 1891 until 1945. After the Second World War, the Italian army switched over to the British Enfield, and many surplus Mannlicher-Carcano rifles were cheaply sold to gun dealers in the United States. The Mannlicher-Carcano is a high-powered rifle firing copper-jacketed bullets at a speed of approximately 2,296 feet per second upon leaving the barrel.

It has been called "crudely made, poorly designed, dangerous and inaccurate...unhandy, crude, [and] unreliable on repeat shots."* While not the best military rifle of that generation (which included the 7.65 Mauser, the .303 Enfield, and the 30-06 Springfield), the Mannlicher-Carcano was more than sufficient for three shots at a slowly moving target at distances between 150 and 263 feet. The cartridges recovered from the sixth floor of the TSBD were manufactured by Western in 1954 as part of four separate production runs totaling four million rounds. Other cartridges from that production run proved reliable—in none of the official tests did examiners have weak loads or misfires.

The rifle has a two-stage trigger that has some slack in the trigger before

---

Mechanix Illustrated (October 1964), quoted in Mark Lane, *Rush to Judgment; A Critique of the Warren Commission's Inquiry into the Murders of President John F. Kennedy, Officer J. D. Tippit, and Lee Harvey Oswald* (New York: Holt, Rinehart & Winston, 1966), f. 123.

the sear mechanism is engaged and the weapon is fired. A two-stage trigger is commonly found on military rifles, unless they have been modified for competitive marksmanship. Such a trigger poses no problem to a shooter who is familiar with the rifle, either by dry-firing or with live ammunition.

By the time the FBI tested the rifle, its telescopic sight was out of alignment, probably owing to the rifle's being disassembled by both the Dallas police and the FBI in their search for fingerprints, although there was also a possible design flaw that prevented the scope from being precisely adjusted. During their limited ballistics tests with the original rifle, FBI investigators had trouble keeping the sight adjusted, causing the weapon to fire high and to the right when the crosshairs were fixed on the target. The elevation did not stabilize immediately after adjustment, but only after the rifle had been fired five or six times. Also, the scope itself was damaged, with a large scrape in the metal toward the rear of the scope tube. This damage could have occurred at some point during the investigation, or possibly when the suspect concealed the weapon on the floor beneath a stack of boxes on the sixth floor of the Texas School Book Depository.

Despite these problems, the FBI ballistics expert, Robert A. Frazier, characterized the C2766 Mannlicher-Carcano as "a very accurate weapon." Frazier said the scope made it easy to aim at a target, and the rifle fired where it was aimed.

A military rifle is generally dependable and accurate, capable of shots well beyond three hundred yards. The farthest shot in the assassination was 263 feet, or less than 100 yards. The C2766 Mannlicher-Carcano was equipped with a four-power scope that would only increase the speed and accuracy with which the gun could be fired at such a distance. I urge anyone who believes these are difficult shots to visit Dealey Plaza and go to the sniper's nest in the Sixth Floor Museum (which is worth a visit anyway). The location of the limousine at the time of the fatal shot is marked by an X on the street pavement, clearly visible from the window. For an experienced shooter firing a weapon he is familiar with, these are fairly easy shots.

Because I had heard so many doubts expressed about the rifle's efficacy, I decided to have tests of my own performed with a similar Mannlicher-Carcano. My friend Dave Gullow is a specialist in antique rifles and ammunition and a long-range competitive rifle shooter who has won several world championships. His company, Buffalo Arms, deals in antique firearms, munitions, and accessories. His own expertise is black powder and antique rifles, firing at distances up to 1,000 yards—or more than ten times the longest shot in the assassination.

Dave bought a Mannlicher-Carcano with plain iron sights. He didn't practice working the bolt or dry-firing extensively prior to the tests. Setting up a target 100 yards away, Dave fired three shots to sight in the rifle. Then he fired a second sequence of three shots at slow fire rate, taking time to aim each shot. These three shots were in a three-inch group, two of which were a half-inch apart. The rifle was accurate.

Then Dave fired the gun for speed. He fired three separate sequences of three shots each. His speeds were 6.75, 4.34, and 5.12 seconds. Each time he shot a group within one foot. All three sequences were within the timing indicated by the Zapruder film (from 6.72 to 8.3 seconds). If he had practiced more with the rifle, he would have significantly increased the accuracy and probably lowered the firing time.

Dave is an excellent shooter, yet he was unfamiliar with the rifle. His first group of three shots proves that the rifle fires where aimed. His subsequent three groups prove that the rifle can be fired with reasonable accuracy in as little as 2.17 seconds between shots.

End of story.

Although the Mannlicher-Carcano might not be the weapon of choice for a professional assassin, it is definitely capable of inflicting all the wounds attributed to it during the time frame indicated by the Zapruder film.

Bullet Yaw

One characteristic of high-velocity military ball round ammunition that will be important in our later examination of the evidence is its tendency to yaw, or wobble off its axis.

There are two types of bullet yaw. The first occurs naturally as the bullet flies through the air. When the bullet exits the rifle barrel, the explosive gases propelling it from behind are now free to expand and move past the bullet. This makes the bullet temporarily unstable, causing it to wobble slightly off center. Over its first 100 yards of flight—if it doesn't hit a solid target—the bullet will yaw slightly in one direction or another, moving in and out of gyroscopic stability in what is called epicyclic motion. After 100 yards, the bullet has a tendency to stabilize and fly straight for another 200 to 300 yards before it loses significant velocity and starts yawing again. This in-flight yaw is relatively minor, and while it might cause a bullet to enter a target at a slight angle, it does not greatly affect accuracy.

The second type of yaw is created when a bullet hits a solid target that pushes the bullet slightly off its rotational axis and disturbs its gyroscopic stability. This can occur to a bullet either by deflection or simply by passing through a mass that is denser than air. Upon hitting a solid target, the gyroscopic stability is affected. As it continues to travel through that target, even if undeflected, the bullet can yaw off its axis and continue until it is completely turned around. This can occur in any direction, depending on minuscule variations of velocity drag or trajectory. Undeflected yaw through soft tissue usually occurs in the first twelve centimeters inside the target. (Please refer to my color illustration "Bullet Yaw and Tumbling" in the center of this book.)

Bullets are designed to fly through the air with as much stability as possible, yet once they enter a target they are made to increase their drag force and expend as much energy as possible within the target, therefore creating the maximum amount of damage. Soft- or hollow-point bullets start to mushroom upon impact. By contrast, military ball rounds are meant to pass through a human body without mushrooming. Instead, the bullet's yaw is the manner by which it increases the damage created along the wound path.

When Robert Frazier shot the Mannlicher-Carcano at targets, he noticed "no evidence at all of tumbling or yaw." Ballistics expert Larry Sturdivan of the Aberdeen Proving Grounds, who performed tests for the Warren Commission, told the HSCA that the Mannlicher-Carcano "was perhaps one of the most stable bullets we have ever done experiments with."

Sturdivan's ballistics tests showed a Mannlicher-Carcano penetrating fifteen inches of 20 percent gelatin composition, designed to resemble human tissue, without appreciable yawing. In similar tests, rounds from an M-14 (7.62) and an M-16 (.223) both showed more yaw, while a soft-point .257 hunting bullet mushroomed upon impact. The Mannlicher-Carcano was found to have "terrific penetrating ability" and to be able to travel relatively straight through soft tissue while retaining more of its initial velocity than other bullets of similar composition or caliber.

In examining wounds inflicted upon humans, if the wound path becomes wider and more erratic and the exit wound is larger, ragged, and even oblong (indicating a bullet leaving the body sideways), we can conclude that the bullet went into a yaw. Also, the placement of bullet fragments in the body, and where they come from on the bullet, can indicate whether the bullet entered nose- or base-first.

The more energy a bullet expends inside its target, either by yawing or deforming, the more damage it causes. A yawing bullet creates more damage along its path than a bullet traveling straight. It also loses energy much more quickly. Once a yaw begins, the bullet encounters significantly more resistance. A through-and-through wound in which the bullet does not wobble creates entry and exit wounds that are roughly the same size and shape. That bullet, on exiting the target, has not expended as much energy along the wound path and will go farther than a bullet that has been yawing and slowed down.

The ballistics evidence from the JFK assassination links the C2766 Mannlicher-Carcano to the crime scene, the wounds inflicted on both victims, the almost entire bullet found at Parkland Memorial Hospital, and the fragments recovered from both victims' bodies and the presidential limousine. Now let's see if there is evidence of another weapon.

CHAPTER 5

The Fatal Shot

THE FATAL WOUND inflicted on President Kennedy came from a shot to the head, clearly visible on frame 313 of Zapruder's film. The sequence can only be described as "graphic." I have seen my share of carnage and have viewed the Zapruder film countless times. With each viewing, it doesn't get easier to see John F. Kennedy die. The scene is all the more poignant as Jacqueline Kennedy cradles her wounded husband the moment the bullet strikes. He is slumping over, helpless in the arms of his wife, when the fatal shot hits him.

Every time I see the sequence, it makes me feel not repulsed or shocked, but outraged. This crime's true nature is revealed as an act of stupid violence. Although the killer's motive may not be essential to solving the crime, you have to ask yourself why someone would do this.

If the Zapruder film doesn't answer all our questions concerning the shot sequence, it does give us an exact reference point for at least one shot. From Zapruder frame 313, we can count backward to the second shot, as late as frame 235 or as early as frame 231. This gives the shooter between 4.3 and 4.5 seconds—seventy-eight to eighty-two frames—or enough time for the Mannlicher-Carcano to be reloaded, aimed, and fired again.

Yet, for all the certainty that the Zapruder film provides concerning the timing of the third shot, it also raises some questions. Critics say that the film provides visual proof that the President was hit from the front right by a gunman firing from the direction of the grassy knoll.

Let's examine the head shot sequence closely to see what it shows us. (The relevant frames of the Zapruder film can be found in the center of this book.)

Frame 312: The point of impact. The bullet, traveling some 2,000 feet per second, enters Kennedy's skull at this moment.

Frame 313: Kennedy's head moves forward as the bullet passes through his skull. Blood and brain tissue are visible at the right front of his head. Vaporized blood and larger solids are seen rising from the head wound. A light-colored object moves toward the front of the vehicle. This could be a skull fragment breaking off from the wound and flying away.

Frame 314: Vaporized blood moves straight up and slightly to the rear. The light-colored object continues up and away from the vehicle, now at a steeper angle.

Frames 315 through 323: The President moves backward very rapidly, thrust into the seat. The cloud of blood and brain matter is now behind him. Here we can clearly see the location of the wound as the right side of the skull. The rear of his head is intact.

The Medical Evidence

All three doctors who examined the President's body during the autopsy and every government-appointed medical expert who later reviewed the autopsy materials and the physical evidence concluded that the fatal head shot was fired from Kennedy's right rear. Even Dr. Cyril Wecht, who hypothesizes that there might have been a second head shot at almost precisely the same moment by a frangible bullet fired from the grassy knoll, acknowledges that a shot from the right rear entered Kennedy's skull and caused fatal trauma.

The autopsy report prepared by Drs. Humes and Boswell initially described the entrance wound to the head as being located above and to the right of the external occipital protuberance (the bump at the center rear of the skull). They made this determination without being able to refer to the X-rays and photographs. Following verbal description by the autopsy doctors, the Warren Commission had a medical artist draw this sketch to represent the wound path in the President's head.

In 1978, when the HSCA forensic medical panel, led by New York City medical examiner Michael Baden, viewed autopsy X-rays and photographs that the Warren Commission had not seen, they determined that Kennedy's head wound was four inches higher than the Warren Commission had described it.

According to the HSCA forensic medical panel, the bullet entered the upper posterior right side of the President's skull approximately one inch to the right of the midline and some four inches above the external occipital protuberance. The bullet proceeded from back to front, causing extensive fractures of the bones on the right side of the skull and damaging a significant amount of brain tissue before exiting through a semicircular

Warren Commission artist's rendering of President Kennedy's head wound.
Courtesy of National Archives.

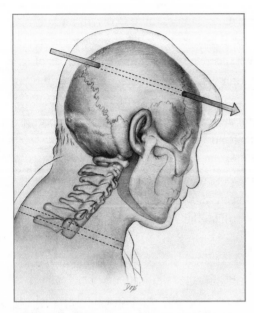

HSCA artist's rendition of President Kennedy's head wound. *Courtesy of National Archives.*

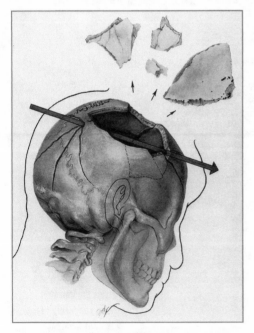

HSCA artist's rendition of President Kennedy's skull trauma. *Courtesy of National Archives.*

defect in the frontal bone of the skull.

Upon entering the skull, the bullet sheared open, leaving a trail of small fragments along its path and breaking up into several larger fragments. The fragmentation of the bullet created a wound path of severe trauma to the President's right cerebral area.

Questions Regarding the Head Wound

Why did the bullet causing Kennedy's head wound fragment extensively, while Commission exhibit 399 remained virtually intact? A copper-jacketed bullet will usually not fragment unless it directly hits a dense object. The Mannlicher-Carcano 6.5-millimeter bullet may remain relatively undamaged when going through tissue or deflecting off bone, but when it hits a solid object head on, the copper jacket frequently shears off and travels separately from the lead core. The skull bone is dense and large, so a bullet normally travels directly through it rather than deflecting to cause a tangential fracture, such as we have seen in Connally's wrist wound. The skull is also round, which causes the propulsive force of a penetrating missile to radiate outwards, often in different directions.

Both the density and the curvature of the skull bone contributed to the bullet's fragmentation upon impact. As the bullet broke up into smaller pieces, these fragments radiated outwards. The increased drag force of these smaller fragments caused them to expend their energy and come to rest along the wound path, while the larger fragments exited the President's skull.

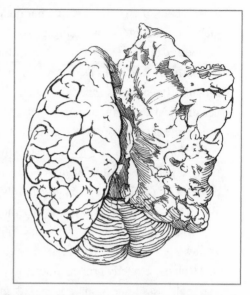

HSCA artist's rendition of President Kennedy's brain trauma. *Courtesy of National Archives.*

Two larger bullet fragments and several very small lead fragments were recovered from Kennedy's head. In addition to these, two fragments later matched to the head wound were recovered from the limousine: Commission exhibit 569, a copper bullet jacket found on the floor, and Commission exhibit 567, a lead core found on the front seat. Out of a 161-grain bullet that hit the President's skull, 65 grains were recovered. The lead core found on the front seat was probably the fragment that hit the windshield, as tests later found traces of lead on the inside of the windshield and the glass was shattered in a manner indicating the missile hit from the inside. The 96 grains that were not recovered probably continued outside of the limousine. One of them could have been the bullet fragment that nicked the curbside and caused a superficial wound to bystander James Tague.

Several more tiny fragments are visible in the X-rays and were probably left in the brain and skull area, although this cannot be determined owing to the fact that the President's brain is missing.

Why is JFK's brain missing? Shortly after the autopsy doctors performed their reexamination, on December 6, 1963, the formalin-set brain was turned over to the Secret Service. The brain was stored in a metal bucket (described in the chain of custody documentation as "a stainless steel container, 7 by 8 inches in diameter, containing gross material") that stayed in a locked file cabinet at the Executive Office Building, until Rear Admiral Burkley, on orders from Robert F. Kennedy, personally transferred the brain to Evelyn Lincoln, President Kennedy's personal secretary. Lincoln kept the brain in her office at the National Archives, although it remained under her control as a representative of the Kennedy family and was not part of any Archives collection. In 1966 all the materials still held by Evelyn Lincoln were officially transferred to the Archives, pursuant to a law passed for the express purpose of forcing the Kennedy family to turn over the autopsy materials. When the materials were physically moved from Lincoln's office to a separate Archives location in October 1966, the brain was discovered missing. Following a lengthy investigation twelve years later, the HSCA concluded that Robert Kennedy probably destroyed the brain and other missing autopsy materials (tissue sections and blood smear slides) or otherwise had them rendered inaccessible. It is assumed that Robert Kennedy did this to hide the fact that his brother had Addison's disease and was using steroids and other drugs like amphetamines and procaine.

Two weeks after the assassination, Robert Kennedy, then the attorney general and the highest-ranking law enforcement officer in the nation, issued a ruling requiring that all correspondence that dealt with his brother's medical records "be regarded as privileged communication, and should not go into the Central Files." This kept the truth regarding JFK's drug use from the public for many years after his death. Yet several historians have documented that President Kennedy received regular visits from Dr. Max Jacobson, a high-society drug dispenser known as "Dr. Feelgood," who injected him with amphetamines. One of Kennedy's personal doctors also gave him procaine injections. Whether or not President Kennedy was taking drugs at the time of his assassination, we will never know. Robert Kennedy was aware of his brother's drug use and Addison's disease. As spokesman for the 1960 presidential campaign, he personally, publicly and repeatedly denied that his brother suffered from the illness. (President Kennedy himself made similar denials.) As far as drug use is concerned, JFK kept it a secret from most people, including some of his own doctors—he had several. In the end, however, these facts are much less important than who killed him. Proper preservation and examination of his brain, as well as other evidence destroyed or suppressed by Robert, would have helped the investigation.

Even without the brain itself—or records of its coronal sectioning—all the medical evidence shows one and only one bullet entering the rear of the skull and exiting the front right side, consistent with a shot fired from the sixth-floor, southeast-corner window of the Texas School Book Depository.

Does the Zapruder film show a frontal head shot? When the Zapruder film was first aired on television by Geraldo Rivera on the March 6, 1975, broadcast of *Goodnight America,* Robert Groden argued that the rearward movement of Kennedy's head following frame 313 was proof that the President was hit by a bullet coming from the grassy knoll. This theory led to viewings of the Zapruder film by congressional leaders and their staffs, with Groden's commentary, and was one of the main reasons the HSCA was formed to reinvestigate the JFK assassination.

While a real-time viewing of the head shot sequence does seem to indicate that the President was hit with some powerful force propelling him rearward, there are several explanations for this phenomenon. These explanations are separate, but not necessarily exclusive, and could have occurred together.

First of all, when a person is shot, the body doesn't always move in the direction of the bullet. It is almost impossible to predict how a body will move immediately after receiving a gunshot wound because there are so many variables: the impact of the bullet itself; the damage it causes to bone, muscle, and nerves; the body position of the victim; the victim's voluntary and involuntary movements, balance, and weight; and gravity and other factors. When John Wayne shoots a bad guy perched on a rooftop, the bad guy pitches over and falls forward, not because this is scientifically accurate but because it makes a good picture. Likewise with the agonal jitterbug we see when Sonny Corleone is machine-gunned to death in *The Godfather.* In considering the reactions of gunshot victims to their wounds, we need to forget Hollywood and focus on the evidence.

The "Jet Effect"

First proposed by physicist Luis Alvarez, and later demonstrated in ballistic experiments performed by Dr. John Lattimer, the jet effect theory posits that the blood and brain tissue exploding from Kennedy's skull would have carried more momentum upon exit than the bullet itself upon entry. An object enters the head with significant energy, pushing tissue and fluid forward and exiting a larger hole. The fluid and tissue push against the air much the same as burning gases push against the air in a jet engine. The jet produces thrust and moves forward. The sudden explosion of energy, fluid, and tissue from the President's head could have created the same effect for a split second. Since the bullet exited the right front of Kennedy's skull, his head would snap back to the left rear.

The Neuromuscular Reaction

Testifying before the HSCA, wounds ballistics expert Larry Sturdivan described the backwards movement of President Kennedy's head as a "mechanical stimulation of the motor nerves." Since the President's brain was severely damaged, both by direct impact with the bullet and by its shock wave, all the motor nerves were stimulated at the same time, creating a neuromuscular reaction clenching all the muscles in his body. When this happens, the strongest muscles predominate. Since the President was sitting down, the clenching of his back muscles, which would have been stronger than the corresponding abdominals, would have caused his entire body to arch backwards.

Hunters often observe neuromuscular reaction when they shoot an animal in the back, neck, or head. The animal can move in any direction, either toward or away from the direction of the bullet. This is not a reaction to the bullet's impact, but a seizure created by damage to the spinal cord and/or severe neurological damage. Sometimes the reaction is so powerful that an animal as large as an elk lying on its stomach can do a complete backflip and land with its legs in the air.

The Acceleration of the Limousine

The driver of the presidential limousine, Secret Service agent William Greer, testified that he "tramped on the accelerator" after glancing over his shoulder and seeing Governor Connally start to fall. He estimated that he looked over his shoulder after the second shot. Greer's supervisor, Roy Kellerman, was in the passenger seat. He testified that the car "leaped forward" when Greer accelerated, although he too could not recall whether this was after the second or third shot. Secret Service agent Clint Hill almost lost his footing while trying to climb onto the back of the limousine shortly after the third shot, indicating that the car accelerated sometime after Kennedy received his fatal wound.

Jacqueline Kennedy's Actions

At the time of the fatal head wound, Jacqueline Kennedy was holding on to her husband, who leaned to the left. Shortly after impact, Kennedy jolted backwards. She could have pulled him toward her. Since Earl Warren never asked Mrs. Kennedy about such details during her deposition, we will never know. These and other questions should have been put to her immediately after the assassination, preferably on Air Force One while they flew back to Washington. The Secret Service should have interviewed all the witnesses while their memory was still fresh, particularly those in the limousine.

Even a close viewing of the Zapruder film does not give us a clear picture of the lateral direction of the President's movement. He appears to be moving forward, then backward and to the left. How far he moved is impossible to tell from viewing a two-dimensional film taken from a fixed perspective.

Other Evidence

All these factors—the jet effect, the neuromuscular reaction, the limousine accelerating, and Jacqueline Kennedy's pulling her husband backwards—could have occurred, together or separately in any combination, to explain why the President's head and body snapped backward in a violent motion shortly after being shot from the right rear.

There is other evidence that corroborates a shot from that direction.

In frame 313, we see a mist that rises from the wound and a light-colored object cast up and forward from the President's skull. This object appears to be moving at about a ten- to- fifteen-degree angle up and away from the President toward the front of the vehicle. There is a visible trail from the wound to the object.

In the next frame, this light-colored object is still seen and the trail is still visible coming from the President's head wound, arching now at a slightly steeper angle. The object seems to be losing energy and nosing over until it has left the frame in frame 315.

The spray of blood and brain tissue flew onto the Connallys in the jump seats in front of the President. Nellie Connally testified to feeling the spray hit her and her husband, as he reclined in her lap. Blood and tissue were found in almost every part of the limousine, front to back. There was blood spatter visible on the windshield during the search of the limousine shortly after the assassination. In the Zapruder film, we see blood and brain landing on the rear trunk, as the limousine drives out from under the spray. When Jackie starts climbing onto the trunk, she is retrieving a piece of her husband's brain, which she later gave to a doctor at Parkland Hospital. Two Dallas police motor officers riding behind the presidential limousine were splattered with blood and tissue. Viewing the Zapruder film, it is clear that the officers drove into the mist, which was hanging momentarily in the air.

Note also how the President's rear skull is visibly intact. A shot from the front would have resulted in massive trauma to the rear of the skull.

ALL THIS EVIDENCE seems to demonstrate that Kennedy was killed by a single shot from the right rear. Now we need to take a closer look at the alleged suspect and see what evidence links him to the crime.

CHAPTER 6

The Suspect

JUST PRIOR to the motorcade's arrival at Dealey Plaza, Arnold Rowland saw a white male of slender build with dark hair in "the second floor from the top" window of the Texas School Book Depository. The man "was holding in his arms what appeared to be a hi [*sic*] powered rifle because it looked like it had a scope on it. He appeared to be holding this at a parade rest sort of position." Rowland asked his wife, "Do you want to see a Secret Service agent?" When she turned to look at the window, the man was no longer visible.

As the motorcade passed down Elm Street, Howard Brennan heard a noise that he thought was a motorcycle backfire or a firecracker. Brennan looked up at the TSBD and saw a man take deliberate aim with a rifle and fire in the direction of the presidential motorcade as it passed. He described the suspect as a white male weighing approximately 165 pounds, five feet ten inches tall, in his early thirties.

Fifteen-year-old Amos Lee Euins was watching the motorcade from the southwest corner of Elm and Houston, facing the TSBD. He saw what he described as a "pipe thing sticking out the window." When he heard the first shot, he thought it was a backfire. Looking around, Euins saw a man's hands on the barrel and the trigger of the rifle. He saw him fire again.

After the first shot, Mrs. Earle Cabell, the wife of the Dallas mayor, looked up toward the TSBD and saw "a projection" sticking out of one of the sixth-floor windows.

Robert H. Jackson, a staff photographer with the *Dallas Times Herald,* was traveling in a press car in the motorcade when he heard three shots. He told the Warren Commission:

> Then after the third shot, I guess all of us were just looking all around and I just looked straight up ahead of me, which would have been looking at the School Book Depository, and I noticed two Negro men in a window straining to see directly above them, and my eyes followed right on up to the window above them and I saw the rifle or what looked like a rifle, approximately half of the weapon, I guess I saw, and just as I looked at it, it was drawn fairly slowly back into the building, and I saw no one in the window with it.

When Malcolm O. Couch, a newsreel cameraman, heard Jackson say he saw the rifle, he looked up at the southeast-corner, sixth-floor window and saw "about a foot of a rifle being—the barrel brought into the window." Thomas Dillard, a photographer with the *Dallas Morning News,* heard Jackson and immediately took a photograph.

Dillard's photo shows Bonnie Ray Williams and Harold Norman, two employees of the Texas School Book Depository, who were watching the motorcade from the fifth floor, along with James Jarman Jr. These were the men referred to by Robert Jackson and Howard Brennan in their statements. Norman was in the extreme southeast window, watching the motorcade. Looking above him, he could see light through the ceiling cracks between the fifth and sixth floors (the flooring was being replaced). In his testimony to the Warren Commission, Norman stated:

> I heard a shot, and then after I heard the shot, well, it seems as though the President, you know, slumped or something, and then another shot and I believe Jarman or someone told me, he said, "I believe someone is shooting at the President," and I think I made a statement. "It is someone shooting at the President and I believe it came from up above us." Well, I couldn't see at all during the time, but I know I

The Texas School Book Depository seconds after shots were heard. *Courtesy of National Archives.*

heard a third shot fired, and I could also hear something sounded like the shell hulls hitting the floor and the ejecting of the rifle.

Williams stated that when he heard the second shot, "it sounded like it was right in the building." The entire building shook and cement dust fell onto Williams's head.

Norman, Jarman, and Williams ran to windows on the west side of the building to see what happened to the motorcade. When they reached a window on the west side, Jarman said to the others, "That shot probably came from upstairs, up over us." Norman replied, "I know it did, because I could hear the action of the bolt, and I could hear the cartridges drop on the floor." The men went downstairs and left the building, where they saw Howard Brennan talking to a police officer. Brennan recognized Norman and Jarman as the men he had seen in the window directly below the shooter, and they related what they had heard to the police.

Motor Officer Marrion Baker located TSBD supervisor Roy Truly, and together they began searching the building. In the second-floor lunchroom, Baker and Truly saw a man standing by the soda machine. "Does this man work here?" Baker asked Truly, who confirmed that he did. Believing that the assassin was not an employee, Baker continued his search, leaving Lee Harvey Oswald to walk across the second floor and exit the building. For several minutes the front door was left unsecured while TSBD employees watched the back door and did not let anyone leave the building from that exit.

Howard Brennan had gotten the best look at the man in the sixth-floor window, and his description was repeatedly broadcast over Dallas police radio, beginning at 12:45. The suspect was white, slender, weighing about 165 pounds, five feet ten inches tall, and in his early thirties.

At approximately 1:15 P.M., Patrolman J. D. Tippit was driving car 78 through the Oak Cliff district of Dallas. He stopped his patrol car on Tenth Street, directly behind a man who was walking away from him on the curb. The man turned around and approached the patrol car. Tippit spoke to him through the open passenger side vent window. Then Tippit got out of the car. The man walked around to the driver's side of the car, drew a pistol, and shot Tippit four or five times, delivering a coup de grâce from close range into Tippit's head as he lay on the street. Tippit died instantly.

The murder was witnessed by William Scoggins, Domingo Benavides, and Helen Markham. They all saw Tippit shot, and they got a good look at the suspect as he left the scene. Benavides saw the suspect empty his gun and throw the used cartridges in some nearby bushes. Benavides then approached the patrol car and, using Tippit's radio, reported the shooting to the Dallas police. After hearing the shots, seven additional witnesses saw the fleeing suspect.

A report of the Tippit shooting and description of the suspect was broadcast by local radio stations. The suspect was described as "a white male about thirty, five feet eight inches, black hair, slender," following the description given by Helen Markham. Johnny Brewer, manager of a shoe store on Jefferson Boulevard, saw a man matching the suspect's description duck into the entrance of his store as a police vehicle made a U-turn on Jefferson. Once the police vehicle had driven away, the man continued down the street. Brewer went outside, where he saw the man enter the Texas

Theater. He asked Julia Postal, the ticket taker, if the man had bought a ticket. "No, by golly, he didn't," she replied. Brewer went into the theater, while Postal called the police.

Some fifteen police officers arrived at the theater. The houselights were turned on, and Brewer was asked to identify the man he had seen on Jefferson—he pointed out someone seated alone in the rear of the main floor, near the right center aisle. Patrolman M. N. McDonald approached the suspect, who rose to his feet and said, "Well, it's all over now," then punched McDonald with his left fist. With his right hand, the suspect reached for a pistol. McDonald was able to grab the gun and keep him from firing. Three other officers assisted McDonald in controlling the suspect—Lee Harvey Oswald.

When Oswald was taken to Dallas police headquarters, detectives were already looking for him, because he had been reported missing from a roll call of employees at the Texas School Book Depository.

Lee Harvey Oswald being taken from the Texas Theater. *Courtesy of National Archives.*

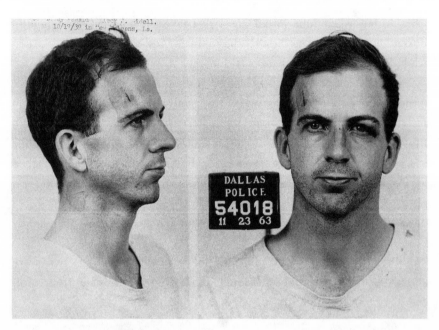

Lee Harvey Oswald's mug shot. *Courtesy of National Archives.*

Oswald was a twenty-four-year-old order filler at the Depository. He had been at work that day. He was a male Caucasian, five foot nine, 140 pounds, with brown hair and blue-gray eyes. An ex-Marine who had gotten an early hardship discharge and then defected to Russia in 1959, Oswald returned to the United States after three years, along with his Russian bride, Marina Prusakova Oswald, and their daughter June. A second daughter, Rachel, had been born on October 20, 1963. Oswald and his wife were living apart. He rented a small room in a boardinghouse in the Oak Cliff neighborhood of Dallas while Marina and their daughters lived with Ruth Paine, a friend who let them stay at her Irving home in return for Russian lessons. Oswald was registered at the boardinghouse under the name O. H. Lee.

When arrested, Oswald was carrying a forged Selective Service card with his photo and the name Alek James Hidell. Among other possessions, Oswald carried a business card from a consular officer at the Soviet embassy in Washington, D.C., and two cards designating membership in the Fair Play for Cuba Committee. One of those cards was signed by A. Hidell, identified as New Orleans chapter president. Oswald had $13.87 cash and was wearing black trousers and a brown "salt and pepper," long-sleeved shirt.

Beginning at 2:30 P.M., Oswald was interrogated by a number of investigators, including Dallas police officers, FBI and Secret Service agents, and a U.S. postal inspector. There were no stenographic or tape recordings of these interrogations, only written memoranda by the interrogators and their later testimony to the Warren Commission.

During these interrogations Oswald denied any knowledge of or participation in the assassination of President Kennedy or the shooting of Officer Tippit. He stated that he was not aware of the fact that Governor Connally had been wounded. He denied owning a rifle and said the only weapon he had shot recently was a .22. He refused to take a polygraph test. When asked if he wished to speak to an attorney, Oswald said that he wanted to be represented by John Abt, a New York City attorney famous for defending the constitutional rights of left-wing activists. After several attempts, Oswald was unable to get the lawyer on the phone. He said that if he could not get Abt, he wished to be represented by a lawyer from the American Civil Liberties Union, of which he was a member. Oswald continued to speak with interrogators while waiting to get legal representation.

The interrogations were interrupted several times in order to place Oswald in lineups for witnesses of the Tippit shooting. He was identified by five witnesses that night. Another witness identified Oswald the next day. Later, three additional witnesses identified Oswald from a photograph, and two more witnesses eventually testified that Oswald resembled the man they had seen.

At 7:05 P.M., Oswald was formally charged with the murder of Officer J. D. Tippit.

Commission exhibit 143 is the pistol Oswald tried to fire when apprehended at the Texas Theater. Four expended .38-caliber cartridge cases (Commission exhibit 594) were found at the scene of Tippit's murder. Two of the cases were manufactured by Western Cartridge and two by Remington-Peters. (It is possible that five shots were fired and one of the cartridges was not recovered, since of the four bullets removed from Tippit, three were Winchester-Western and one was Remington-Peters.) All four cartridges were determined to have been fired from Oswald's pistol, to the exclusion of all other weapons.

Because Oswald's revolver had been rechambered to shoot .38 Special ammunition, the barrel was slightly too large. This made the bullets wobble

Four .38 special cartridges found at the Tippit crime scene
CE 594
FBI Ex. C47 - C50

The revolver found on
Oswald when he was arrested.
Courtesy of National Archives.

Cartridges recovered
from the Tippit crime
scene. *Courtesy of National
Archives.*

down the barrel, and therefore they did not contain consistent rifling marks that ballistics experts could match to any pistol. Even consecutive bullets test-fired from Oswald's revolver could not be matched. The four .38 Special lead bullets recovered from Tippit's body had the same rifling characteristics as Oswald's revolver—five lands and grooves and a right twist. One ballistics expert hired by the Warren Commission matched a bullet from Tippit's body to Oswald's revolver, but the FBI expert could only state that the bullets "could have been fired" from the gun. Four cartridges were found in the revolver's cylinder. Two of those cartridges were manufactured by Western Cartridge Company, and two were manufactured by Remington-Peters. Five additional Western .38 Special cartridges were found in Oswald's trouser pocket.

Oswald claimed to have bought the pistol in Forth Worth. Investigators soon determined that it was bought from a mail-order house in Los Angeles for $10 cash and shipped to A. J. Hidell at a post office box rented by Oswald. Handwriting analysis determined that Oswald had filled out the order form, signing both the Hidell signature and that of a fictitious witness, D. J. Drittal, attesting that the person ordering the gun was a U.S. citizen and had not been convicted of a felony. The revolver was identified by Marina Oswald as belonging to her husband.

Paraffin tests on Oswald's hands revealed traces of nitrate consistent with the residue on the hands of a person who had recently handled or discharged a firearm. Paraffin tests on his right cheek were negative. These tests are suggestive, but not determinative, of having recently fired a gun, as a suspect can pick up nitrates by other means. And negative results do not prove that a suspect did not fire a weapon. The usefulness in paraffin tests is mostly limited to interrogation, where investigators try to provoke incriminating statements from the suspect following such tests.

Oswald said he did not own a rifle. When presented with the rifle found on the sixth floor of the Texas School Book Depository, Oswald said it was not his. The FBI determined that the C2766 Mannlicher-Carcano was part of a shipment of surplus Italian military weapons purchased for resale by Klein's Sporting Goods in Chicago. The company's records showed that the rifle C2766, with a mounted scope, was shipped on March 20, 1963, to A. J. Hidell at the same post office box rented by Lee Harvey Oswald where the pistol had been delivered.

Confronted with this evidence, Oswald said it was not true.

Marina Oswald stated that her husband owned a rifle. Although she could not positively identify the Mannlicher-Carcano, she said it looked like the weapon he owned. She later said that shortly after learning that the president had been assassinated near the building where her husband worked, she went out to Ruth Paine's garage to see if Lee's rifle was there. She saw the blanket in which he kept his rifle and assumed the rifle was still inside.

When Dallas police came to the Paine residence later that afternoon, Ruth Paine let them in. The police asked if Oswald had any weapons at her house. Paine said no, then translated the question for Marina, who told them that there was a rifle wrapped in a blanket in the garage. When they went to the garage and picked up the blanket, it was empty. Oswald denied owning a rifle that had been kept wrapped in a blanket in Ruth Paine's garage. Eventually, four additional witnesses reported having seen Oswald's rifle: George and Jeanne De Mohrenschildt, their daughter Alexandra, and their son-in-law Gary Taylor.

When asked about the Selective Service card issued to Alek James Hidell found in his wallet, Oswald stated that he had picked it up in New Orleans while working for the Fair Play for Cuba Committee.

He denied ever receiving a package in his post office box addressed to Hidell. He also denied receiving the rifle at that address. When postal inspector H. D. Holmes confronted Oswald with evidence that A. J. Hidell was listed on a post office box that Oswald had rented in New Orleans, he replied: "I don't know anything about that." When asked why he was registered under the name O. H. Lee at the North Beckley Street boardinghouse, Oswald said that the landlady made a mistake. The boardinghouse register showed that Oswald had signed O. H. Lee in his own hadwriting.

Interrogated concerning his political views, Oswald stated, "I am a Marxist, but I am not a Marxist-Leninist." He said that he didn't think the death of President Kennedy would help Cuba much, because "someone else would take his place" whose views would be the same. Asked what he thought of President Kennedy and his family, Oswald said, "I have no views on the President. My wife and I like the President's family. They are interesting people. I have my own views on the President's national policy. I have a right to express my views, but because of the charges I do not think I should comment further."

When asked to account for his whereabouts around the time of the assassination, Oswald told investigators that he took his lunch break around noon and went to the first-floor lunchroom to eat a cheese sandwich and an apple he had brought with him that morning. He claimed to have eaten with two black coworkers, one of them named "Junior." James Jarman, nicknamed "Junior," said he did not eat lunch with Oswald, or see him after noon. Oswald said that at some point he went to the second floor to buy a Coca-Cola.

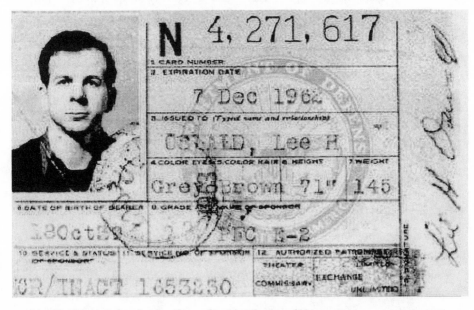

Identification cards found on Lee Harvey Oswald at the time of his arrest. *Courtesy of National Archives.*

He claimed to be on the first floor when the presidential motorcade passed by the building. After eating lunch, he went outside, where he talked to foreman Bill Shelley for five or ten minutes and then went home. Shelley denied seeing Oswald anytime after noon. At another point during the interrogation, Oswald said that because of all the confusion, he decided that there would be no more work that afternoon, so he took a bus home, changed his clothes, and went to a movie. When confronted later with evidence that he had taken a cab, he admitted that he had left the bus and then taken a cab to the 500 block of North Beckley.

In interviews with Oswald's coworkers, investigators determined that Oswald was given a ride to work that morning by Buell Wesley Frazier, who stated that Oswald had brought a long package wrapped in brown paper. When Frazier asked what the package contained, Oswald said it held curtain rods for his room.

Confronted with this during the interrogation, Oswald denied bringing any package to work with him that morning other than his lunch sack. He denied telling Buell Wesley Frazier he was carrying curtain rods.

Although they lived apart, Oswald usually visited Marina and their daughters at the Paine residence on weekends. The night before the assassination, he had spent the night there. When asked why he went to the Paine residence, Oswald stated that there was a party for the Paine children planned that weekend and he preferred not to be there. In fact, the party had taken place the weekend previous.

All these denials indicate consciousness of guilt. If Oswald had not been involved in the assassination, then he might reasonably be expected to explain his actions and movements during and after the assassination, his use of pseudonyms, his ownership of the rifle, the package he was seen carrying to work, and other discrepancies. The fact that he could not account for where he was at the time of the assassination, that the rifle apparently belonged to him yet he denied owning it, that he had already been caught in several lies (the curtain rod story, his false ID and pseudonym at the boardinghouse, eating lunch with "Junior," and speaking with Bill Shelley shortly after the assassination)—all indicate that he had something to hide. This didn't prove guilt, but it was a good start to continued interrogation, as the questioners could use these demonstrable falsehoods to gain leverage against the suspect, as long as he continued to talk.

At 11:26 P.M., Oswald was charged with the murder of President John F. Kennedy.

Shortly after 1:10 A.M., Dallas police got a warrant to search the residence of Ruth Paine. Discovered in this search were two photos of Oswald carrying a rifle similar in appearance to the Mannlicher-Carcano, wearing a pistol in a holster on his waist, and holding the periodicals *The Militant* and *The Worker*. Confronted with these photos, Oswald claimed they were fakes. He once again denied owning a rifle.

Investigators determined that the photographs had been taken in the backyard of a house on Neely Street in Dallas, where Oswald and his wife lived in the spring of 1963. Oswald denied ever living there. When told that friends had reported visiting Oswald and his wife at that address, Oswald said they must have been mistaken.

The morning of November 25, Dallas police were planning to transfer Oswald from police headquarters to the county jail. Since his shirt had been taken to the FBI crime lab for tests, Oswald was wearing only a T-shirt. He asked for something warmer and was given a choice of clothing from his possessions. Oswald selected a worn

Photos of Oswald posing with rifle, pistol, and revolutionary periodicals in the backyard of the Neely Street home. *Courtesy of National Archives.*

black sweater. The Dallas police wanted to show that Oswald had not been mistreated, so they invited some fifty journalists to the underground garage of the Police and Courts Building to film and interview Oswald during the transfer. Seventy-five Dallas police officers secured the area.

At 11:21 A.M., Oswald exited the jail office, handcuffed to Detective T. K. Leavelle. Seeing the crowd of journalists, Leavelle told Oswald, "If someone tries to shoot you, I hope he's as good a shot as you are." As the suspect was led toward the truck that would take him to jail, a local strip-club owner named Jack Ruby stepped out from the crowd of journalists. He drew a .38-caliber revolver and shot Oswald once in the stomach. Oswald was taken to Parkland Hospital, where he was declared dead at 1:07 P.M., forty-eight hours almost to the minute after President Kennedy died.

Jack Ruby would be tried and convicted of Oswald's murder and sentenced to death. Ruby claimed that he shot Oswald in order to protect the President's family from a possible trial. In 1966 Ruby would be granted a new trial, after a court ruled that statements he made immediately after Oswald's murder should not have been allowed as evidence. By then he was already sick with cancer of the liver, brain, and lungs. Ruby would die in prison on January 3, 1967.

With Ruby's murder of Oswald, the JFK investigation started going sideways. What might have looked like a slam-dunk case was now becoming a mystery.

CHAPTER 7

The Case Against Oswald

IF OSWALD HAD LIVED and gone to trial, what would have been the state's case against him?

Although the assassination of President Kennedy and the wounding of Governor Connally were separate crimes from the murder of J. D. Tippit, I will examine them together, since the Tippit murder can be considered as an attempt to avoid arrest for the Kennedy assassination.

Ballistic Evidence

Oswald bought the C2766 Mannlicher-Carcano and the .38 revolver under a false name. They were both sent to a post office box that he rented, and the order forms were filled out in his handwriting. His wife recalled seeing both weapons in his possession and took photographs of him with them. The C2766 Mannlicher-Carcano was determined to have fired the bullets that killed President Kennedy and wounded Governor Connally, to the exclusion of any other weapon. The .38 Smith & Wesson revolver that Oswald was carrying at the time of his arrest was matched to all four cartridges found at the Tippit crime scene, to the exclusion of any other weapon.

Fingerprints

A palm print lifted from the underside of the barrel of the C2766 Mannlicher-Carcano, partially beneath the stock, was found to match Oswald's right palm print.

A fingerprint and palm print lifted from the handmade paper bag discovered next to the southeast-corner, sixth-floor window of the Texas School Book Depository matched the left index fingerprint and right palm print of Lee Harvey Oswald. The palm print was on the bottom of the paper bag, indicating that he had carried the bag supported by his right hand. (The materials used to construct the bag matched paper and tape from the Texas School Book Depository shipping room and would have been available to Oswald prior to the shooting.)

On boxes arranged in the southeast-corner, sixth-floor window of the TSBD, Oswald's right palm print, right index fingerprint, and left palm print

Locations where Oswald's prints were found in the sniper's nest. *Courtesy of National Archives.*

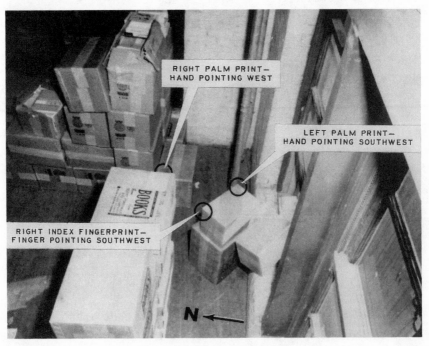

APPROXIMATE LOCATION
OF WRAPPING-PAPER BAG

N

Location where a paper bag was found in the sniper's nest. *Courtesy of National Archives.*

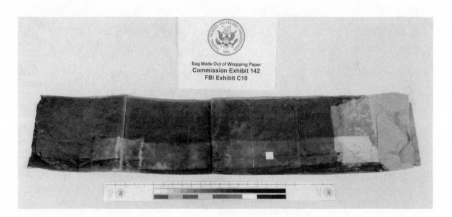

Bag Made Out of Wrapping Paper
Commission Exhibit 142
FBI Exhibit C10

Paper bag found in the sniper's nest. *Courtesy of National Archives.*

were recovered. Although it is no surprise to find Oswald's prints in an area where he regularly worked, the freshness of these prints on cardboard (which does not retain latent prints for very long) indicates that he left them close to the time of the assassination, and the location of these prints suggests his position in the sniper's nest.

Fibers

Several cotton fibers were recovered from a crevice between the butt plate and the wooden stock of the C2766 Mannlicher-Carcano. These fibers were compared to fibers taken from the shirt Oswald was wearing when he was arrested in the Texas Theater. The colors, shades, and twist of these two groups of fibers were found to be similar. During his interrogation Oswald claimed to have changed his shirt after returning home. However, the bus transfer he received at 12:36 P.M. was still in the pocket of the shirt he was wearing when arrested.

Eyewitness Evidence

While Howard Brennan did not make a positive identification of Oswald during a live lineup the night of the assassination, he did tell investigators that Oswald was the one most resembling the man he saw with a rifle in the sixth-floor window. We call this a 50–60 percent identification. Brennan later said that he believed the assassination was a "Communist activity," and since he was the only eyewitness, he feared that he and his family might not be safe. Brennan also later testified that he could have positively identified Oswald. (Although some critics claim that Brennan had poor eyesight, in fact, he was farsighted, which would have enabled him to see better at that distance. A sandblasting accident also damaged his sight, yet it occurred months after the assassination.)

Other witnesses from Dealey Plaza were unable to identify Oswald as the man they saw with a rifle in the Texas School Book Depository window.

A total of eleven eyewitnesses identified Oswald at or near the Tippit murder scene.

Other Assassination Attempts

Although she did not offer this information during her initial interviews with law enforcement officials, Marina Oswald later admitted that her husband had previously tried to assassinate General Edwin Walker, a right-wing political figure who lived in Dallas. Since being fired from his command of a NATO division by President Kennedy for distributing political literature to his troops, Walker had been a vocal critic of both Kennedy and the civil rights movement.

On April 10, 1963, Oswald left the house shortly after dinner. When he did not come home after several hours, Marina began to worry. On his desk she found a note he had written in Russian, telling her what to do in case he didn't return. The note didn't describe what he was planning to do, but it clearly indicated that Oswald expected to be killed or captured. "If I am alive and taken prisoner, the city jail is located . . ."

Oswald returned around 11:30 P.M. He told Marina that he had fired a shot at General Walker but didn't know whether he had hit him. The next morning, when Oswald learned that Walker had not been injured, "he was very sorry that he had not hit him," according to his wife. He told her that he had buried the rifle, and he did not retrieve it until several days after the shooting. He also showed Marina a notebook he had made in preparation for

Photo of General Walker's house found among Oswald's possessions. *Courtesy of National Archives.*

Commission Exhibit No. 573
C148

Bullet recovered from
General Walker's house.
Courtesy of National Archives.

the shooting, which included photos of Walker's house. Oswald eventually destroyed the notebook, but not three photographs of Walker's home that were found among his possessions at the North Beckley boardinghouse. (These photos were later determined by the HSCA photographic panel to have been taken by Oswald's Imperial Reflex camera, as were the backyard photos.)

On the evening of April 10, 1963, General Walker was sitting at his desk, working on his taxes, when he heard what he thought was a firecracker. A bullet had been fired at him from outside his house. The bullet had nicked the bottom of the window frame and been slightly deflected, so it just missed Walker's head and embedded itself in the wall.

Above is a photo of the bullet recovered from that shooting. Warren Commission exhibit 573 is a 6.5-millimeter, copper-jacketed, lead-core bullet. It has four lands and four grooves with a right-hand twist. Owing to its damaged condition, neither the FBI nor the HSCA firearms panel could match it to the C2766 Mannlicher-Carcano, even though it shared similar characteristics to the bullets fired from that weapon. When the bullet was submitted to neutron activation analysis by Dr. Vincent Guinn for the HSCA, he matched it to the unfired bullet ejected from the C2766 Mannlicher-Carcano.

Marina Oswald told of another incident two weeks after the Walker shooting, when her husband said he was going out to see the Vice President. There is some confusion as to whether Oswald was referring to Vice President Johnson or former vice president Richard Nixon. Marina thought her husband meant Nixon, because Lee had read about Nixon's anti-Castro policies in the newspaper that morning, but Nixon was not in Dallas. Johnson, however, was to visit Dallas the next day. Oswald put on his best suit and took his pistol. Marina reminded him that he had promised not to do anything like the Walker incident again. The two fought, and Marina physically kept him from leaving the house, locking him in the bathroom for some time.

The Walker shooting and the Vice President incident, whatever the details, show that Lee Harvey Oswald had planned and attempted an assassination prior to November 22, 1963. He expressed no regret about the Walker shooting, except that he had missed his target. After retrieving his rifle from wherever he had hidden it, Oswald began practicing more often, shooting live ammunition outside the house and dry-firing at home.

Means, Opportunity, and Motive

Three things a homicide investigator looks for when considering a suspect are means, opportunity, and motive. These elements demonstrate whether the suspect is physically capable of committing the crime, was available in time and place, and had a reason to do it. While not constituting proof, these elements allow us to exclude suspects who lack them. If we have the right suspect, means, opportunity, and motive help us see more clearly how the crime occurred.

Means

Means refers to whether a suspect has the physical capacity to commit the crime. Oswald owned the C2766 Mannlicher-Carcano. It was found on the sixth floor of the Texas School Book Depository. Prior to that, the rifle was last seen wrapped in a blanket in Ruth Paine's garage. Oswald spent the night of November 21–22 at the Paine house. He could have taken the rifle from the garage sometime before going to work on the morning of November 22 and wrapped it in brown paper he had brought from the Depository. He was seen by Buell Wesley Frazier and Linnie Mae Randle carrying a long package wrapped in brown paper and placing it in the backseat of Frazier's car. When they arrived at the Texas School Book

Depository, Frazier saw him carry the package into the building. Although Oswald told Frazier that the package contained curtain rods, the boarding-house room where Oswald lived already had curtain rods. There were no curtain rods found anywhere in the Texas School Book Depository that could have belonged to Oswald. He had not mentioned curtain rods to either Marina or Ruth Paine. And he denied making the curtain rod statement to Frazier. If there were curtain rods in the package, why would he deny telling Frazier this?

Oswald's rifle was found in the sniper's nest where his prints were lifted from the rifle itself and from several boxes, including one apparently used as a gun rest. The rifle was ballistically matched to the bullets and fragments determined to have caused the wounds to President Kennedy and Governor Connally. So far, Oswald had the means in regards to physical possession of the murder weapon at the crime scene. Did he have the ability to make the shots that killed President Kennedy and wounded Governor Connally?

In the Marine Corps, Oswald qualified as a sharpshooter, which ranks between marksman and expert in the Corps' scale of shooting proficiency. Even if he wasn't a very good marksman by U.S. Marine standards, we must keep in mind that those are extremely high standards. Like all Marines, Oswald underwent extensive training and practice in shooting a rifle. The shots fired from the southeast-corner, sixth-floor window of the Texas School Book Depository ranged from 150 to 263 feet in distance, at a slow-moving target traveling away from the shooter. Using a four-power scope and firing from a kneeling position with the rifle resting on a stack of boxes, any experienced civilian shooter, much less an ex-Marine who was familiar with the weapon, would find these to be easy shots.

During the FBI test shootings, it was determined that the telescopic sight was not properly adjusted, and following adjustment, it took several shots to stabilize. Not wanting to fire too many rounds through the weapon and pos-sibly alter the rifling marks, the FBI marksmen performed their tests with the scope slightly off. As a result, the rifle fired consistently high and to the right. Still, the shots were grouped closely together. The FBI tests proved that the rifle was accurate in terms of shooting where it was aimed. (Separate bench-firing tests performed at the Aberdeen Proving Grounds showed the rifle's dispersion to be normal for a high-powered rifle. In other words, the gun was as accurate as its shooter.)

Damage to the scope could have occurred when the rifle was dismantled during the search for fingerprints, or it could have been due to a defect in the scope mount. We do not know the condition of the telescopic sight when the crime occurred. Even if the scope was not precisely aligned at that time, the difference between the sighted and actual target is not enough to make the shooter miss entirely and could possibly even have aided Oswald in making the shots. FBI tests estimated that at its worst, the rifle fired five inches high and five inches to the right at 100 yards—clearly within the kill zone, particularly if Oswald was sighted in at the center of Kennedy's upper torso, as his Marine Corps training would have taught him to aim at a human target.

Oswald could have been aware of the sighting defect and adjusted his aim accordingly. Since he was reported by his wife to have practiced firing the rifle with live ammunition, we can assume he sighted in his scope or, if unable to do so, learned how to fire accurately by compensating for its inaccuracy. Or Oswald could have adjusted the scope in such a manner that it was accurate for his method of shooting but not others'. Each shooter has his own way of holding and aiming a rifle. Perhaps Oswald's was idiosyncratic. Finally, there is the possibility that Oswald ignored the scope altogether and aimed through the iron sights, with the target visible beneath the mounted scope.

Either way, Oswald could have made the shots. If he used the scope, that device aimed the weapon for him. All he had to do was put the crosshairs on the target and squeeze the trigger. If he didn't use the scope, his Marine Corps training with the peep sights of the M-1 was sufficient preparation for these shots, even if they differ from the military blade and "V" sights of the Mannlicher-Carcano. I don't believe he did use the iron sights, because it would have made the shots more difficult and probably taken him longer to aim. Using iron sights, the target is a blur and the sights are clear. Using a scope, both the target and sights are clear. Still, this possibility has to be taken into account.

The Mannlicher-Carcano has minimal recoil compared to other military rifles, making it a good weapon for rapid-fire shooting. The recoil does not elevate the muzzle that far off the target, and it does not jar the shooter nearly so much as a higher-powered rifle.

According to his wife, Oswald often practiced dry-firing as he sat on his porch at night. Dry-firing is an extremely important, and often neglected, aspect of firearms training. It helps the shooter become familiar with a weapon's sights and trigger draw and allows him to practice aiming and firing much more often than he could if he were using live ammunition. He can also practice in an environment, such as the home, where he would not be able to discharge the weapon.

One benefit that dry-firing has over shooting live ammunition is that the shooter usually will not develop the habit of flinching or jerking the trigger in anticipation of the weapon's recoil. This gives him a better chance at a well-placed first shot. If the recoil surprises the shooter, this only happens once the bullet has left the barrel. The first shot is the most important and usually the most accurate.

According to eyewitness statements, the medical and ballistic evidence, and analysis of the Zapruder film, the three shots were fired within a time span of 4.8 to 8.3 seconds, depending on the shot sequence. Was it possible for Oswald to have accurately fired that rifle three times within that amount of time?

If he shot from the sixth floor of the Texas School Book Depository, Oswald would have been able to see the limousine from the time it turned onto Houston Street. He might have lost sight of it as it passed directly beneath him turning onto Elm, but whether or not the tree at the corner of Elm Street obstructed his view, Oswald had ample time to prepare the first shot. After that, he had at least 4.8 seconds to get off the next two rounds.

With the rifle barrel resting in the crease in the box found in the windowsill, Oswald was aiming a stable weapon, making the shots much easier than if he had been shooting offhand. The target was moving away from him at a steady speed of approximately eleven miles an hour. The fact that the target was moving away down his line of sight made it easier for him to track it, and he would probably not have to give it any lead. If he was aiming point of aim/point of impact, the rifle shooting high would aid in accurately placing a shot at the target moving into the bullet.

When the FBI conducted its tests to determine whether Oswald's Mannlicher-Carcano could have been fired quickly and accurately enough for Oswald to have made all three shots, the agents, though experienced marksmen, were not familiar with this particular rifle. They had not practiced with the weapon prior to testing it, and they were each given the chance to fire only a handful of rounds. A shooter more familiar with the action of the bolt on the Mannlicher-Carcano and more practiced in aiming it at targets would have been able to fire the weapon more rapidly and accurately than these expert marksmen, who had never used it before. Indeed, the FBI marksmen stated that their unfamiliarity with the two-stage trigger of the Mannlicher-Carcano made it difficult for them to shoot as quickly and accurately as they might have with a different weapon or if they had had more time with the C2766.

Even though FBI ballistics expert Robert Frazier was unfamiliar with the Mannlicher-Carcano and the scope was maladjusted and possibly damaged, he was able to fire three shots in 4.6 seconds with an approximately three-inch spread at 25 yards. (This translates to a one-foot spread over 100 yards—not precision accuracy, but close to the kill zone.) With more practice, Frazier felt he could have fired with greater accuracy, although not any faster, since he determined that 4.6 seconds for three shots was firing as quickly as the bolt could be operated.

Oswald's possession of the rifle, his familiarity with it, his Marine Corps training, and the weapon's sufficient accuracy all gave him the means to commit this crime.

Opportunity

Opportunity refers simply to the suspect's availability for the crime. Lee Harvey Oswald had worked as an order filler in the Texas School Book Depository since October 16, 1963. He got the job through Buell Wesley Frazier, a neighbor of Ruth Paine's. Linnie Mae Randle, Frazier's sister, had told Paine on October 14 that there might be a job opening at the Depository and gave her the number of supervisor Roy Truly. Paine called Truly and told him that she had a friend who was looking for work. Truly said he would speak to the man if he came down to the Depository. Paine called Oswald at the boardinghouse but was unable to get ahold of him because she didn't know he was registered under the name O. H. Lee. When Oswald called the Paine residence later that day, Ruth told him about the possible job opening at the Depository. Oswald applied for the job the next day, October 15. He was hired and began the following day. Oswald's work at the Depository took him between the sixth floor, where he gathered books, and the first floor, where he delivered them to the shipping room.

On the morning of November 22, Oswald was seen in the building by several employees. Charles Givens saw Oswald on the sixth floor shortly before noon. He asked Oswald if he was going downstairs for lunch. Oswald replied in the negative, then asked Givens to close the gate when he got downstairs, so Oswald could call the elevator back up to the sixth floor.

Bonnie Ray Williams was eating lunch on the sixth floor from 12:00 to 12:18. He left plastic wrapping, chicken bones, and a soda bottle found later that day. He did not see Oswald during that period. It is possible that Oswald was already in the sniper's nest, hidden by the stacks of boxes. Or he could have waited for Williams to finish his lunch and go down to the fifth floor to watch the motorcade with Jarman and Norman. Either way, Oswald had time to be in position and ready to fire well before the motorcade passed.

There were some questions raised as to whether Oswald could have been elsewhere in the building when the motorcade passed. He was seen by TSBD supervisor Roy Truly and Dallas police motor officer Marrion Baker in the second-floor lunchroom about ninety seconds after the shots were fired. Mrs. Robert Reid, clerical supervisor at the TSBD, saw Oswald thirty to forty-five seconds later on the second floor as he walked toward the front stairs.

It would have been easy for Oswald to shoot the President from the sixth-floor sniper's nest, discard his rifle in the northwest corner, and then take the stairs down to the second floor in time to encounter Truly and Baker and be seen by Mrs. Reid after buying a Coca-Cola and walking across the second floor.

Three journalists separately witnessed a white male roughly fitting Oswald's description exiting the TSBD as they entered. Robert McNeil, then a correspondent for NBC, Pierce Allman, program director at WFAA-TV in Dallas, and Terry Ford, WFAA-Radio's promotion director, all reported asking a young white male where the telephone was located. One of these encounters could have been with Oswald, since he told his interrogators that as he was leaving the building he directed a man with short hair and a suit, whom he took to be Secret Service, toward a telephone. William Lovelady, another TSBD employee who resembled Oswald, was also nearby.

Upon leaving the building, Oswald walked east on Elm Street for seven blocks. At the corner of Elm and Murphy he got on a bus, which would have taken him to the Oak Cliff neighborhood where he lived. However, the bus

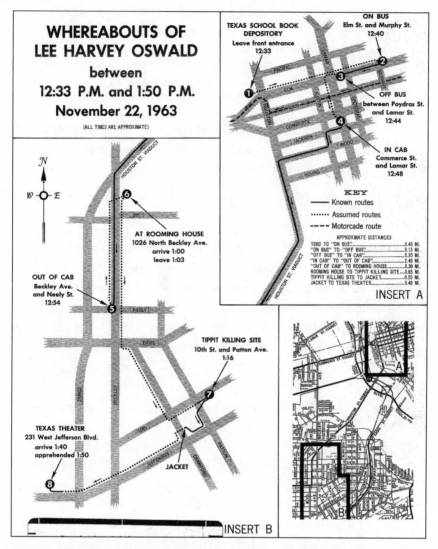

WHEREABOUTS OF LEE HARVEY OSWALD
between
12:33 P.M. and 1:50 P.M.
November 22, 1963
(ALL TIMES ARE APPROXIMATE)

TEXAS SCHOOL BOOK DEPOSITORY
Leave front entrance
12:33

ON BUS
Elm St. and Murphy St.
12:40

OFF BUS
between Poydras St. and Lamar St.
12:44

IN CAB
Commerce St. and Lamar St.
12:48

KEY
—— Known routes
•••••• Assumed routes
– – – Motorcade route

APPROXIMATE DISTANCES
TSBD TO "ON BUS".............................0.40 MI.
"ON BUS" TO "OFF BUS"......................0.15 MI.
"OFF BUS" TO "IN CAB".......................0.20 MI.
"IN CAB" TO "OUT OF CAB".................2.40 MI.
"OUT OF CAB" TO ROOMING HOUSE......0.30 MI.
ROOMING HOUSE TO TIPPIT KILLING SITE....0.85 MI.
TIPPIT KILLING SITE TO JACKET...........0.20 MI.
JACKET TO TEXAS THEATER................0.40 MI.

INSERT A

N
W — E

AT ROOMING HOUSE
1026 North Beckley Ave.
arrive 1:00
leave 1:03

OUT OF CAB
Beckley Ave. and Neely St.
12:54

TIPPIT KILLING SITE
10th St. and Patton Ave.
1:16

TEXAS THEATER
231 West Jefferson Blvd.
arrive 1:40
apprehended 1:50

JACKET

INSERT B

Oswald's movements after the assassination. *Courtesy of National Archives.*

was tied up in traffic, owing to the confusion at Dealey Plaza. Oswald requested and got a transfer (which was found later in his shirt pocket) and exited the bus. He then walked to the Greyhound bus station, where he took a cab driven by William Whaley. Oswald was driven to the 500 block of North Beckley; then he walked to his boardinghouse at 1026 North Beckley. The housekeeper, Earlene Roberts, was watching a television report on the assassination when she saw Oswald enter in unusual haste. She told him, "Oh, you're in a hurry," but Oswald did not reply. He went to his room, staying no longer than three or four minutes. He had entered the house in his shirtsleeves and left zipping up a jacket. A few seconds later Mrs. Roberts saw him standing at a bus stop in front of the house on the east side of Beckley.

Oswald was next seen at the southeast corner of Tenth Street and Patton Avenue, just prior to the Tippit shooting. Twelve witnesses put him at or near the Tippit crime scene when the murder was committed.

Motive

Motive is a secondary consideration, especially in an assassination, where, like serial killing or mass murder, the motives are primarily psychological and therefore not essential to connecting the suspect to the crime. In a rage-based killing motivated by jealousy, for example, it is helpful, even necessary, to link the suspect with the victim. (Sometimes that link exists only in the suspect's imagination.) However, in an assassination, where the victim is murdered to satisfy the psychological urges and/or political beliefs of the suspect, motive is not only unnecessary for the solution of the case but often a question that will forever remain unanswered and may distract investigators from other subjects more pertinent to the solution of the crime.

Lee Harvey Oswald fits the profile of a presidential assassin so perfectly that many people have assumed that he was framed by conspirators seeking to pin the crime on a stereotypical malcontent. Although he was married with two small children, Oswald was socially isolated. He was a failure as a Marine, and when he defected to the Soviet Union, he failed at that too. He returned home to a series of entry-level jobs that usually ended in his being fired. His extreme political views seemed to be more an expression of his personal frustration than of any kind of philosophical or moral convictions. His propensity for violence was demonstrated by repeated physical abuse of his wife, his attempt to shoot General Walker, the murder of Officer J. D. Tippit, and his attempt to shoot another police officer when arrested in the Texas Theater.

Why would Oswald have shot President Kennedy? Was it desire for a place in history, envy of a man more powerful than he could ever dream of being, political convictions, or psychopathology? We can speculate endlessly without reaching any real conclusions. Perhaps it was all of these motives, and possibly more.

THE EVIDENCE AGAINST Lee Harvey Oswald in the assassination of President Kennedy, the wounding of Governor Connally, and the murder of Officer Tippit is extremely powerful. We can link Oswald to both murder weapons and to both crime scenes; he had means and opportunity, and his motive is understandable, at least in a clinical sense. There is no exculpatory evidence that outweighs the accumulated proof against him. He has no alibi. No credible witnesses place him anywhere outside of the crime scenes when they occured.

After considering all the evidence against Oswald, we can conclude that he was involved in the assassination. Now the question is—did he act alone?

CHAPTER 8

The Lone Gunman

LEE HARVEY OSWALD was born on October 18, 1939, in New Orleans. His father had died two months earlier, leaving his mother, Marguerite, to raise Lee, his brother, Robert, and his half-brother, John Pic, by herself. Oswald's childhood was difficult and unstable. At seventeen, he joined the Marines, where his career was less than stellar. He did not get along with other enlisted men and often antagonized his superior officers. Two incidents resulted in separate courts-martial—first when he shot himself with an unauthorized pistol, and later when he drunkenly tried to provoke his sergeant into a fight. While still a Marine, he began studying Russian on his own, and he continued his reading of Marxist texts and periodicals, which he had begun doing when he was fifteen. He was given a hardship discharge three months prior to his scheduled separation date, ostensibly to care for his mother, who had suffered an injury at work. Instead of staying with Marguerite, Oswald traveled to Russia.

In Moscow, Oswald announced his wish to defect, claiming to be in possession of certain military secrets. U.S. embassy personnel, including a CIA operative, tried to persuade Oswald not to turn in his passport and renounce his citizenship, but they didn't seem too worried that Oswald would transmit any important information. (Oswald had been stationed at Atsugi, Japan, where U-2 planes took off for high-altitude surveillance of the Soviet Union and Communist China, but he did not have top-security clearance, nor is there any indication that he transmitted military secrets to the Soviets.)

The Soviet officials first denied Oswald's request to defect. He then attempted suicide by cutting his wrists. They finally allowed Oswald to stay in the country, giving him a relatively swank apartment in Minsk, a job in a radio factory, and a salary supplement from "the Red Cross" (which came, in fact, from the Soviet government's fund for helping defectors, since they were good propaganda). This was pretty standard treatment for a defector from the West.

For the first time in his life Lee Harvey Oswald had a pretty good job, a nice place to live, a social life, and even girlfriends. However, he grew bored with the Soviet Union and disgruntled with Soviet communism, which he documented in his "Historic Diary" and other writings. After meeting and marrying Marina Prusakova, he decided he wanted to move back to the States. Oswald was allowed to return, along with his wife and their baby daughter June. This too is unremarkable, as any returned defector was seen as a propaganda coup.

Oswald was broke and needed a loan from the State Department to pay for his trip (which eventually he repaid). When he and Marina arrived in New York, he was disappointed that there were no reporters waiting to interview him, only a representative from the Traveler's Aid Society, who helped them get a hotel room in Times Square for the night. They continued on to Dallas, where they stayed with Oswald's brother, Robert, and then his mother, Marguerite, for brief spells, until they found their own apartment. In Dallas, Oswald got a job with Jagger-Chiles-Stovall, a printing firm. He was fired in early April 1963, a few days before he tried to kill General Edwin Walker.

In criminal investigations, you often see the wife or girlfriend of the suspect providing the evidence that clinches the case, whether they do this out of spite, self-protection, or without even knowing it. From Marina's testimony, we see Oswald meticulously preparing the Walker murder attempt. He documented the event in a blue loose-leaf notebook, as if for posterity, including the schedule of the bus he would have to take to Walker's house, because he didn't know how to drive. Several days after the failed shooting, Oswald retrieved his rifle and burned most of the contents of his notebook, leaving a photo of Walker's house, as well as the backyard photos, among their possessions. One day shortly after the shooting, when their friend George De Mohrenschildt, a Russian-born geologist with ties to the CIA, came to the house, he asked, jokingly, "Lee, how did you miss Walker?"

Lee looked at Marina, horrified that she might have told De Mohrenschildt about the Walker shooting. Although he had not been serious when he said it, De Mohrenschildt realized that Lee might in fact have been involved. A few days later De Mohrenschildt and his wife moved to Haiti for five years on a long-planned business venture. They never saw Lee Harvey Oswald again.

Oswald gave one of the backyard photos to De Mohrenschildt shortly before the Walker attempt. "Hunter of fascists, ha, ha, ha!" is written on the back of that photograph, in Russian and in what experts have determined was Marina's handwriting. De Mohrenschildt later signed the photograph himself to prove ownership. It indicates how seriously Marina and De Mohrenschildt took Oswald's political activities.

De Mohrenschildt's work for the CIA was limited to debriefings by the domestic contacts division, which routinely questioned cooperative businessmen who traveled abroad. He committed suicide in 1977, shortly after being called to testify before the HSCA. He had already given extensive testimony to the Warren Commission, been institutionalized for mental illness, and attempted suicide on least four prior occasions.

If De Mohrenschildt had been cultivating Oswald for the CIA, the Walker shooting would have scared off any professional spook. And if he had any conspiratorial relationship with Oswald, why did he sign the backyard photograph and keep it in his possession? Finally, if he had prior knowledge of the Walker shooting, why joke about it in front of Marina?

The larger question raised by the Walker shooting is how it fits into a conspiracy to assassinate President Kennedy. I believe the act reveals Oswald to have been completely out of anyone's control and a liability to any operation requiring secrecy. Claims that the Walker shooting was part of the conspiracy, either to frame Oswald or to show him capable of assassination, fall apart when you see how his wife's testimony, the photograph of Walker's house, and the ballistic evidence proving the bullet was fired from the C2766 Mannlicher-Carcano (which wasn't determined until the second round of neutron activation analysis by the HSCA) all fit together to show that

Oswald was guilty of this crime and most probably did it alone. Since when do conspiracies require the shooter to take a bus to the victim's house carrying a rifle under his raincoat?

Two weeks after the Walker attempt, the Oswalds decided to move to New Orleans, in part because Marina was afraid that Lee would try again to shoot the general. When their marriage faltered in New Orleans, Marina went to live with Ruth Paine in Irving, Texas.

Oswald's stay in New Orleans has generated so much speculation that it is difficult to keep in mind exactly what evidence linked him to possible conspiratorial elements there in the first place. According to the Warren Commission, Oswald embarked upon a mission to establish his bona fides as a revolutionary activist in order to impress Castro's government and get a visa to that country. Marina told the Commission that her husband's pro-Cuba activities were "primarily for purposes of self-advertising. He wanted to be arrested. I think he wanted to get into the newspapers, so that he would be known." At one point Oswald tried to convince Marina to help him hijack a plane to Cuba. She refused.

Oswald created a local chapter of the Fair Play for Cuba Committee, whose members included himself and his alias, Alek Hidell. He wrote a series of letters to Fair Play leaders and prominent American Communists, making exaggerated claims about the local chapter and his political activities. He tried to "infiltrate" the anti-Castro Cubans, but on August 9, when one of them saw Oswald on the street passing out pro-Castro leaflets, a fight almost broke out and Oswald was arrested for disturbing the peace. Upon his release, local radio and television programs invited Oswald to debate the Cuban question. Oswald clearly enjoyed the attention, despite the fact that it was negative, even hostile. The newspapers wrote brief articles on the incident, which he added to his scrapbook.

The day he was arrested, Oswald's leaflets were stamped with the address 544 Camp Street, which happened to be a separate entrance for the Newman Building at 531 Lafayette Street, where Guy Bannister had his office. Bannister was a former FBI agent in charge of the Chicago office turned rabid anti-Communist working in the murky fringes between CIA black ops, anti-Castro counterrevolutionaries, and local organized crime. There is no evidence that Oswald ever had a Fair Play for Cuba office. (He used two other addresses on the leaflets he had handed out on previous occasions.)

Perhaps he put that address on his leaflets that day in order to antagonize the anti-Castro Cubans who frequented Bannister's office. Perhaps he had seen a FOR RENT sign in the building on his way to work as a greaser of coffee-processing machines. The problem is that the address on the flyer is the only documented connection between Oswald and Guy Bannister, David Ferrie, Clay Shaw, or anyone allegedly involved in the conspiracy that Jim Garrison spun out over a period of several years.

In 1955 Oswald had been a cadet in the New Orleans Civil Air Patrol unit that David Ferrie served as commander. But Ferrie had been suspended from Civil Air Patrol from 1954 to 1958 for giving political lectures to his cadets. Aside from a few questionable witnesses who say they saw Oswald, Ferrie, and Shaw together, there is no other evidence of their association, much less of their having plotted a conspiracy to assassinate the President.

Entire books have been written exposing the Jim Garrison investigation and his trial of Clay Shaw. Edward Jay Epstein's *Counterplot* and the relevant chapter in Posner's *Case Closed,* as well as the trial transcripts available online at historymatters.com, demonstrate how far Oliver Stone's version of Jim Garrison strays from the truth. Critics might say that while Garrison made some mistakes, at least he meant well and was headed in the right direction. Yet from Garrison's years of investigation, and later reinvestigations by the HSCA and countless independent researchers, not another shred of hard evidence has surfaced connecting Oswald to any assassination conspiracy in New Orleans.

One investigative trail that Garrison did not follow was in his own backyard. New Orleans crime boss Carlos Marcello is said to have made statements wishing the Kennedys dead. Robert Blakey, among others, considers Marcello a prime suspect for the JFK assassination. David Ferrie and Guy Bannister did private investigation work for Marcello. (Ferrie was in court with Marcello the day Kennedy was shot.) Oswald's uncle, Dutz Murret, was a small-time bookie with connections to the Marcello crime family.

These are connections that might have proved important if there had been evidence to connect Marcello or other New Orleans mobsters to the assassination. After an extensive investigation of a possible Mafia conspiracy (which is what its chief counsel believed happened), the HSCA could not find any hard evidence linking organized crime to the JFK assassination.

On September 25, 1963, Oswald left New Orleans by bus, arriving in

Mexico City the morning of the twenty-seventh. He visited the Cuban embassy and asked for a visa to travel there. He showed embassy officials his scrapbook of press clippings, correspondence, and backyard photos. The Cubans processed Oswald's visa application but told him he needed either permission from the Soviet Union or a Soviet visa in order to enter Cuba. Oswald went to the Soviet embassy. The Cuban officials had been in contact with the Soviets already concerning Oswald's request, so the Soviets were no doubt expecting him. They told Oswald that a visa application would take several weeks. Oswald didn't have that much time. His

Surveillance photo of the Cuban embassy in Mexico City—the man who the CIA thought was Lee Harvey Oswald. *Courtesy of National Archives.*

Mexican tourist visa was due to expire, and he was running low on cash. He hung around Mexico City for a few days, visiting tourist sights and returning to both embassies to inquire about his visa applications, before giving up and taking the bus back to Dallas.

Several critics have argued that Oswald did not visit Mexico City and that all his actions were a sophisticated cover story created by an "Oswald double." These allegations are based, for the most part, upon a photograph taken by the CIA outside the Soviet embassy on September 27.

Obviously, this man is not Lee Harvey Oswald. Yet the CIA thought it was and sent the photo to the FBI immediately after the assassination. The fact that the CIA didn't know what Oswald looked like is a pretty clear indication that they didn't have any contact with him and were probably not running him as some kind of agent, whether in an assassination attempt on the President or some other clandestine affair. This simple case of mistaken identity has taken on a life of its own, spawning theories of an Oswald double who could have been anywhere in the world at any time, thus lending credibility to eyewitnesses claiming to have seen Oswald firing rifles at shooting ranges, test-driving cars, accepting large cash payments from suspicious individuals, or meeting with the FBI, the CIA, anti-Castro Cubans, and so on. Any sighting of Oswald reported after the assassination can now be accepted as either legitimate evidence of his presence somewhere or the Oswald double adding another anecdote to the legend.

Returning to Dallas, Oswald stayed in the YMCA until he found a room in a boardinghouse, where he was kicked out by the landlady because the FBI had come around inquiring about him. (If he had been an FBI informant or intelligence operative, agents would not have contacted his landlady.) He moved to the North Beckley boardinghouse, where he registered under a pseudonym to avoid FBI contacts.

Oswald still hadn't given up on Cuba, however. He wrote the Soviet embassy in Washington and told them that he was sorry he hadn't been able to stay in Mexico City; he couldn't extend his travel visa unless he gave authorities his real name. (Oswald had traveled to Mexico under his real name.) The fact that he would write such a letter to the Soviet embassy, casually lying about the use of a false identity at a time when the FBI was routinely intercepting mail to Soviet and Communist addresses, indicates what professional spies would call a lack of tradecraft.

A couple of weeks prior to the JFK assassination, Oswald attended a meeting of the American Civil Liberties Union with Michael Paine, the estranged husband of Ruth Paine, and Marina, who had just given birth to their second daughter, Rachel. On the way to the meeting Oswald whispered to Marina, "If only Michael knew what I wanted to do to Walker! Wouldn't he be scared!" Clearly, Oswald wanted to impress people, including his wife and their acquaintances.

His movements and actions in the days leading up to the assassination deserve some scrutiny. The motorcade route was published in the *Dallas Morning News* and the *Dallas Times-Herald* on November 19. That day the *Times-Herald* ran an article describing President Kennedy as having "all but invited the Cuban people today to overthrow Fidel Castro's Communist regime and promised prompt U.S. aid if they do."

Marina and Ruth Paine had tried to call Oswald at the boardinghouse on Sunday, November 17. They asked for Lee Harvey Oswald, but since he was registered under a false name, they were told that no one by that name lived there. When Oswald called the next day, Marina was furious that he was using a pseudonym. She hung up the phone, and when Lee tried calling again, she refused to speak with him.

That week Oswald spent every night until the eve of the President's visit at the boardinghouse. He did not receive any phone calls. He normally called Marina twice a day, but that week he did not call her again after Monday. During his entire stay at the boardinghouse, Oswald never had any visitors and was never seen going out at night, except on one occasion to wash his clothes at a Laundromat across the street.

At the Texas School Book Depository on the morning of November 21, Oswald asked Buell Wesley Frazier for a ride to Irving after work. He said he needed to get some curtain rods for his apartment. Oswald arrived at the Paine house around 5:00 P.M. He had not called ahead, as he always did. He always visited on weekends, never during the week. The couple hadn't spoken since their fight that Monday. Oswald told Marina that he was lonely and wanted to make peace, but she was still angry with him over his use of a pseudonym and feared he still had dreams of going to Cuba and being a revolutionary. He played with his two daughters. Several times he suggested that Marina and the girls come back to live with him. She said it was not a good idea.

When Ruth Paine came home around 5:30, she was surprised to see Oswald. She told him the President was coming to town the next day. Oswald replied, "Ah, yes." Then he walked away.

At dinner, Marina brought up the President's visit and asked if Lee knew which route the motorcade would take. He said he didn't know much about it. After dinner, Oswald watched television by himself. He went to bed around 9:00 P.M.

At some point after Oswald had gone to bed, Ruth Paine noticed a light on in the garage. She assumed that Oswald had gone out there to get something.

The next morning Oswald woke up and made his own breakfast. He said good-bye to Marina, but did not kiss her. When she got up, Marina found that he had left $170 and his wedding ring on the bureau next to the bed.

Following his arrest, Oswald told reporters at the Dallas police headquarters that he was just a patsy. The possibility that Oswald was framed by a larger conspiracy has been the focus of much speculation. I see only two such possibilities:

1. Oswald brought a rifle to the Texas School Book Depository.
2. Someone took the rifle from Ruth Paine's garage and planted it in the Depository.

If Oswald brought a rifle to work the morning that the President was scheduled to drive by in a motorcade, this shows involvement in a planned assassination. Oswald knew about the motorcade. There is no innocent explanation.

If Oswald did not bring the rifle to work that morning, what was in the package seen by Buell Wesley Frazier and Linnie Mae Randle? Why did he go to Ruth Paine's the night before? Why did he leave $170 and his wedding ring with Marina?

The murder of Officer J. D. Tippit is another fact that argues against an innocent Oswald being framed by a conspiracy. Whether Tippit stopped Oswald because he fit the description broadcast by the Dallas Police or just because Oswald was acting suspiciously will never be known and really doesn't matter. Tippit stopped his car, and Oswald shot him. Then Oswald ran away, dumping the cartridges and reloading his pistol.

These are the actions of a criminal seeking to avoid apprehension. Could Tippit have stopped Oswald because he, Tippit, was part of the conspiracy? That seems unlikely, since Tippit was shot before it was determined that Oswald was no longer at the Texas School Book Depository. Even if there was a massive conspiracy involving several Dallas police officers who had foreknowledge of the assassination and were involved in a plot to kill Oswald immediately afterwards, no one knew Oswald had left the building, gone home, and then walked to Tenth Street.

Where was Oswald going when he left the North Beckley boardinghouse with his revolver and $13.87 cash? Some have speculated that he was planning to take a bus to the Greyhound station and then travel on to Mexico. (He had just enough money for a one-way fare.) Another possibility is that Oswald was on his way to the house of a former FBI informant whose revelations had brought the Texas Communist Party close to ruin. The informant lived on Tenth Street, just a couple of blocks away from where Tippit stopped Oswald. Perhaps Oswald was looking to commit one last violent act before he was arrested or killed. A news story concerning the information ran in the *Dallas Times-Herald* the same day that the motorcade route and the article on Kennedy and Castro were published. On the same page as the informant story was an article about John Abt, the New York civil liberties lawyer whom Oswald tried to retain following his arrest.

Two days after the assassination, Jack Ruby shot Oswald while he was in the custody of the Dallas police. Ruby consistently and emphatically denied any involvement in a conspiracy. When he testified before members of the Warren Commission in Dallas, the first thing Ruby said, even before taking the oath, was that he wanted a polygraph.

MR. RUBY: I would like to be able to get a lie detector test or truth serum of what motivated me to do what I did at that particular time, and it seems as you get further into something, even though you know what you did, it operates against you somehow, brainwashes you, that you are weak in what you want to tell the truth about and what you want to say, which is the truth.

His testimony continues in much the same vein: the more he tries to explain, the more he winds up confusing everyone, including himself. However, Ruby was clear about one thing: he wanted everyone to believe that he acted alone. Ruby repeatedly expressed the fear that since people suspected him of killing Oswald as part of a larger conspiracy, they thought he was therefore involved in Kennedy's assassination. His statements to the Commission are those of a man who was deeply paranoid and possibly schizophrenic or even psychotic. By the time of his death, Ruby was clearly insane, ranting about anti-Semitic conspiracies and attempting suicide on several occasions.

So why did Ruby kill Oswald?

"I wanted to be a hero," Ruby said just after the shooting, "but I guess I screwed up."

When the assassination took place, Ruby was at the *Dallas Morning News,* discussing the purchase of advertising space for his nightclub. Ruby might have visited Parkland Hospital shortly afterwards, as he was seen by a veteran reporter who knew him. That night he attended a news conference in the Dallas Police and Courts Building held by Chief Jesse Curry and District Attorney Henry Wade. When Wade referred to the pro-Castro organization Oswald belonged to as the "Free Cuba Committee," Ruby was one of those present who corrected the DA, telling him it was "Fair Play for Cuba." To stay close to the action, Ruby claimed to be working as a reporter for a local radio station, but no one seems to have asked for his credentials.

In the forty-eight hours following the assassination, Ruby was distraught, even hysterical, traveling around Dallas on various errands and visits, following developments on the news, and staying awake with the help of Preludin, a diet pill. Around 11:05 Sunday morning, Ruby drove to the Western Union station and parked across the street, leaving his dog, Sheba, in the car. At 11:17, he wired $25 to Karen Carlin, one of his strippers, who had called him that morning asking for a loan. (Since Ruby had closed his nightclub following the assassination, Carlin hadn't worked and was short on cash.) Then he walked to the Police and Courts Building. At exactly 11:21, Oswald came out of the elevator. Ruby had just arrived. In the confusion attending Oswald's expected transfer, Ruby had been able to enter the basement of the police headquarters and mix with the group of journalists without attracting suspicion, as he had done for the past couple of days.

Oswald's transfer had been scheduled for 10:00 A.M., but postal inspector Harry Holmes came by the police headquarters and interrogated him for an hour. Also, Oswald had requested something warmer to wear. If these delays had not occurred and the transfer had gone off as scheduled, Ruby would have arrived too late to shoot Oswald. And if Ruby had been ordered by someone to shoot the man who just killed the president, why did he first stop off at Western Union and wire $25 to a stripper? As Ruby himself told the Warren Commission: "You wouldn't have time enough for any conspiracy."

Ruby often carried a gun, as well as large amounts of cash. (He had $2,000 on him when he shot Oswald.) He claimed to have gone to Western Union, seen the crowd outside the police headquarters, and decided to take a look for himself. In his testimony, he repeatedly said that the shooting had not been premeditated. If Ruby was planning to shoot Oswald, why would he take his dog and then leave it in the car, knowing he would probably not return?

The hypothesis that Ruby shot Oswald to silence him is a perfectly natural suspicion, but at some point it has to be supported by the evidence. After extensive investigation, the HSCA found no evidence that Jack Ruby was connected to an assassination conspiracy, even though they believed that he was.

If Oswald had stood trial and been convicted, there still might have been questions about a possible conspiracy. This occurred with the assassination of Martin Luther King: James Earl Ray was convicted, and the HSCA later determined that while Ray was the lone gunman, there was probably a conspiracy behind him.

One result of Oswald's unexpected death is that his life has become more mysterious and more important in retrospect. Some authors have seen in Oswald's actions the deliberate creation of a legend or cover story to hide the fact that he was a top-secret operative for the CIA, or KGB, or perhaps a double agent. That's giving Oswald far too much credit, according to those who knew him best.

George De Mohrenschildt told the Warren Commission, "I never would believe that any government would be stupid enough to trust Lee with anything."

In her HSCA testimony, Marina Oswald said her husband could not have been part of a conspiracy because he didn't get along with other people.

Yuri Nosenko, a KGB agent who defected to the United States shortly after the assassination, told his CIA interrogators that Soviet intelligence "didn't want Oswald from the beginning." This was confirmed when Oswald's KGB file was made available after the fall of the Soviet Union. Although he was the subject of surveillance—standard procedure for a defector from the West—Oswald was never contacted by the KGB, according to these files (which also confirm that he didn't turn over military secrets).

In a homicide investigation, we must listen to the evidence and follow where it leads, even if it contradicts our gut feelings or everything we believe to be true. Through all the different scenarios, only two pieces of evidence stand out that are suspicious enough to support a conspiracy theory. The first is the acoustics evidence developed by the HSCA. The second is Commission exhibit 399, the Magic Bullet. I will examine each in turn.

CHAPTER 9

The House Select Committee on Assassinations

THE HOUSE SELECT COMMITTEE on Assassinations was created in September 1976 as a result of widespread skepticism regarding the finding of the Warren Commission that Lee Harvey Oswald was solely responsible for the JFK assassination. Representative Tom Downing (R-Va.), who was to be the Committee's first chairman, said: "In the case of President Kennedy, I am convinced there was a conspiracy involved."

Downing retired before the investigation got off the ground, and Henry Gonzales (D-Tex.), who had been in the motorcade, took over as chairman. Richard Sprague, an assistant DA from Philadelphia who had worked under Arlen Specter, was named chief counsel. Sprague and Gonzales fought over funding and investigative methods, and both of them wound up resigning. Representative Louis Stokes (D-Ohio) took over as chairman, and Robert Blakey, a Justice Department lawyer who specialized in organized crime and had been close to Robert Kennedy, was appointed chief counsel. The HSCA was to investigate the assassinations of both JFK and Martin Luther King Jr.

In the early stages of its investigation, the HSCA met with several of the prominent critics of the Warren Commission. Independent researcher Mary Ferrell told the Committee that she had located a copy of the Dictabelt recording of the Dallas Police Department radio traffic from November 22, 1963. Apparently, this tape contained the entire shot sequence at Dealey Plaza, as a police officer had mistakenly keyed his microphone and left it in the on position.

The original Dictabelt recording had languished in a locked file cabinet in the Dallas Police Department, which thought that the sequence recorded by the open microphone had been at another location minutes after the assassination and therefore had no evidentiary value. The HSCA located the original Dictabelt and submitted it to Bolt, Beranek and Newman (BBN), a team of acoustic experts who identified four separate sound impulses, which are not audible when one listens to the recording. The experts concluded that these four sound impulses were rifle shots.

To determine if these sound impulses were gunshots and where they might have originated, Bolt, Beranek, and Newman performed a reenactment on August 20, 1978. They placed microphones every eighteen feet in thirty-six locations throughout Dealey Plaza and had sharpshooters fire Mannlicher-Carcanos from the southeast-corner, sixth-floor window of the Texas School Book Depository and behind the stockade fence above the grassy knoll (where a pistol was also fired) to see if they could match the sound impulses and echo patterns they found on the Dictabelt recording. According to BBN's analysis of the reenactment, the first, second, and fourth shots were fired from the Texas School Book Depository. And there was a 50 percent chance that the third shot had been fired from behind the grassy knoll.

This made the HSCA rethink the entire shot sequence. The Committee investigators timed the Dictabelt recording against the Zapruder film, starting from frame 313 as the last shot in the four-shot sequence and counting backwards. (They also tried with frame 313 as the third shot, but that didn't work, since it contradicted the evidence that the fatal wound was fired from the right rear.) According to the HSCA's new scenario, the first shot was fired from the Texas School Book Depository at frame 160, missing the limousine and its occupants entirely. The second shot was fired from the Texas School Book Depository at frame 190, wounding both Kennedy and Connally. The third shot was fired from the grassy knoll at frame 297, missing the limousine and its occupants entirely. Then at frame 313, the head shot that killed President Kennedy was fired from the Texas School Book Depository.

Seeking corroboration for this shot sequence from the Zapruder film, HSCA medical and photographic experts closely examined the film for "jiggle analysis" and signs of "severe external stress" exhibited by the two victims.

Jiggle analysis was based on the conclusion that blurred sequences in the film were the result of Abraham Zapruder's reacting to the sound of a gunshot and jiggling the camera. There are a handful of blurred sequences, some of them lasting for several frames. The HSCA found jiggle at the frames corresponding to their timing of the shot sequence, even though they admitted the limits of their own conclusions: "The possibility that other blurs on the film might be attributable to Zapruder's reactions to gunshots could not be confirmed or dismissed without additional data." Indeed, the blurred sequences might or might not have had anything to do with the gunshots. Zapruder's camera had a tendency to expose some frames of film farther away from the aperture, resulting in a blurred image. Also, Zapruder, who suffered from vertigo, had his secretary stand close to steady him. He could have jiggled the camera before or after the gunshots or in reaction to echoes bouncing across Dealey Plaza.

The HSCA also found signs of severe external stress that appeared to corroborate the new shot sequence. In frames 162 to 167, Governor Connally moves his head from left to right. At frame 200, President Kennedy stops waving, and over the next two frames his head moves rapidly to the left. (Also, according to the HSCA, Kennedy and Connally's bodies were aligned in such a way as to make the single bullet trajectory possible.) There was no visual corroboration necessary for the grassy knoll at frame 297, since the shot missed. And the head shot at frame 313 was a visible hit.

Hoping to find other corroborating evidence, the HSCA subjected all the photographs taken at Dealey Plaza to intense scrutiny—and in many cases, enhancement—to see if they could find any evidence of a gunman on the grassy knoll. They found nothing.

A lack of corroborative evidence was not the only problem with the HSCA's revised shot sequence. If the acoustic evidence was valid, then the first and second shots were only 1.66 seconds apart. Warren Commission ballistics expert Robert Frazier had testified that it took 2.3 seconds to load, aim, and fire the C2766 Mannlicher-Carcano.

HSCA chief counsel Robert Blakey conducted a test in which

Washington, D.C., police marksmen fired a Mannlicher-Carcano (the C2766 was in poor condition and could not be used) at targets placed 143, 165, and 266 feet away. They found that they could fire more accurately and more rapidly using the open iron sights rather than a four-power scope. (The marksman firing at Dealey Plaza during the acoustics reenactment had used the open iron sights and had no problem hitting the sandbags positioned on Elm Street.) None of the D.C. sharpshooters could fire more quickly than 2.1 seconds between shots. Finally, Blakey and his assistant counsel, Gary Cornwell, each took the weapon and fired by point aiming. Cornwell was able to fire two shots within 1.2 seconds. Blakey was able to fire two shots in 1.5 seconds. Even though all shots missed their targets, Blakey was satisfied that their test proved two accurate shots were possible within 1.66 seconds.

Also, the revised shot sequence appeared to contradict earlier assumptions concerning the availability of the target. The Secret Service, and later the Warren Commission, had determined that the live oak tree at the east end of Elm Street had obscured Kennedy from the shooter's sight between Zapruder frames 166 and 207, with only a small window of availability around frames 185 and 186. If the shot was fired from the sniper's nest at frame 190, the target would have been almost completely obscured by the tree. The earlier shot, at frame 160, would have been taken before the target was even available to the shooter, according to the Warren Commission's reenactment, where Kennedy's stand-in was not visible until frame 161. Even if the shooter fired anticipating his target, the tree was not yet in the way, and he would be firing down onto the limousine. How could he have missed the limousine and all its occupants?

Prior to the August 20 reenactment, the HSCA had hired another group of experts, Mark Weiss and Ernest Aschkenasy of Queens College, to independently review BBN's acoustical data. After BBN presented its conclusions from the reenactment, the Committee asked Weiss and Aschkenasy "if they could go beyond what [BBN] had done to determine with greater certainty if there had been a shot from the grassy knoll." Weiss and Aschkenasy examined both the Dictabelt and the reenactment data and determined within a 95 percent probability that the third shot had been fired from the grassy knoll.

The HSCA still didn't know whose radio had been keyed on. Two days before hearings were concluded, they brought in H. B. McLain as a witness. McLain was a Dallas motor officer who had been riding to the left of the vice presidential limousine. After his location in the motorcade was established as conforming to the estimated location of the open microphone that recorded sound impulses during the reenactment found to be similar to those on the Dictabelt, McClain was asked if his microphone had been stuck in the on position that day.

MR. MCCLAIN: Not that I know of.

MR. CORNWELL: Do you know whether or not it would have been possible for your microphone to have been stuck in the open position without your knowledge?

MR. MCCLAIN: Yes, sir; it has before.

McLain said that shortly after the shots were fired, he heard Chief Jesse Curry on the radio telling officers to proceed to Parkland Hospital. If his radio had been stuck in the on position, McClain said he would not have heard the transmission. He was asked whether it was possible that he had overheard Curry's transmission from the radio of a nearby motor officer. McClain stated that this was very possible.

When he testified, McClain hadn't heard the recording. (Preparing McClain for testimony, HSCA staff showed him photos of the motorcade, but told him he didn't need to listen to the Dictabelt.) Once he did hear the tape, McClain said it could not have been his radio transmitting, because his foot-activated siren would have been heard as soon as he accelerated, along with the rest of the motorcade as it rushed to Parkland Hospital. (Photographs confirm that he arrived at Parkland along with the other motor officers.) McClain also remembered hearing all the conversation on the tape, which seemed to him impossible if his microphone had been stuck.

As late as December 13 the HSCA's findings had read: "The committee finds that the available scientific evidence is insufficient to find that there was a conspiracy to assassinate President Kennedy." Everybody seemed ready to sign off on the conclusion that Lee Harvey Oswald was the assassin and that he had acted alone. The forensic medical panel had endorsed the single bullet theory. The HSCA had determined that the autopsy photographs and X-rays were authentic, as were the backyard photographs. The

Committee had disproved several specific conspiracy theories, and it had found no evidence that anyone other than Lee Harvey Oswald was involved.

On December 29, the acoustics evidence was presented as Weiss, Aschkenasy, and McLain all testified in open hearings. The Committee had to scrap its original findings draft, and on the same day, after a long debate that did not satisfy all the Committee members, it approved a nine-page summary of the essential findings and then adjourned. When the HSCA findings were published on July 17, 1979, they stated:

> Scientific acoustical evidence establishes a high probability that two gunmen fired at President John F. Kennedy. Other scientific evidence does not preclude the possibility of two gunmen firing at the President.... The committee believes, on the basis of the evidence available to it, that President John F. Kennedy was probably assassinated as a result of a conspiracy. The committee was unable to identify the other gunman or the extent of the conspiracy.

Despite its belief in a conspiracy, the HSCA had not changed its opinion concerning Oswald's responsibility for the President's death.

A. Lee Harvey Oswald fired three shots at President John F. Kennedy. The second and third shots he fired struck the President. The third shot he fired killed the President.
  1. President Kennedy was struck by two rifle shots fired from behind him.
  2. The shots that struck President Kennedy from behind him were fired from the sixth-floor window of the southeast corner of the Texas School Book Depository building.
  3. Lee Harvey Oswald owned the rifle that was used to fire the shots from the sixth-floor window of the southeast corner of the Texas School Book Depository building.
  4. Lee Harvey Oswald, shortly before the assassination, had access to and was present on the sixth floor of the Texas School Book Depository building.
  5. Lee Harvey Oswald's other actions tend to support the conclusion that he assassinated President Kennedy.

So who were Oswald's co-conspirators? The HSCA stated that while it believed that anti-Castro Cubans and the Mafia, as groups, were not involved in President Kennedy's assassination, "the available evidence does not preclude the possibility that individual members [of both groups] may have been involved."

Several Committee members dissented from the findings. Christopher Dodd (D-Conn.) had a problem with the timing of the shots. If the acoustics evidence was valid and the first and second shots were 1.66 seconds apart, Dodd asked, how could Oswald have fired them? He suggested that perhaps the grassy knoll shooter had fired the second shot and that the acoustics experts were wrong in locating it as originating from the Texas School Book Depository. Dodd remained convinced that there was a conspiracy and a shooter on the grassy knoll, but he wanted the acoustics evidence studied more closely. Samuel Devine (R-Ohio) and Robert Edgar (D-Penn.) both felt that the acoustics evidence was not enough to support a "high probability of a conspiracy." Harold Sawyer (R-Mich.) stated his belief that "there are far too few, if any, established or verified facts in this entire acoustical scenario." In his dissent, Sawyer pointed out that Weiss and Aschkenasy's contribution to the evidence was a series of mathematical computations based upon Dr. James Barger's earlier givens, most notably the location of the open microphone based on the reenactment. Barger, who worked for BBN, in turn, endorsed Weiss and Aschkenasy's finding of a 95 percent probability of a grassy knoll gunman. Sawyer described the acoustics findings as "three experts who were all in agreement with each other, one of whom had somewhat inexplicably drastically modified his earlier testimony to conform with that of the other two on the basis of merely an exercise in mathematics."

Acknowledging that its investigation had left some important questions unanswered, the HSCA asked the Justice Department to continue the investigation into President Kennedy's assassination.

Since the Dictabelt analysis was the only evidence indicating a conspiracy, the Justice Department's investigation began and ended with two scientific reevaluations of the acoustics studies and the original recording. First the FBI found, in a report issued December 1, 1980, that the evidence presented to the HSCA "did not scientifically prove that the Dictabelt recording...contains the sounds of gunshots or any other sounds originating in Dealey Plaza."

Around the same time that the FBI report was being prepared for release, the National Academy of Sciences appointed a panel of twelve scientists, formally titled the National Research Council Committee on Ballistics Acoustics but commonly known as the Ramsey Panel, for its chairman, Norman Ramsey of Harvard. After two years of study, the Ramsey Panel found the HSCA work "seriously flawed."

According to the Ramsey Panel, the HSCA experts did not demonstrate that there had been a grassy knoll shot, and they also found that there was "no acoustic basis" for their claim of a 95 percent probability of that shot. The sound impulses that the experts identified as gunshots were located on a portion of the Dictabelt that was recorded after the assassination had already taken place.

"In some of these analyses," the panel concluded, "desirable control tests were omitted, some of the analyses depended on subjective selection of data, serious errors were made in some of the statistical calculations, incorrect statistical conclusions were drawn and analysis methods used were novel in some aspects."

The panel examined the theory first proposed by Ohio rock drummer Steve Barber, who had spent hours listening to a record of the Dictabelt transmission he got in *Gallery* magazine. Barber heard cross-talk on the recording that indicated the section of the tape under consideration was recorded several minutes after the assassination. The Ramsey Panel found that Barber was correct. The cross-talk proved conclusively that the Dictabelt segment had been recorded after the assassination, most probably by a motor officer waiting at the Dallas Trade Mart. The Ramsey Panel acknowledged that further studies could be performed but argued against them, since the evidence against a grassy knoll shot "is already so strong that the Committee believes the results to be expected from such studies would not justify their cost."

Since the Ramsey Panel report was issued, independent studies have both confirmed the HSCA's acoustics experts and contradicted them. The results of a new round of government-sponsored tests on the acoustics evidence had not been made public when this book went to press.

James Bowles was the Dallas police communications supervisor in charge of the Dictabelt recordings in 1963. He listened to and transcribed the original tapes before turning them over to the FBI. Bowles, who went on to become sheriff of Dallas County, did not hear any shots on the tapes. He described the sound impressions found by the HSCA experts as "super-sonic," meaning that they were impressions that did not register any sound. And he said that such impressions were found throughout the Dictabelt, a fact the HSCA experts admitted. This caused Bowles to wonder why they selected four of these impressions and decided they were gunshots. Gunshots were often heard on police radio recordings, and they were easily heard and recognizable as gunshots. Indeed, the reenactment gunshots, according to Bowles, sounded like gunshots, not the inaudible sound impressions that they were matched to by the HSCA experts. Bowles felt that it was much more likely that these sounds were artifacts created by the stylus being placed onto the fragile Dictabelt, quite possibly by the FBI when it first attempted to transcribe the radio traffic of that day, prior to returning it to Bowles. (The feds could not make sense of much of the police jargon used over the radio.)

The HSCA conspiracy scenario stands or falls on the accuracy of its acoustics evidence. Robert Blakey himself told a journalist, "If the acoustics come out that we made a mistake somewhere, I think that would end [talk of a conspiracy in the case]." *

I can't say which side is right on the science, but the only possible cor-roborating evidence I can find are the earwitness reports. Twelve percent of the 178 witnesses at Dealey Plaza reported hearing shots fired from the direction of the grassy knoll (28 percent identified the Texas School Book Depository at the source of the shots). Nearly half (44 percent) could not determine the source of the shots. The vast majority of earwitnesses reported hearing three shots (88 percent, according to Gerald Posner, and 83 percent according to Josiah Thompson).

Dr. David Green, a consultant for BBN, conducted a separate test during the HSCA reenactment to evaluate the accuracy of earwitness reports of source direction for the gunshots in Dealey Plaza. Two sound experts were blindfolded and asked to locate the direction of the shots fired from both the Texas School Book Depository and the grassy knoll. The experts were able to correctly identify the source direction of 90 percent of the shots. Of

*Gerald Posner, *Case Closed: Lee Harvey Oswald and the Assassination of JFK* (New York: Random House, 1993), p. 457 note.

course, they were expecting the shots and knew they were coming from only two directions. As a result, Green concluded, "It is difficult to draw any firm conclusions relative to the reports of witnesses in the plaza as to the possible locus of the assassin." Green also stated, "It is hard to believe a rifle was fired from the knoll," since such a shot would be easy to localize.

If there had been a shot from behind the grassy knoll, it would have been heard clearly by the witnesses, and the shooter would have been seen immediately after the shot was fired, if not before. Even shots fired from the sixth floor of the Texas School Book Depository, sixty feet above the street and hundreds of feet away from the witnesses, were easy for many earwitnesses to localize and led to several eyewitness observations of a man holding a rifle.

For earwitnesses farther away from the source of a gunshot, Dealey Plaza can be an acoustical echo chamber. Sounds bounce off the large buildings to the north and east and echo toward the open spaces to the south and west. Looking at the location of witnesses and their reports concerning the source of gunfire, we see that most witnesses citing the Texas School Book Depository as the source were near that building, while the grassy knoll witnesses were closer to the other end of Dealey Plaza. This observation tends to support the conclusion that grassy knoll witnesses were hearing echoes. It could also explain why some witnesses (fewer than 5 percent) reported hearing four or more shots and why four witnesses thought the shots came from more than one location.

When considering earwitness reports, we must keep in mind exactly what the witnesses are saying. Determining the source direction of gunshots is not a direct observation. It is something more like a guess based on certain impressions and experience. And since it does not imprint on the mind like visual observation, witness reports of sounds are even more subject to variation over time, especially in a dramatic public event like the assassination of a president.

That's not to say that earwitness reports should be ignored or discounted. They should be given their proper weight and considered in the context of other evidence. The HSCA set up its acoustics reenactment with one shooter behind the grassy knoll, because of earwitness statements (and the persistent belief among critics that this was a shooter's location). Once the data were analyzed, they appeared to support the theory of a grassy knoll shooter. Did the acoustical analysis actually test the hypothesis or simply attempt to confirm it? To me, the acoustic evidence and the earwitness statements are not independent of each other, and therefore not corroborative.

None of the original witness statements report seeing a suspect with a weapon behind the stockade fence. Those witnesses whose stories have improved over time are simply not credible. And the few credible eyewitness reports of something behind the stockade fence ("a puff of smoke" or "some kind of commotion") are much less powerful than the combined and corroborated testimony of the eyewitnesses seeing and hearing the shots from the direction of the Texas School Book Depository, along with the ballistics evidence collected from the sixth floor of that building and the medical evidence that both Kennedy and Connally were shot only from the right rear.

If you're still not convinced, visit Dealey Plaza and walk around. Everything is still there, except that the foliage has grown thicker and the Stemmons Freeway sign has been moved. The parking lot behind the stockade fence above the grassy knoll is visible from several positions all over the Plaza. If a gunman had been standing behind the fence, he would have been clearly visible to eyewitnesses. Someone would have seen him, and his form would be readily apparent (not some blur) in photographs taken during the assassination. Abraham Zapruder himself was just fifteen to twenty feet away from where the gunman was supposed to be standing. From their position on top of the short wall, Zapruder and his secretary, Marilyn Sitzman, could look over the fence into the parking lot. Several other witnesses were nearby. I find it difficult to believe that a gunman could have set up behind the fence, fired at least one shot, and gotten away without being apprehended or at least photographed.

The grassy knoll is a terrible position for a sniper. He would have been low, with a bad angle toward the target. His only shot opportunity would have been when the limousine crossed directly in front of him. If he had shot earlier, he would have struck the windshield and probably one of the other passengers. Even if successful with this one shot, his exposed location and proximity to witnesses would have made it highly probable that he would be observed, photographed, and apprehended.

The HSCA acoustics evidence and the Committee's grassy knoll scenario raise the following questions:

1. Why would conspirators wanting to frame someone in the Texas School Book Depository shoot Kennedy from another direction?
2. Why not use a silencer?
3. Why choose a location where the gunman could fire only one shot?
4. Why choose a location where the gunman could be easily observed?
5. Why were no bullets, fragments, or spent cartridges found?
6. How could the gunman miss not only President Kennedy but the limousine and everybody else in the line of fire?

Often forgotten in the debate over the acoustics evidence is the fact that the HSCA endorsed many of the Warren Commission's most controversial findings, including the strange trajectory of the Magic Bullet. If there is any hard evidence of a conspiracy in the JFK assassination, it is Commission exhibit 399.

CHAPTER 10

The Magic Bullet

CERTAIN PIECES of evidence defy explanation (like the acoustics evidence). Other pieces of evidence demand explanation. You cannot solve the JFK assassination without accounting for Commission exhibit 399, the Magic Bullet—where it came from, what it did, and how it ended up where it was found. I would even argue that this bullet is the only piece of evidence that demands such attention.

Sometimes one piece of evidence is enough to solve a murder. The bloody glove I found behind the guest cottage on O. J. Simpson's Rockingham estate, which contained the blood of both victims as well as that of Simpson himself, is one example. Account for that evidence, and you solve the case. In the JFK assassination, the Magic Bullet proves either that Lee Harvey Oswald shot President Kennedy and Governor Connally or that he was framed by a larger conspiracy. With the stakes so high, it's no wonder that every detail about this bullet is hotly contested, beginning with its discovery on a stretcher in Parkland Hospital.

When the limousine arrived at the hospital, Governor Connally was put on a stretcher and wheeled into trauma room 2, directly across the hall from trauma room 1, where President Kennedy was taken.

Once it was determined that he should go into surgery, Connally was taken to operating room 5 on the second floor. There Connally was transferred onto the operating table, and the stretcher was wheeled out and left in the elevator. Shortly after 1:00 P.M., Darrell Tomlinson, the hospital's senior engineer, went to the vestibule to answer a call for someone to operate the elevator. He saw a stretcher inside the elevator and wheeled it out, pushing it against the wall on the first floor. At that time he noticed a second stretcher nearby. Sometime later, when Tomlinson returned to the vestibule, he saw one of the stretchers blocking the entrance to the elevator, so he pushed it back against the wall. When the stretcher hit the wall, a bullet rolled out from beneath the mattress. Tomlinson notified O. P. Wright, chief of security for Parkland Hospital, who came and viewed the bullet with Tomlinson. Wright contacted an FBI agent, who refused to take custody of the bullet. Wright then found Secret Service agent Richard Johnsen, who put the bullet in his pocket and later gave it to his boss, James Rowley, along with a written report stating approximately where and when the bullet was discovered and noting: "It could not be determined who had used this stretcher or if President Kennedy had occupied it." Rowley gave the bullet to the FBI, which maintained control of it during the investigation.

The assumption that this bullet came from President Kennedy lasted until the day after the autopsy, when Commander James Humes spoke with Dr. Malcolm Perry and discovered that the tracheotomy had been cut into an existing bullet wound, which Humes then concluded had been caused by the exit of the bullet that entered Kennedy's back.

At Parkland Hospital, the President had remained on his stretcher, heavily stained with blood and tissue, until death was pronounced. Then he was placed in a coffin procured from a local funeral home. The coffin containing the President's body was driven from Parkland Hospital to Love Field, where it was placed on Air Force One and taken back to Washington.

Although Tomlinson's testimony to the Warren Commission shows some confusion, on either his part or on the part of Arlen Specter, who was examining the witness, it is clear that the bullet did not come from Kennedy's stretcher, which had been stripped and cleaned shortly after his body was removed and was never in the elevator or first-floor vestibule between Kennedy's arrival and the discovery of the bullet.

The chain of custody was less than ideal, and the general handling of this important piece of evidence was sloppy. But does this invalidate

Commission exhibit 399 as evidence? Not at all. In a court of law, the defense might argue that should it be excluded as evidence (and they might win). However, when a detective is trying to solve a murder, the exclusionary rule does not apply. Evidence is not always found by detectives or police officers. Often it is discovered by civilians who do not have training in evidence handling or crime-scene protection. Even cops can mishandle evidence, whether through negligence, inattention, or simple unawareness of its presence. As a result, much evidence is walked over, kicked, played with, sat on, or in some way compromised long before anyone realizes its value. When these mistakes are made, it's much better to document the discovery of evidence and chain of custody honestly rather than try to "clean up" any problems along the way. Any attempt to ignore links in the chain of custody or gloss over the mishandling of evidence is flirting with disaster. Often the fear of suspicion creates suspicion, and cops who cover up innocent mistakes, like routine mishandling of evidence, later find themselves accused of not-so-innocent things like planting evidence.

Before we get to the question of whether or not the bullet was planted, first let's assume it's a valid piece of evidence and see what connection it might have with the crime.

The bullet in question is an expended 6.5-millimeter, copper-jacketed, lead-core bullet. It was fired from the C2766 Mannlicher-Carcano found on the sixth floor of the Texas School Book Depository. The tests matching this bullet to that rifle were conducted first by the FBI and then reconfirmed by the HSCA firearms panel. By neutron activation analysis, the bullet was matched not only to the C2766 Mannlicher-Carcano but also to the bullet found in the chamber of that rifle and the three empty cartridges recov-

CE 399, the Magic Bullet.
Courtesy of National Archives.

The Magic Bullet viewed from the rear. *Courtesy of National Archives.*

ered from the floor nearby. Those bullets were all from the same manufacturer and lot number, as were the large fragments recovered from the presidential limousine. The fragments were also 6.5-millimeter Mannlicher-Carcano bullets, yet differences in metallic composition proved that Commission exhibit 399 was not the source of the fragments. Mohair wool fibers embedded in its base were found to be microscopically consistent with mohair wool fibers taken from Governor Connally's suit and the wound in his wrist. Several lead fragments retrieved from Governor Connally's wrist were determined, by neutron activation analysis, to match the lead core from the base of the Magic Bullet.

At first glance, the bullet appears almost intact, aside from a small piece of copper taken from its nose by the FBI for comparison tests. Turning the bullet over and examining it from back to front, however, you see that the lead core has extruded from the bullet's base and lost some of its mass. Also, the missile has been flattened and is slightly bent.

Even with the damage to the bullet's base and lead core, it looks remarkably undeformed considering all the wounds it was alleged to have caused.

1. It entered Kennedy's upper back, passed through his neck, and exited just below his Adam's apple.
2. It entered Connally's back, shattered his fifth rib, collapsed his right lung, exited just below his right nipple, entered his right wrist, fractured his radius, exited the wrist, and lodged superficially in his left thigh.

WHY IS COMMISSION EXHIBIT 399 SO IMPORTANT?

1. The bullet is a highly identifiable piece of evidence that was ballistically connected to the C2766 Mannlicher-Carcano discovered on the sixth floor of the Texas School Book Depository and proved to be owned by Lee Harvey Oswald.

2. The bullet points to Oswald as the lone assassin. Two other bullet fragments found in the limousine are found to be similar in composition. They are both fragments from 6.5 Mannlicher-Carcano Western cartridges. Together, these fragments do not weigh enough to account for an entire second bullet, but it has been determined that they came from the same bullet. There was only evidence of two bullets (the Magic Bullet and the fragments) recovered from either the limousine or the victims.

3. Since the bullet was reportedly discovered on Connally's stretcher and bullet fragments from Kennedy's head wound were matched ballistically to the same gun that fired it, this bullet links Oswald, the sniper's nest, the rifle, and both victims.

This is the single bullet theory—the controversial hypothesis that both Kennedy and Connally were shot by the same bullet, Commission exhibit 399. If the single bullet theory is not confirmed by the evidence, many believe, Oswald could not have been the lone gunman.

The single bullet theory was born of a necessity that early investigators had not even considered. As a result of their initial inquiries, both the FBI and Secret Service had separately concluded that the assassin fired three shots: the first hit Kennedy in the upper back, the second caused all of Connally's wounds, and the third caused Kennedy's fatal head wound.

The Warren Commission decided that, "for the sake of the historical record," it needed to be more precise about the shot sequence. Commission staffers Norman Redlich, Melvin Eisenberg, and Arlen Specter, along with FBI agents Lyndal Shaneyfelt (a photographic expert) and Leo Gauthier (a visual aids expert) and Secret Service inspector Thomas Kelley, examined the Zapruder film together on January 27, 1964. They watched the film several times and also examined it frame by frame. As a result of this viewing, investigators concluded that the visible reactions of Kennedy and Connally appeared too close together in time to have been caused by two bullets fired from the Mannlicher-Carcano.

The FBI calculated that the Zapruder film ran at an average speed of 18.3 frames per second. (This was later independently confirmed by Bell Howell labs.) On the film, Kennedy is obscured by the Stemmons Freeway sign for a period of about thirteen frames (210 to 223). When Kennedy emerges from behind the sign at frame 224, he is already reacting to his first wound. His shoulders hunch forward and his hands rise toward his throat.

At this time, Governor Connally does not appear to be injured. In fact, there is no visible indication that Connally has been shot until frame 237, some seven-tenths of a second later, when his shoulder buckles, his hair is disheveled, his mouth opens, and he appears to be gasping for breath. (Please refer to the color reproductions of Zapruder frames 224 and 237 in the center of this book.)

Was it possible that Kennedy had been shot earlier than frame 224 and therefore hit by a separate bullet than the one that wounded Connally? The Secret Service had already reenacted the assassination in Dealey Plaza in early December 1963 and determined that an oak tree on the southeast corner of Elm Street obscured the view from the sniper's nest from frame 166 to frame 207. According to the Secret Service, the earliest that Kennedy could have been shot was frame 207. After speaking with Connally and his doctors, Warren Commission staffers decided that the latest the Governor could have been hit was frame 240. (The Governor thought it was frame 235.) Therefore, the longest possible time between shots was only thirty-three frames, or 1.8 seconds.

Since the Mannlicher-Carcano is a bolt-action rifle, the shooter has to open the bolt, pull it back, push it forward, and aim again before firing a second shot.

Could the assassin have shot both Kennedy and Connally within 1.8 seconds? This is a question the Warren Commission attempted to answer with a series of tests using FBI marksmen firing the C2766 Mannlicher-Carcano. With the first bullet already in the chamber, the marksmen fired three shots as quickly as possible. It took 4.6 seconds to 9 seconds to fire three shots. FBI agent Robert A. Frazier, who made the shots in 4.6 seconds, later testified that he achieved this result "firing this weapon as fast as the bolt can be operated." The Commission decided that it was possible to fire three bullets from the Mannlicher-Carcano in 4.6 seconds. That translated to 2.3 seconds, or forty-two frames, between each shot.

All the evidence pointed to three shots. Three empty cartridges had been found on the sixth floor of the Texas School Book Depository. According to a vast majority of the eyewitnesses, only three shots had been fired. Aside from a crack on the inside of the windshield, which was assumed to have been caused by a fragment from the head shot, and a dent in the windshield trim, which investigators weren't even certain had been caused by a bullet, there were no bullet holes or marks on the presidential limousine. Warren Commission investigators believed that if any bullet had struck the limousine or its occupants, it would have been recovered. Since the Magic Bullet and the fragments found in the limousine appeared to be from only two separate bullets, they determined that only two bullets had struck either the limousine or its occupants. If three bullets were fired, one of them must have missed the limousine entirely. They speculated that this bullet could have been deflected by a leaf or twig from the oak tree at the corner of Elm Street. Also, several eyewitnesses reported seeing a ricochet, and one of them, bystander James Tague, was wounded by what appeared to be a bullet fragment or chunk of concrete chipped off a nearby piece of curbing by an errant missile. If one shot missed and the third shot hit President Kennedy in the head, then the second shot would have had to inflict Kennedy's neck wounds and all of Connally's wounds as well.

Assistant counsel Arlen Specter, whose day job was assistant district attorney in Philadelphia, was responsible for "the facts of the assassination"—that is, everything that happened from the time of the first shot through the autopsy. His immediate superior, former New York City police commissioner Francis W. H. Adams, was busy with his own law practice, so all the work fell on Specter's shoulders. Chief Justice Earl Warren had decided that the investigation in Dallas should be held off until Jack Ruby's trial was concluded, so as not to adversely affect that procedure. As a result, Specter was not able to do much work on the shot sequence until March 15, the day after the Ruby verdict. The deadline for his chapter of the Warren Report was June 1.

Specter began by talking with the doctors who had performed Kennedy's autopsy. He told them about the closeness in time between the reactions of Kennedy and Connally. Commander James J. Humes speculated that both men could have been hit by the same bullet.

Testifying before the Commission on March 16, 1964, Humes introduced

Zapruder frame 224. *Courtesy of Sixth Floor Museum*

Zapruder frame 237. *Courtesy of Sixth Floor Museum*

Zapruder frame 238. *Courtesy of Sixth Floor Museum*

Zapruder frame 312. *Courtesy of Sixth Floor Museum*

Zapruder frame 313. *Courtesy of Sixth Floor Museum*

Zapruder frame 314. *Courtesy of Sixth Floor Museum*

Zapruder frame 315. *Courtesy of Sixth Floor Museum*

Zapruder frame 316. *Courtesy of Sixth Floor Museum*

Zapruder frame 317. *Courtesy of Sixth Floor Museum*

Zapruder frame 318. *Courtesy of Sixth Floor Museum*

Zapruder frame 319. *Courtesy of Sixth Floor Museum*

Zapruder frame 320. *Courtesy of Sixth Floor Museum*

Zapruder frame 321. *Courtesy of Sixth Floor Museum*

Zapruder frame 322. *Courtesy of Sixth Floor Museum*

Zapruder frame 323. *Courtesy of Sixth Floor Museum*

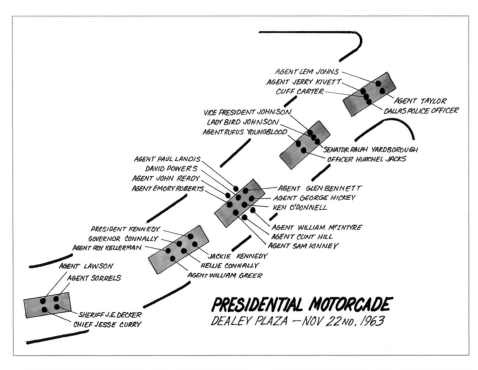

PRESIDENTIAL MOTORCADE
DEALEY PLAZA — NOV 22ND, 1963

AGENT LEM JOHNS
AGENT JERRY KIVETT
CLIFF CARTER
AGENT TAYLOR
DALLAS POLICE OFFICER

VICE PRESIDENT JOHNSON
LADY BIRD JOHNSON
AGENT RUFUS YOUNGBLOOD
SENATOR RALPH YARDBOROUGH
OFFICER HURCHEL JACKS

AGENT PAUL LANDIS
DAVID POWERS
AGENT JOHN READY
AGENT EMORY ROBERTS
AGENT GLEN BENNETT
AGENT GEORGE HICKEY
KEN O'DONNELL

PRESIDENT KENNEDY
GOVERNOR CONNALLY
AGENT ROY KELLERMAN
AGENT WILLIAM McINTYRE
AGENT CLINT HILL
AGENT SAM KINNEY

AGENT LAWSON
AGENT SORRELS
JACKIE KENNEDY
NELLIE CONNALLY
AGENT WILLIAM GREER

SHERIFF J.E. DECKER
CHIEF JESSE CURRY

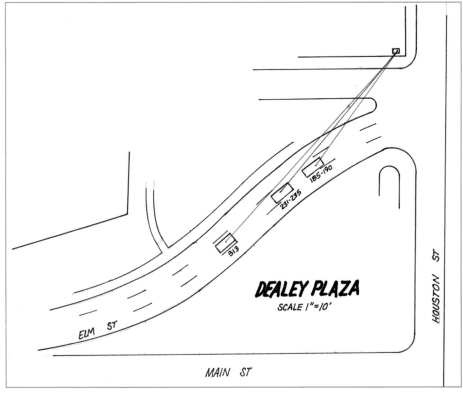

DEALEY PLAZA
SCALE 1" = 10'

ELM ST

MAIN ST

HOUSTON ST

313
231-235
185-190

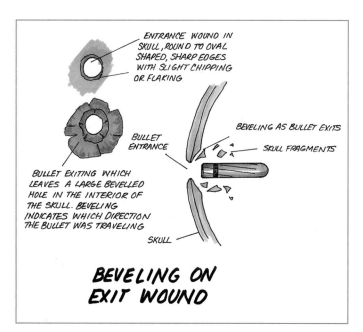

ENTRANCE WOUND IN SKULL, ROUND TO OVAL SHAPED, SHARP EDGES WITH SLIGHT CHIPPING OR FLAKING

BEVELING AS BULLET EXITS

SKULL FRAGMENTS

BULLET ENTRANCE

BULLET EXITING WHICH LEAVES A LARGE BEVELLED HOLE IN THE INTERIOR OF THE SKULL. BEVELING INDICATES WHICH DIRECTION THE BULLET WAS TRAVELING

SKULL

BEVELING ON EXIT WOUND

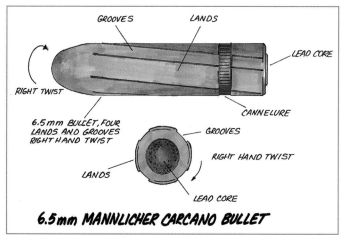

GROOVES

LANDS

LEAD CORE

RIGHT TWIST

6.5mm BULLET, FOUR LANDS AND GROOVES RIGHT HAND TWIST

CANNELURE

GROOVES

RIGHT HAND TWIST

LANDS

LEAD CORE

6.5mm MANNLICHER CARCANO BULLET

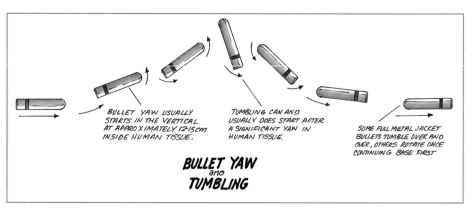

BULLET YAW USUALLY STARTS IN THE VERTICAL AT APPROXIMATELY 12-15cm INSIDE HUMAN TISSUE.

TUMBLING CAN AND USUALLY DOES START AFTER A SIGNIFICANT YAW IN HUMAN TISSUE.

SOME FULL METAL JACKET BULLETS TUMBLE OVER AND OVER, OTHERS ROTATE ONCE CONTINUING BASE FIRST

BULLET YAW and TUMBLING

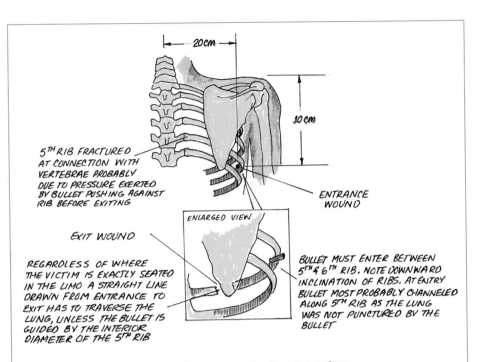

20cm

10cm

5TH RIB FRACTURED AT CONNECTION WITH VERTEBRAE PROBABLY DUE TO PRESSURE EXERTED BY BULLET PUSHING AGAINST RIB BEFORE EXITING

ENTRANCE WOUND

ENLARGED VIEW

EXIT WOUND

REGARDLESS OF WHERE THE VICTIM IS EXACTLY SEATED IN THE LIMO A STRAIGHT LINE DRAWN FROM ENTRANCE TO EXIT HAS TO TRAVERSE THE LUNG, UNLESS THE BULLET IS GUIDED BY THE INTERIOR DIAMETER OF THE 5TH RIB

BULLET MUST ENTER BETWEEN 5TH & 6TH RIB. NOTE DOWNWARD INCLINATION OF RIBS. AT ENTRY BULLET MOST PROBABLY CHANNELED ALONG 5TH RIB AS THE LUNG WAS NOT PUNCTURED BY THE BULLET

HSCA CONNALLY BULLET WOUND PLACEMENT

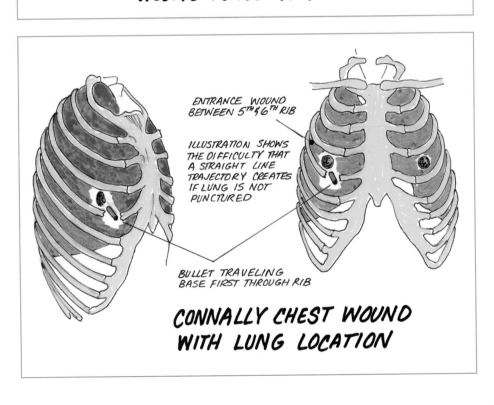

ENTRANCE WOUND BETWEEN 5TH & 6TH RIB

ILLUSTRATION SHOWS THE DIFFICULTY THAT A STRAIGHT LINE TRAJECTORY CREATES IF LUNG IS NOT PUNCTURED

BULLET TRAVELING BASE FIRST THROUGH RIB

CONNALLY CHEST WOUND WITH LUNG LOCATION

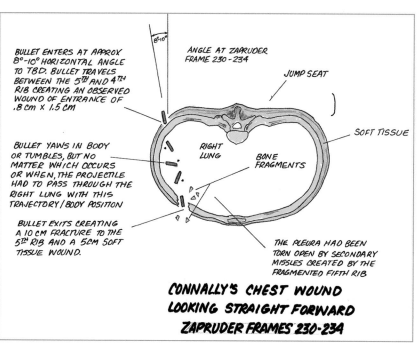

BULLET ENTERS AT APPROX
8°-10° HORIZONTAL ANGLE
TO TBD. BULLET TRAVELS
BETWEEN THE 5TH AND 4TH
RIB CREATING AN OBSERVED
WOUND OF ENTRANCE OF
.8 CM x 1.5 CM

8°-10°

ANGLE AT ZAPRUDER
FRAME 230-234

JUMP SEAT

SOFT TISSUE

BULLET YAWS IN BODY
OR TUMBLES, BUT NO
MATTER WHICH OCCURS
OR WHEN, THE PROJECTILE
HAD TO PASS THROUGH THE
RIGHT LUNG WITH THIS
TRAJECTORY/BODY POSITION

RIGHT
LUNG

BONE
FRAGMENTS

BULLET EXITS CREATING
A 10 CM FRACTURE TO THE
5TH RIB AND A 5CM SOFT
TISSUE WOUND.

THE PLEURA HAD BEEN
TORN OPEN BY SECONDARY
MISSLES CREATED BY THE
FRAGMENTED FIFTH RIB

**CONNALLY'S CHEST WOUND
LOOKING STRAIGHT FORWARD
ZAPRUDER FRAMES 230-234**

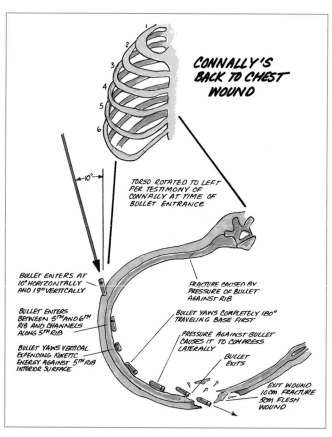

**CONNALLY'S
BACK TO CHEST
WOUND**

1
2
3
4
5
6

10°

TORSO ROTATED TO LEFT
PER TESTIMONY OF
CONNALLY AT TIME OF
BULLET ENTRANCE

BULLET ENTERS AT
10° HORIZONTALLY
AND 19° VERTICALLY

FRACTURE CAUSED BY
PRESSURE OF BULLET
AGAINST RIB

BULLET ENTERS
BETWEEN 5TH AND 6TH
RIB AND CHANNELS
ALONG 5TH RIB

BULLET YAWS COMPLETELY 180°
TRAVELING BASE FIRST

PRESSURE AGAINST BULLET
CAUSES IT TO COMPRESS
LATERALLY

BULLET YAWS VERTICAL
EXPENDING KINETIC
ENERGY AGAINST 5TH RIB
INTERIOR SURFACE

BULLET
EXITS

EXIT WOUND
10CM FRACTURE
5CM FLESH
WOUND

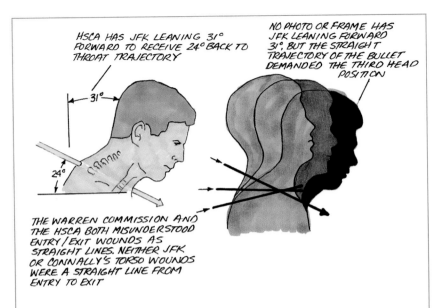

HSCA HAS JFK LEANING 31° FORWARD TO RECEIVE 24° BACK TO THROAT TRAJECTORY

31°

24°

NO PHOTO OR FRAME HAS JFK LEANING FORWARD 31°, BUT THE STRAIGHT TRAJECTORY OF THE BULLET DEMANDED THE THIRD HEAD POSITION

THE WARREN COMMISSION AND THE HSCA BOTH MISUNDERSTOOD ENTRY/EXIT WOUNDS AS STRAIGHT LINES. NEITHER JFK OR CONNALLY'S TORSO WOUNDS WERE A STRAIGHT LINE FROM ENTRY TO EXIT

HSCA DIAGRAM OF JFK HEAD POSITION AND POSSIBLE TRAJECTORY ANGLES

ARLEN SPECTER DEMONSTRATES "SINGLE BULLET" TRAJECTORY AFTER RE-ENACTMENT

CONNALLY TESTIFIED HE IS TURNING LEFT NOT RIGHT WHEN HE IS FIRST HIT

BULLET TO JFK'S BACK ENTERS AT AN ANGLE OF 18° FROM RIGHT TO LEFT NOT LEFT TO RIGHT

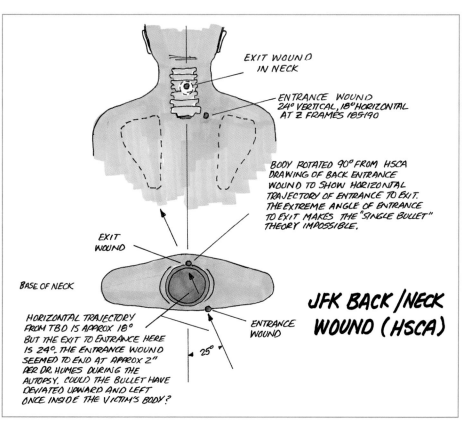

EXIT WOUND
IN NECK

ENTRANCE WOUND
24° VERTICAL, 18° HORIZONTAL
AT 2 FRAMES 185-190

BODY ROTATED 90° FROM HSCA
DRAWING OF BACK ENTRANCE
WOUND TO SHOW HORIZONTAL
TRAJECTORY OF ENTRANCE TO EXIT.
THE EXTREME ANGLE OF ENTRANCE
TO EXIT MAKES THE "SINGLE BULLET"
THEORY IMPOSSIBLE.

EXIT
WOUND

BASE OF NECK

HORIZONTAL TRAJECTORY
FROM TBD IS APPROX 18°
BUT THE EXIT TO ENTRANCE HERE
IS 24°. THE ENTRANCE WOUND
SEEMED TO END AT APPROX 2"
PER DR. HUMES DURING THE
AUTOPSY. COULD THE BULLET HAVE
DEVIATED UPWARD AND LEFT
ONCE INSIDE THE VICTIM'S BODY?

25°

ENTRANCE
WOUND

JFK BACK / NECK WOUND (HSCA)

PLACING CONNALLY
EXTREMELY TO THE LEFT
COULD SOLVE THE ALIGNMENT
HORIZONTALLY IF CONNALLY
IS TURNING TO THE LEFT
NOT RIGHT

ENTRANCE
WOUND

ANGLE OF BULLET
HORIZONTALLY

WARREN COMMISSION SEATING POSITIONS

JFK IS PLACED FAR TO THE
RIGHT. EVEN WITH THE
GENEROUS PLACEMENT OF
THE VICTIMS THE "SINGLE BULLET"
TRAJECTORY DOES NOT ALIGN
VERTICALLY AND HORIZONTALLY

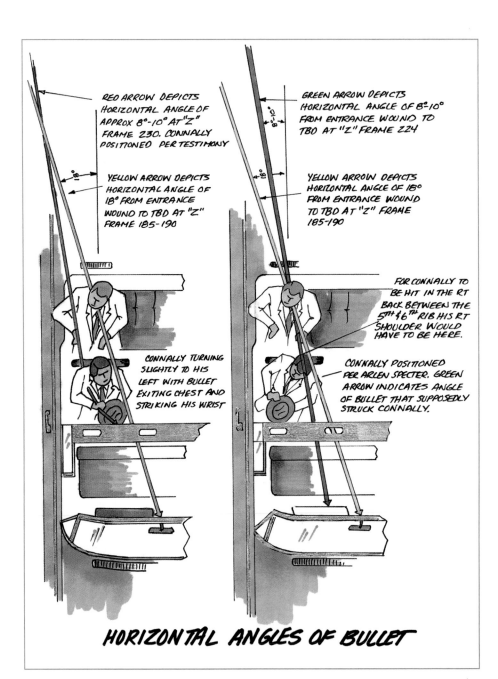

HORIZONTAL ANGLES OF BULLET

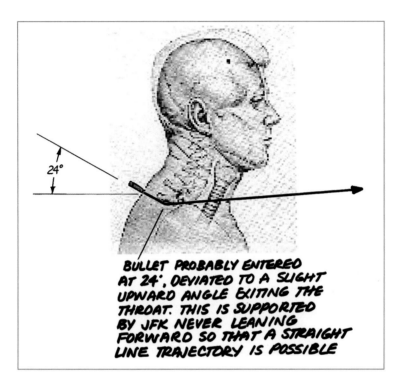

BULLET PROBABLY ENTERED
AT 24°. DEVIATED TO A SLIGHT
UPWARD ANGLE EXITING THE
THROAT. THIS IS SUPPORTED
BY JFK NEVER LEANING
FORWARD SO THAT A STRAIGHT
LINE TRAJECTORY IS POSSIBLE

FROM THE TIME THE MOTORCADE
TURNS FROM HOUSTON ONTO ELM
JFK IS SEATED AS IN THIS
ILLUSTRATION. THE FIRST SHOT AT
"Z" FRAME 185-190, AT NO TIME
DOES JFK LEAN 31° FORWARD

CONNALLY IS SEATED PRIOR
TO THE FIRST SHOT AS
DEPICTED BELOW EXCEPT HE
IS HOLDING HIS HAT IN HIS
RIGHT HAND.

SEAT AND BODY POSITIONS AT "Z" 185-190

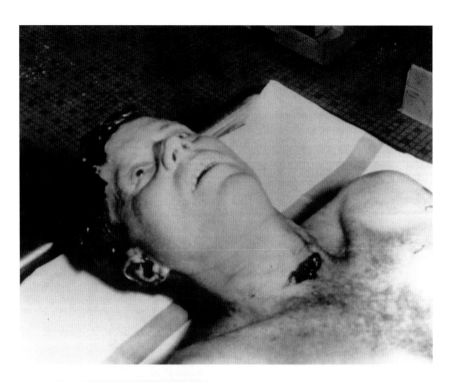

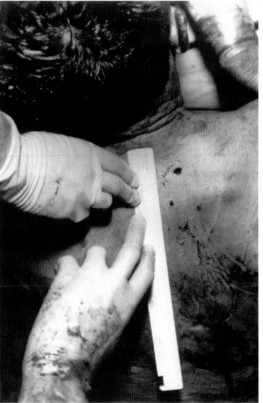

While some critics claim that these photographs from Kennedy's autopsy have been altered, they correspond to the medical evidence, sworn testimony, and the HSCA artist's renditions of Kennedy's wounds. This photograph shows the exit wound in Kennedy's throat that had been widened into a tracheotomy incision at Parkland Hospital.

The rear entry wound in Kennedy's upper back is considerably lower than originally described by the Warren Commission. The bullet had to travel in a slightly upward overall trajectory to exit beneath his Adam's apple, meaning it was deflected or yawed within his body. Note how the rear of his head is intact.

The massive trauma to the right of Kennedy's skull is evident in the photographs to the right and below. A flap of scalp hanging down in the rear might have led some doctors at Parkland Hospital to describe the trauma as located in the back of the head. This was the only position in which most doctors at Parkland saw Kennedy.

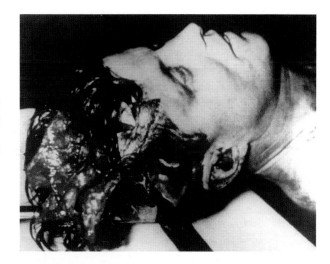

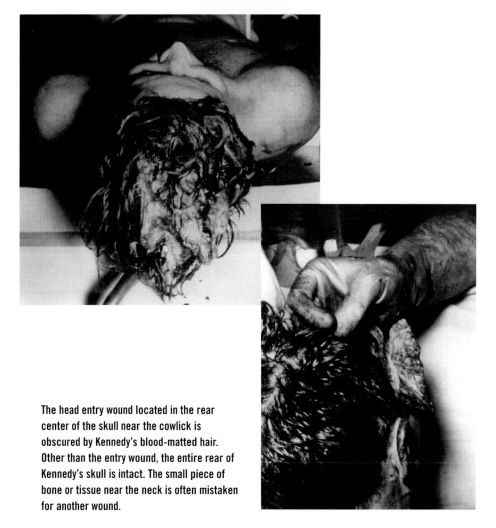

The head entry wound located in the rear center of the skull near the cowlick is obscured by Kennedy's blood-matted hair. Other than the entry wound, the entire rear of Kennedy's skull is intact. The small piece of bone or tissue near the neck is often mistaken for another wound.

In James Altgens's photograph taken just after the second shot, the windshield is undamaged.
AP/WideWorld Photos

Altgens's next photograph, taken just after the third shot, shows that the windshield is cracked.
AP/WideWorld Photos

the single bullet theory into the public record. When Humes told the Commission that the bullet entering Kennedy's back had apparently exited from his throat, Specter said, "That is the subject of some theories I am about to get into. That is an elusive subject, but Dr. Humes has some views on it."

Later on in his testimony, Humes stated, looking at a still photo of Zapruder frame 230, "I see that Governor Connally is sitting directly in front of the late President, and suggest the possibility that this missile, having traversed the low neck of the late President, in fact traversed the chest of Governor Connally."

Kennedy's autopsy had been Commander Humes's first medico-legal forensic examination. He had not even seen Connally's wounds but only reviewed reports from Parkland Hospital. Yet his theory appeared to solve the timing problem that Arlen Specter had been wrestling with ever since viewing the Zapruder film in January.

Still, the theory raised a troubling question: if a single bullet hit both Kennedy and Connally, why didn't the two men show visible reactions at the same time? Even at a diminished velocity, after passing through Kennedy's back and throat, the bullet would still have been traveling some 1,700 to 1,900 feet per second (according to Specter's estimates). At this speed, it would cross the twenty-four inches between the men in less than a single Zapruder frame. Why did Connally show no reaction until more than a second later?

Was it possible, Specter asked Humes, that the bullet hit Connally without his immediately knowing it? He responded:

I believe so. I have heard reports, and have been told by my professional associates of any number of instances where people received penetrating wounds in various portions of the body and have only the sensation of a slight discomfort or slight slap or some minor difficulty from such a missile wound. I am sure he would be aware that something happened to him, but that he was shot, I am not certain.

When Governor Connally testified before the Commission on April 22, he appeared to contradict Humes's speculation. Connally described hearing the first shot, and then following a "very, very brief span of time," feeling a second shot "like someone had hit me in the back." How did Connally know it was the second shot that hit him? Because he heard the first shot, and the last, but he didn't hear the one that wounded him. Knowing that a rifle bullet travels faster than the speed of sound, Connally concluded that he was hit by the bullet before the sound of the gunshot reached him. Therefore, he must have been struck by the second shot. Prior to his testimony, Connally viewed the Zapruder film along with his wife and Texas attorney general Waggoner Carr. Upon viewing both the film and individual slides, Connally decided he was hit at frame 231. The vividness with which he described the pain of being hit—"as if someone doubled his fist and . . . hit you right in the back"— and his doctor's description of a shattered rib and sucking chest wound made it seem unlikely that Connally would have had a delayed reaction.

Nellie Connally's testimony was even more emphatic. Seated in the driver's side jump seat, she actually saw the President react to his first wound before she saw her husband shot. When Specter asked at which Zapruder frame she believed her husband was shot, Mrs. Connally estimated it to be frame 229 or the next three or four frames.

Arlen Specter remained convinced of the single bullet theory despite the Connallys' testimony—which he himself took. When Specter's theory was initially floated among Warren Commission staffers, "at first, some lawyers were incredulous," assistant counsel Melvin Eisenberg told Edward Jay Epstein.* Specter argued that the single bullet theory was the only way to account for the evidence, particularly in light of the Zapruder film, and he embarked upon a series of tests in order to prove it.

---

*Edward Jay Epstein, *Inquest: The Warren Commission and the Establishment of Truth*, in *The Assassination Chronicles* (New York: Carroll and Graf, 1992), p. 126.

CHAPTER 11

The Warren Commission
Reenactment

ONE OF THE MOST OBVIOUS PROBLEMS with the single bullet theory was the relatively undamaged condition of the bullet after it allegedly caused seven wounds, including the smashing of ten centimeters of Connally's fifth rib and the breaking of his right radius into three pieces. Hoping to overcome objections to the theory raised by his own Warren Commission colleagues, Arlen Specter supervised ballistics tests on April 27, 1964. These tests attempted to demonstrate that if the bullet had been slowed down by hitting Kennedy first, it could have caused Connally's wounds without severe deformation to the missile. Specter wanted to see whether passing through so many solid targets would actually make the bullet more likely to remain relatively undeformed.

Since the bullet that passed through Kennedy's back and neck apparently did not hit any bones (prevented from viewing the X-rays, Specter was not certain of this), it could have exited without suffering any significant deformation. And once the bullet was slowed down exiting Kennedy's throat, it could have gone into a yaw and entered Connally's back lengthwise, striking his fifth rib at an angle. As the yaw continued upon exiting Connally's chest, the bullet would enter his wrist base-first, fracturing his right radius with a tangential strike at a severely reduced speed. Then it would hit his left thigh with just enough energy (some 700 feet per second) to pierce the skin and imbed itself in the soft tissue above his knee. If this sequence of events occurred, it was possible that the bullet remain relatively intact.

Specter couldn't re-create the entire wound sequence, so he attempted to demonstrate that a similar bullet fired directly into bone would cause more damage and be significantly more deformed than Commission exhibit 399. During the April 27 tests, bullets were fired from a Mannlicher-Carcano into anesthetized goats and the wrists of cadavers.

Commission exhibit 856, fired into a cadaver's wrist, suffered much more damage than Commission exhibit 399. This bullet was a direct hit, impacting nose-first into the radius bone, which was shattered, while Connally's radius was fractured by a more tangential impact.

If these ballistic tests would cause problems for the Warren Commission once the results were made public (owing to a misunderstanding of the experiment's intent), they appeared to support Specter's hypothesis that a

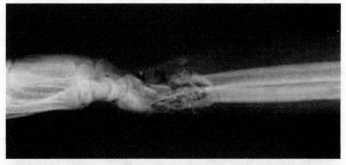

(Above) 6.5-millimeter Mannlicher-Carcano bullet fired directly into a cadaver's wrist. *Courtesy of National Archives.*

(Above right) X-ray of the cadaver's wrist. *Courtesy of National Archives.*

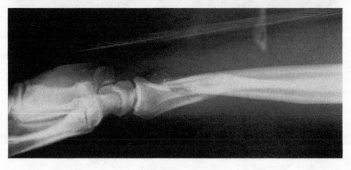

(Right) X-ray of Governor Connally's wrist wound. *Courtesy of National Archives.*

bullet that had not passed through another solid target would probably have undergone more extensive deformation than Commission exhibit 399.

Specter still hoped to view the autopsy photographs and X-rays in order to see whether that evidence supported his theory. Secret Service inspector Thomas Kelley had asked Robert Kennedy for permission to view the material, and Kennedy had refused. On April 30, Arlen Specter wrote a memo to general counsel J. Lee Rankin, stating that it was "indispensable that we obtain the photographs and X-rays" in order to "determine with certainty whether shots came from" the Texas School Book Depository. Specter's memo warned that the artist's renderings might be inaccurate and that the Commission needed to review these materials in order to establish the source direction of all three shots.

This and subsequent requests to view the photographs and X-rays were refused by Earl Warren, who decided that he alone would look at them. After having seen the photographs and X-rays, Warren decided that they should not become part of the investigation, because the Commission would then be obliged to make them part of the public record.

Denied access to this vital evidence, and with his single bullet theory under continued attack by other Commission staffers, Specter proposed a full reenactment of the assassination at the crime scene. Rankin had doubts about the project, fearing that "an over-enthusiastic lawyer" could "make the facts fit the hypothesis."* Specter later said that the Commissioners were opposed to the reenactment "because they felt it would look bad at this late date to show that the basic facts were not known."** (Specter's draft of the final report chapter was due June 1.) Eventually the Commissioners agreed to the reenactment, on the condition that Rankin supervise it.

Since the presidential limousine was not available, the reenactors used the follow-up car, a 1956 Cadillac. The presidential limousine was a 1961 Lincoln Continental stretch limousine, measuring twenty-one feet in length. It had a rear bench seat that was higher than the two jump seats. By comparison, the Cadillac is a much smaller and narrower vehicle. It does not have jump seats.

The reenactment team made adjustments to compensate for the differ-

---

*Edward Jay Epstein, *Inquest: The Warren Commission and the Establishment of Truth,* in *The Assassination Chronicles* (New York: Carroll and Graf, 1992), p. 130.
**Ibid

Kennedy's stand-in, with marks where the shots were thought to have hit. *Courtesy of National Archives.*

ences in size and dimension between the two vehicles. Because of the vertical difference of ten inches between the two automobiles, they made both stand-ins sit higher. The jump seats were three inches lower than the backseat, yet Connally was an inch and a half taller than Kennedy, so the reenactors decided that Kennedy was seated an inch and a half higher than Connally during the motorcade. (This was changed to three inches by the HSCA when it performed a trajectory analysis.) The jump seats of the presidential limousine had 5.5 inches of clearance between their outer edge and the door, while the rear bench seat was flush against the door. Since the Cadillac did not have jump seats, the Governor's stand-in was moved to his left.

The differences in vehicle size, height, interior space and design, and the relative positioning of the two victims were not the only variables that had changed since November 22, 1963. The tree that reportedly blocked the assassin's view from the sixth-floor window from frames 166 to 207 would have had thicker foliage after growing another five months (being a live oak, it did not drop its leaves in autumn). The wind, weather, and light conditions were also different.

The reenactment began at 6:00 A.M. on May 24. (They started early so as not to interfere too much with morning traffic.) With J. Lee Rankin and

FBI agent Lyndal Shaneyfelt aims the Mannlicher-Carcano camera. *Courtesy of National Archives.*

Arlen Specter alongside him, FBI firearms expert Robert A. Frazier knelt in the southeast window of the sixth floor of the Texas School Book Depository, aiming a Mannlicher-Carcano at a chalk mark on the back of the President's stand-in.

Norman Redlich observed from the street. Secret Service agent George W. Hickey steered the car as it was pushed along the motorcade route. FBI agents sat in for President Kennedy and Governor Connally. Leo J. Gauthier and Lyndal L. Shaneyfelt, also FBI agents, lined up the car's position with specific frames of the Zapruder film. Then Shaneyfelt went to the sniper's nest and, using a film camera mounted on top of a Mannlicher-Carcano to capture the view through the scope, took a series of pictures corresponding to crucial Zapruder frames.

The photographic montages created by the Warren Commission from the reenactment are rich sources of evidence, showing crucial Zapruder frames from the shooter's perspective, as well as documenting angles and distances measured by the reenactors.

Zapruder frame 161 was the first position at which the shooter could see the target after turning onto Elm Street.

PHOTOGRAPH FROM ZAPRUDER FILM

PHOTOGRAPH FROM RE-ENACTMENT

PHOTOGRAPH THROUGH RIFLE SCOPE

DISTANCE TO STATION C	95.6 FT.
DISTANCE TO RIFLE IN WINDOW	138.2 FT.
ANGLE TO RIFLE IN WINDOW	26°52'
DISTANCE TO OVERPASS	391.5 FT.
ANGLE TO OVERPASS	0°07'

FRAME 166

At frame 166, the target began to be obscured by the oak tree. *Courtesy of National Archives.*

A slight opening in the foliage appeared around frame 186. *Courtesy of National Archives.*

PHOTOGRAPH FROM ZAPRUDER FILM

PHOTOGRAPH FROM RE-ENACTMENT

PHOTOGRAPH THROUGH RIFLE SCOPE

DISTANCE TO STATION C	116.3 FT.
DISTANCE TO RIFLE IN WINDOW	156.3 FT.
ANGLE TO RIFLE IN WINDOW	24°03'
DISTANCE TO OVERPASS	371.7 FT.
ANGLE TO OVERPASS	+0°03'

FRAME 186

PHOTOGRAPH FROM ZAPRUDER FILM

PHOTOGRAPH FROM RE-ENACTMENT

PHOTOGRAPH THROUGH RIFLE SCOPE

DISTANCE TO STATION C	136.6 FT.
DISTANCE TO RIFLE IN WINDOW	174.9 FT.
ANGLE TO RIFLE IN WINDOW	21°50′
DISTANCE TO OVERPASS	350.9 FT.
ANGLE TO OVERPASS	-0°12′

FRAME 207

At frame 207, the target emerged from beneath the tree. *Courtesy of National Archives.*

At frame 210, Kennedy disappeared from Zapruder's view. *Courtesy of National Archives.*

PHOTOGRAPH FROM ZAPRUDER FILM

PHOTOGRAPH FROM RE-ENACTMENT

PHOTOGRAPH THROUGH RIFLE SCOPE

DISTANCE TO STATION C	138.9 FT.
DISTANCE TO RIFLE IN WINDOW	176.9 FT.
ANGLE TO RIFLE IN WINDOW	21°34′
DISTANCE TO OVERPASS	348.8 FT.
ANGLE TO OVERPASS	+0°22′

FRAME 210

PHOTOGRAPH FROM ZAPRUDER FILM

PHOTOGRAPH FROM RE-ENACTMENT

PHOTOGRAPH THROUGH RIFLE SCOPE

DISTANCE TO STATION C .... 153.8 FT.

DISTANCE TO RIFLE IN WINDOW .... 190.8 FT.

ANGLE TO RIFLE IN WINDOW .... 20°11′

DISTANCE TO OVERPASS .... 334.0 FT.

ANGLE TO OVERPASS .... +0°26′

FRAME 225

At frame 225, Kennedy emerged from behind the sign, visibly injured. *Courtesy of National Archives.*

Six frames later was the earliest that Connally and his doctors felt he could have been injured. *Courtesy of National Archives.*

PHOTOGRAPH FROM ZAPRUDER FILM

PHOTOGRAPH FROM RE-ENACTMENT

PHOTOGRAPH THROUGH RIFLE SCOPE

DISTANCE TO STATION C .... 159.0 FT.

DISTANCE TO RIFLE IN WINDOW .... 196.0 FT.

ANGLE TO RIFLE IN WINDOW .... 19°47′

DISTANCE TO OVERPASS .... 329.0 FT.

ANGLE TO OVERPASS .... +0°28′

FRAME 231

PHOTOGRAPH FROM ZAPRUDER FILM

PHOTOGRAPH FROM RE-ENACTMENT

PHOTOGRAPH THROUGH RIFLE SCOPE

DISTANCE TO STATION C	162.3 FT.
DISTANCE TO RIFLE IN WINDOW	199.0 FT.
ANGLE TO RIFLE IN WINDOW	19°26'
DISTANCE TO OVERPASS	326.8 FT.
ANGLE TO OVERPASS	+0°30'

FRAME 235

Frame 235 was the latest Connally and his doctors felt he could have been injured.
Courtesy of National Archives.

Frame 240 was the latest Arlen Specter believed Connally could have been injured.
Courtesy of National Archives.

PHOTOGRAPH FROM ZAPRUDER FILM

PHOTOGRAPH FROM RE-ENACTMENT

PHOTOGRAPH THROUGH RIFLE SCOPE

DISTANCE TO STATION C	167.8 FT.
DISTANCE TO RIFLE IN WINDOW	204.3 FT.
ANGLE TO RIFLE IN WINDOW	19°01'
DISTANCE TO OVERPASS	320.4 FT.
ANGLE TO OVERPASS	+0°34'

FRAME 240

PHOTOGRAPH FROM NIX FILM

PHOTOGRAPH FROM RE-ENACTMENT

PHOTOGRAPH FROM ZAPRUDER FILM

PHOTOGRAPH FROM RE-ENACTMENT

PHOTOGRAPH THROUGH RIFLE SCOPE

DISTANCE TO STATION C	230.8 FT.
DISTANCE TO RIFLE IN WINDOW	265.3 FT.
ANGLE TO RIFLE IN WINDOW	15°21'
DISTANCE TO OVERPASS	260.6 FT.
ANGLE TO OVERPASS	+1°28'

FRAME 313

PHOTOGRAPH FROM MUCHMORE FILM

PHOTOGRAPH FROM RE-ENACTMENT

Frame 313, the final reenactment montage. *Courtesy of National Archives.*

After taking these still photographs, the reenactors drove the limousine down the parade route, filming three trips in black-and-white and one in color. Then they went to a nearby railway garage, where a photograph was taken demonstrating the single bullet theory. A rod was used to represent the trajectory of the path of the bullet traveling the average downward angles of the sniper's nest to the target between frames 210 and 225 and to show how the bullet could have passed from Kennedy's neck into Connally's back.

This may appear to confirm at least the possibility of the single bullet theory, but differing variables between the event and its reenactment tend to diminish the latter's evidentiary value.

To take just one example, in the reenactment photo corresponding to Frame 207, Connally's stand-in is seated approximately ten to twelve inches to the left of the door. The photo depicts the two victims in possible alignment for the single bullet theory. Yet in a subsequent reenactment photo corresponding to frame 225, Connally's stand-in has moved back to his right, against the car door. Is the Warren Commission trying to say that in

Arlen Specter demonstrates the single bullet trajectory following the reenactment.
Courtesy of National Archives.

the space of eighteen frames (almost exactly one second) Connally changed position so that he would be in line to receive the shot exiting the President's neck?

It is difficult, maybe even impossible, to stage reenactments accurately enough for them to be considered evidentiary. Perhaps a reenactment such as the one performed in Dallas on May 24, 1964, would have been helpful to establish whether certain trajectories, timings, and placements of the car and the victims were possible. Reenactments are not evidence but show-and-tell displays to demonstrate what you believe occurred at a crime scene or to corroborate other evidence. One example of a useful reenactment was the test performed by Arlen Specter and other Warren Commission investigators to see whether someone standing on the fifth floor directly below the sniper's nest could have heard the Mannlicher-Carcano bolt working and cartridges falling on the floor if someone was shooting on the floor above. During the reenactment, people on the fifth floor clearly heard both sounds, corroborating the testimony of Harold Norman, who reported having heard the rifle bolt being worked and cartridges landing on the plywood above his head.

Specter's reenactment was made necessary by doubts concerning the single bullet theory. Those doubts remained even during the testimony following the reenactment. When asked by Specter whether he thought a single bullet caused Kennedy's back/throat wound and all of Connally's wounds, Robert Frazier testified:

> I would certainly say it was possible but I don't say that it probably occurred because I don't have the evidence on which to base a statement like that. . . . We are dealing with hypothetical situations here of placing people in cars from photographs which are not absolutely accurate. They are two dimensional. They don't give you the third dimension. They are as accurate as you can accurately place the people but it isn't absolute. Secondly, we are dealing with the fact that we don't know whether, I don't know technically, whether there was any deviation in the bullet which struck the President in the back, and exited from his front. If there were a few degrees deviation then it may affect my opinion as to whether or not it would have struck the Governor. We are dealing with an assumed fact that the Governor was in front of the President in such a position that he could have

taken. So when you say would it probably have occurred, then you are asking me for an opinion, to base my opinion on a whole series of hypothetical facts which I can't substantiate.

Here is one of the most important participants in the reenactment clearly stating the limits on such an exercise. Frazier went on to say that the only time he was certain that either man was hit was frame 313, where the President was obviously struck in the head.

This is how the Warren Report characterized Frazier's testimony quoted above:

> The bullet that hit President Kennedy in the back and exited through his throat most likely could not have missed both the automobile and its occupants. Since it did not hit the automobile, Frazier testified that it probably struck Governor Connally. The relative positions of President Kennedy and Governor Connally at the time when the President was struck in the neck confirm that the same bullet probably passed through both men.

Two pages later, following a lengthy analysis of the single bullet's hypothetical trajectory, the Report stated: "The alinement [sic] of the points of entry was only indicative and not conclusive that one bullet hit both men."

The ambivalence with which the Warren Report treated the single bullet theory was the result of internal disagreement as to whether it was true. This controversy plagued the Commission all the way up until its deadline and was never successfully resolved.

CHAPTER 12

The Science of Magic

O N JUNE 7, Arlen Specter walked Earl Warren and Gerald Ford through the crime scene at Dealey Plaza, showing them how the single bullet theory could have worked. Upon their return to Washington, both Warren and Ford endorsed the theory. Allen Dulles and John McCloy also went along. Still, three members of the Commission, Richard Russell, John Sherman Cooper, and Hale Boggs, had serious reservations.

All three men had been present for Connally's testimony—it had been one of the rare occasions when all the Commissioners heard a witness testify. The three dissenting Commissioners were walked through the crime scene in early September, not by Specter but by other Warren Commission staffers. After the walk-through, all three remained unconvinced. On September 16, Senator Russell wrote a dissent that he wanted published as a footnote to the Warren Report, stating, in part, "I do not share the finding that President Kennedy and Governor Connally were hit by the same bullet."

On September 18, the Commission held an emergency executive session to discuss the controversy and try to come to an agreement about the shot sequence. Unlike every other executive session, this meeting was not transcribed, or at least the transcription was not preserved. A very brief set of typed minutes is the only documentation of this meeting that remains in the National Archives, and these records were not released until the 1990s. The minutes do not mention the single bullet controversy. However, we do know, thanks to testimony, memoirs, and tape-recorded conversations among the Commissioners, that the executive session was taken up by a lengthy argument over the single bullet theory. Earl Warren refused to include Russell's dissent as part of the Report and insisted that the Commission's findings be unanimous. Everybody seemed to agree that Lee Harvey Oswald was the assassin and that he acted alone (years later Russell would say that he believed there had been a conspiracy), yet the three southern congressional leaders would not allow the single bullet theory to contradict the sworn testimony of Texas governor John Connally and his wife, Nellie.

During a long debate that John McCloy called "the battle of the adjectives," the Commissioners wrangled over the verbiage they would use to describe the evidence for the single bullet theory. Gerald Ford wanted to say "compelling." Russell said he would sign off on "credible." Eventually they reached a compromise with "persuasive," which was then upgraded to "very persuasive." Here is the Warren Report's conclusion regarding the single bullet theory:

> Although it is not necessary to any essential findings of the Commission to determine just which shot hit Governor Connally, there is very persuasive evidence from the experts to indicate that the same bullet that pierced the President's throat also caused Governor Connally's wounds. However, Governor Connally's testimony and certain other factors have given rise to some difference of opinion as to this probability but there is no question in the mind of any member of the Commission that all the shots which caused the President's and Governor Connally's wounds were fired from the sixth floor window of the Texas School Book Depository.

Later, Arlen Specter told *Life* magazine that "the dominant thinking with many people right up to the time the Report was published" was that Kennedy and Connally had been hit with separate bullets. This dispute was not resolved by the language used in the Report, despite the fact that the dissenting Commissioners signed their names to it. "Conclusions," Gerald Ford

said, "were the work of the Commission." President Johnson and Earl
Warren wanted those conclusions to be unanimous. If Russell, Cooper, and
Boggs disagreed with the Commission's findings, they were expected to
keep it to themselves.

In a phone call to Johnson on September 18, 1964, shortly before the
Warren Report was issued, Senator Richard Russell told his former senate
protégé that while he was satisfied with the Report in general, he still wasn't
convinced by the single bullet theory.

> RUSSELL: Well, they were tryin' to prove that [the] same bullet that
> hit Kennedy first was the one that hit Connally... went through
> him and through his hand, [and] his bone, into his leg and every-
> thing else. Just a lot of stuff there... I hadn't... couldn't...
> didn't hear all the evidence, and cross-examine all of 'em. But I
> did read the record. So I just, ah... I don't know, I was the only
> fella [commissioner] there that even... *practically,* that sug-
> gested any change whatever in what the staff had got up. This
> *staff* business always scares me. I like to put my *own* views
> down. But we got you a pretty good report.
>
> JOHNSON: Well, what difference does it make which bullet got
> Connally?
>
> RUSSELL: Well, it don't *make* much difference. But they said that
> they believe... that the Commission believe[s] that the same bul-
> let that hit Kennedy hit Connally. *Well, I don't believe it!*
>
> JOHNSON: I don't either.
>
> RUSSELL: And so I couldn't sign it. And I said that Governor
> Connally testified di-*rectly* to the contrary, and I'm not going to
> *approve* of that. So, I finally made 'em say there was a difference
> in the Commission, in that part of 'em [a few Commissioners]
> believed that that wasn't so. 'Course, if a fella [Lee Harvey
> Oswald] was accurate enough to hit Kennedy right in the neck on
> *one* shot, and knock his head off in the *next* one when he's
> leanin' up against his wife's head and not even wound *her*...
> why, he didn't miss *completely* with that *third* shot. But accord-
> ing to *that* theory, he not only missed the whole automobile but
> he missed the *street!* Well, a man [who's] a good enough shot to

put two bullets right into Kennedy, he didn't miss the whole automobile—

JOHNSON: Hmm.

RUSSELL:—nor the street. But anyhow, that's just a little thing, but we—

JOHNSON: What's the net of the whole thing? What [does] it say? That Oswald did it, and he did it for any *reason?*

RUSSELL: Well, just that he was a general misanthropic fella...that he'd...had never been satisfied anywhere he was on earth, in Russia or here, and that he had a desire to get his name in history and all. I don't think you'll be displeased with the whole report. It's too long, but it's a...whole volume.

JOHNSON: Unanimous?

RUSSELL: Yes, sir.

JOHNSON: Hmm.

RUSSELL: I tried my best to get in a *dis*-sent, but they'd come round and trade me out of it by givin' me a little old thread of it.

JOHNSON: Hmm.*

Senator Cooper told Edward Jay Epstein: "There was no evidence to show both men were hit by the same bullet."** And he never changed his mind. Fourteen years later Cooper testified before the HSCA: "I must say, to be very honest about it, that I held in my mind during the life of the Commission, as I have since, that there had been three shots and that a separate shot hit Connally."

When the Warren Report was published, critics pounced on the single bullet theory as the weakest link in the case against Oswald. Controversy over the single bullet theory cast suspicion over the entire Warren Commission investigation and its findings. The critics believed that the reenactment had been designed not for the investigators to learn what might have happened but to establish "scientific" evidence for the single bullet theory and to convince a majority of the Commissioners. By working backwards

---

*Max Holland, *The Kennedy Assassination Tapes* (New York: Knopf, 2004), pp. 250–51.
**Edward Jay Epstein, *Inquest: The Warren Commission and the Establishment of Truth* (New York: Viking Press, 1966), pp. 149–50.

from hypothesis to proof, Arlen Specter was able to create a scenario in which the single bullet theory was possible.

Shortly after the assassination, Fidel Castro performed his own reenactment in Cuba, to see whether Lee Harvey Oswald could have acted alone. He decided that it was not possible.

More than a decade after the Warren Commission investigation, the HSCA reconsidered the evidence with much greater technological expertise at its disposal. When the HSCA was initially convened, many expected it to disprove the single bullet theory. Yet the HSCA forensic medical panel concluded that only two bullets struck Kennedy and Connally and that one bullet was responsible for all of Kennedy's nonfatal wounds and all of Connally's wounds. The panel was led by Dr. Michael Baden, then New York City medical examiner, and included some of the nation's top forensic pathologists. Dr. Cyril Wecht, medical examiner for Allegheny County, Pennsylvania (which includes the city of Pittsburgh), was the lone dissenter. Before reaching its conclusion regarding the single bullet theory, the panel examined evidence, including the X-rays and autopsy photographs, that had not been available to previous investigators, including the Warren Commission's own staff.

In addition to this newly available evidence, the HSCA also commissioned a trajectory analysis by Thomas Canning, a NASA rocket scientist who had developed a highly sophisticated technique of measuring back from wounds toward the source of the shot. One of the virtues of Canning's work, according to the HSCA, was that "the investigative procedures and analyses in this instance were governed by the hypothesis that there was no other evidence... concerning the source of the shots."

That means Canning didn't consider, for example, the fact that the rifle and the three empty cartridges were discovered on the sixth floor of the Texas School Book Depository. Yet Canning wasn't working blind. The forensic medical panel provided him with precise locations of the victims' wounds. Photographic enhancements and analysis by the photographic panel were used to determine where and how the two victims were seated in the limousine. The placement of the limousine was determined by a photogrammetric analysis conducted by the U.S. Geological Survey.

Since the HSCA had determined that "all of the available scientific evidence indicated that President Kennedy and Governor Connally were struck by a total of two bullets," the Committee had Canning measure out three separate trajectories, one from each of Kennedy's wounds and another from Connally's wound to Kennedy's exit wound. And since the Committee had already established, based on analysis of the acoustics evidence, that the single bullet struck the two victims at frame 190, Canning was given this frame as the time and location of the shot.

Canning's trajectory analysis determined that all the wounds suffered by Kennedy and Connally were caused by two shots fired from the southeast corner of the sixth floor of the Texas School Book Depository. He also supported the single bullet theory by concluding that if the bullet passed through Kennedy's upper body without being deflected, it would have gone on to hit Connally in the back.

Yet Canning himself admitted that an error in calculation of just one inch at the wound projected over 150 feet could throw the calculations off by 30 feet at the source of the shot. Since the single bullet theory requires two separate trajectories (one from the sniper's nest to Kennedy's back, another from Kennedy's throat to Connally's back), the margin for error increases correspondingly.

More recently, three very sophisticated reenactments have endorsed the single bullet theory. Failure Analysis Associates, a private firm that creates visual displays for courtroom presentation, performed a computer reenactment of the JFK assassination for the American Bar Association's 1992 mock trial of Lee Harvey Oswald. Their take on the single bullet theory had Kennedy and Connally hit at frames 223 to 224.

The second major computer reenactment was called "Secrets of a Homicide." Created by computer animator and JFK researcher Dale Myers, the reenactment was featured on an *ABC News* prime-time special aired November 20, 2003, and titled "The Kennedy Assassination—Beyond Conspiracy." Myers's model also has the single bullet hitting at frames 223 to 224.

Introducing the computer reenactment, Peter Jennings called it "stunning technology that will make it clear precisely what happened." According to Myers, Governor Connally's visible reactions to being shot include his torso pitching forward, his head pitching rearward, and the right lapel of his jacket flipping outward. This last reaction is supposed to be a result of a bullet passing through his jacket. Yet the bullet exited Connally's jacket well below the lapel, which could easily have flipped up in the wind. (Failure

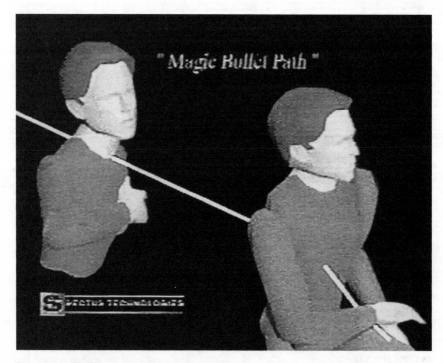

The single bullet theory according to Failure Analysis Associates. *Courtesy of Exponent.*

Analysis also cited this "lapel flip" as an indication that Connally was hit around frames 223 to 224.)

Anatomical Surrogate Technologies (AST) of Adelaide, Australia, performed a ballistic reenactment of the single bullet theory for the Discovery Channel's 2004 documentary *Unsolved History: The JFK Assassination.* While AST spent a great deal of effort on creating surrogate models for Kennedy and Connally, it based its reenactment on a flawed assumption that, ironically, points out a serious problem with the single bullet theory.

When re-creating all the measurements and locations to the greatest degree of possible accuracy, AST had the entry wound on Connally's back measuring nearly three centimeters, or roughly the entire length of Commission exhibit 399. Dr. Robert Shaw's original operative record describes the Governor's back entry wound as "approximately three centimeters in its longest diameter." In his Warren Commission testimony, Shaw described it as "a small wound approximately a centimeter and a half in its greatest diameter. It was roughly elliptical."

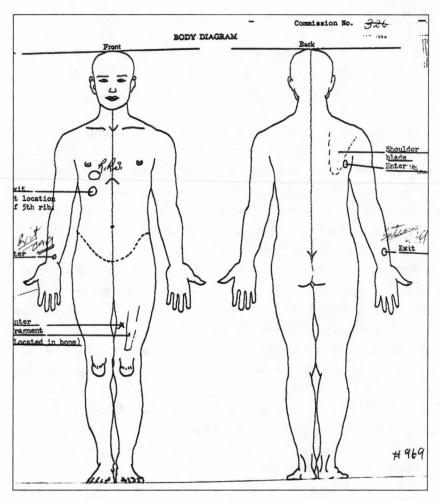

Commission No. 326

BODY DIAGRAM

Front   Back

Shoulder
blade
Enter

xit
t location
f 5th rib

xit
ter

nter
ragment
(Located in bone)

Exit

969

Dr. Robert Shaw's sketch describing Governor Connally's wounds. (Shaw corrected the placement of the chest exit wound to move it closer to the right nipple.) *Courtesy of National Archives.*

When interviewed by Dr. Charles Petty of the HSCA's forensic medical panel, Shaw confirmed the smaller dimensions of the Governor's back entry wound and drew a diagram with both entrance and exit wounds shown actual size.

As a result of this new information, the HSCA forensic medical panel determined that:

> The rear entrance wound was not 3 centimeters [in diameter] as indicated in one of the operative notes. It was a puncture-type wound, as if a bullet had struck the body at slight declination [i.e., not at a right

angle]. The wound was actually approximately 1.5 centimeters in diameter. The ragged edges of the wound were surgically cut away, effectively enlarging it to approximately 3 centimeters.

Yet, in support of the single bullet theory, Dr. Michael Baden testified that the HSCA medical forensic panel had concluded that, "based on the enlarged nature of the entrance perforation in the Governor's back,...the bullet was wobbling when it struck him and had to have struck something before striking the Governor." During his testimony, Baden entered Shaw's original and revised reports but did not state the measurements of either thoracic wound. Examining Connally's scars himself in 1978, Baden reported observing "a two-inch long sideways entrance" in his back (two inches is about five centimeters). Of course, this scar was much larger than the original entrance wound. In his testimony and reports, Dr. Robert Shaw described debriding the necrotic tissue at the edges of the wound, which would have resulted in a larger scar than the original entrance wound.

Dr. Frederick Light, a wounds ballistics expert at the Aberdeen Proving Grounds, had testified before the Warren Commission that while he believed the single bullet theory to be "probably the most likely" explanation, Connally's entrance wound did not necessarily indicate a yawing bullet. Light believed that the bullet entered at an oblique angle "just in the nature of the way the shoulder is built."

At eight millimeters by fifteen millimeters, Connally's back entrance wound is no more elliptical than either of JFK's entrance wounds. Kennedy's back wound measured seven by four millimeters, and his head entry wound measured six by fifteen millimeters. The variation between these three wounds can be accounted for by the different body parts they hit and their angle to the bullet upon impact. Also, the small size and round shape of the original exit wound in Kennedy's throat, according to the Parkland Hospital doctors, indicate that the bullet was neither deformed nor yawing significantly as it left the President's body.

The assumption that Governor Connally's back wound measured three centimeters made a big difference when Anatomical Surrogate Technologies conducted its reenactment using two human surrogates made of gelatin and simulated bone and skin. A 6.5-millimeter Mannlicher-Carcano was fired at mannequin torsos, which were aligned so that a bullet traveling in a straight line would cause wounds roughly similar to those accounted for by the single bullet theory. (When you see the reenactment on television, it is clear that the alignment does not resemble the two men's positions in the limousine, as the Kennedy surrogate is much higher than the Connally one; also, the entry wound on Kennedy's back appears higher and farther to the right than the autopsy photo indicates.)

Because it had only one set of surrogates, AST performed several preliminary tests to line up the targets and make sure the trajectories worked. One of its primary considerations was the bullet entering Connally's back at a yaw. Bullets fired into mannequin torsos exited Kennedy's throat and entered Connally's back almost at a full yaw. Satisfied that the trajectories were correct, AST fired its single bullet.

The bullet entered Kennedy's back and exited his throat, but when it entered Connally's back at a full yaw, it smashed both the fifth and sixth ribs. By the time it entered the gelatin and simulated bone representing Connally's wrist, the bullet did not have sufficient energy to break the radius. It exited the wrist and bounced harmlessly off the simulated thigh tissue, completely spent.

Unintentionally, this reenactment demonstrated that a bullet entering Connally's back at a full yaw would have hit two of his ribs. (I explore this point later in more detail.) Also, it proved that Commission exhibit 399 would not have had enough energy to pass through fourteen centimeters of soft tissue in Kennedy's upper body and then go on to cause all of Connally's wounds. The bullet resulting from the AST test was severely deformed. Although it did not mushroom, the entire missile was bent and flattened.

The problem with the AST reenactment and every other reenactment is that they try to replicate the unique. There is no way that anyone can re-create with any precision exactly what happened in Dealey Plaza that day. Bullets do unpredictable things. So do human bodies. And attempting to line them up in a certain way to "prove" how the assassination occurred is an exercise in futility. All the Warren Commission needed to do was have one person stand in the southeast-corner, sixth-floor window of the Texas School Book Depository and another stand on Elm Street in the approximate positions of the limousine when the shots were fired. Once it was determined that the assassin had a clear shot and that the trajectories from the wounds were found to roughly measure back to the sniper's nest, no more reenactment was necessary.

Trying to nail down every detail of the shot sequence, Arlen Specter created evidence that cast doubt on the Warren Commission's findings and established a level of specificity concerning the shot sequence that now any credible investigation must achieve. This is the only murder case I know of in which every moment of every bullet has had to be accounted for and reenacted. Now any solution to this case must answer all these questions.

In discussing the Warren Commission's inability to match results that resembled the Magic Bullet in any of its various ballistics tests, Dr. Michael Baden told the HSCA that the majority of the forensic panel believed that "the injuries sustained by Governor Connally and President Kennedy, and the trajectory and the ballistics could not be precisely duplicated...there were myriads and myriads of ways the experiment could be done wrong and only one way it could be done right—and if by chance it were done right once we wouldn't know it or be able to prove it."

The HSCA considered having a series of its own ballistics tests conducted to see whether the single bullet theory was possible. It solicited a proposal from a private laboratory, which expressed its professional view that efforts to replicate the assassination would always be subject to theoretical questioning, since no material reacts in the exact manner of live human tissue when bullets are fired into it. Even this objection assumes that such tests could be valid if only the original target material was available (live humans).

It is not just the question of garbage in/garbage out (although that is a problem). The larger mistake committed by these reenactments is that they attempt to render human judgment unnecessary. Evidence only makes sense in the context of other evidence, evaluated by human beings based on their experience, knowledge, and common sense. Even the most sophisticated technological models can only suggest what happened. It is the responsibility of an investigator to evaluate this information, not bow before it. If every murder investigation relied on reenactments to prove exactly what happened, every law enforcement agency would be broke in a matter of weeks. Detectives do this every day, out in the rain and the dark and the cold of the street. They stand where the killer and victim stood, and they figure out what happened, without relying on NASA rocket scientists or computer visuals.

But the JFK assassination is a different kind of investigation. The level of detail necessary to solve this case and the doubt an investigative hypothesis faces are higher than for any other murder in history.

Controversy over the single bullet theory continues to this day. It is the most compelling argument made by critics of the Warren Commission, and the one piece of evidence that neither side can ignore. The case has not yet been conclusively made that Commission exhibit 399 caused all those wounds. Until this question is answered, the Kennedy assassination remains unsolved.

CHAPTER 13

Arguing with the Evidence

THE THREE MAJOR ARGUMENTS against the single bullet theory are:

1. The condition of the bullet
2. Eyewitness statements
3. The bullet's alleged trajectory

Although critics have focused a great deal of attention on Commission exhibit 399's relatively undamaged condition, it actually presents the weakest argument against the single bullet theory. A high-powered rifle firing a military ball round can hit several solid targets without deforming, particularly if it strikes the targets tangentially and is progressively slowed down by passing through each target.

The Mannlicher-Carcano fires 6.5-millimeter military ball rounds. In accordance with the 1925 Geneva Convention, all military bullets are covered with metal jackets, usually copper or steel, designed to keep the bullet from deforming as it passes through a human body. (This provision was meant to avoid some of the crippling nonfatal wounds created by lead bullets so common during World War I.)

According to a classic textbook on gunshot wounds:

This photo shows Kennedy's well-developed upper back muscles. *Courtesy of the Library of Congress.*

Military bullets, by virtue of their full metal jackets, tend to pass through the body intact, thus producing less extensive injuries than hunting ammunition. Military bullets usually do not fragment in the body or shed fragments of lead in their paths. Because of the high velocity of such military rounds as well as their tough construction, it is possible for such bullets to pass through more than one individual before coming to rest. These bullets may be almost virginal in appearance after recovery from the body.*

Let's consider the wounds of each victim separately.

Kennedy was struck in the soft tissue of the upper back. Owing to the steroids he took in treatment for adrenal insufficiency, as well as his exercise regime (which included swimming), Kennedy's muscles in this area were very developed, which is evident in the photo above.

Passing through fourteen centimeters of soft tissue in the President's

---

*Vincent J.M. Di Maio, *Gunshot Wounds: Practical Aspects of Firearms, Ballistics, and Forensic Techniques, 2nd ed.* (Boca Raton, Fl. CRC Press: 1999), p. 176.

back and neck, the bullet reportedly hit no bones or other hard objects, although it is possible that the bullet nicked Kennedy's first thoracic vertebrae. The exit wound was estimated by Dr. Malcolm Perry to have been three to five millimeters, approximately the same size as the entrance wound and the diameter of the bullet. (Sometimes wounds are smaller than the bullet itself because the skin stretches upon impact and then snaps back; this can even happen to bones as thick as the skull.) By all accounts, the exit wound indicated an undeformed bullet.

No bullet fragments were recovered from either the entrance or exit wound. No fragments are visible on the X-rays. (In 1968, a panel of medical experts convened by the Attorney General Ramsey Clark noted what appeared to be metal fragments in Kennedy's upper body X-ray, but the HSCA medical experts determined that these were photographic artifacts.) Small traces of copper were found on the back of Kennedy's suit jacket, but nothing was detected on the buttonhole tears or necktie nick. If the bullet's copper jacket had split open, there would probably have been lead and/or copper traces at the points of exit.

After traversing the soft tissue of Kennedy's back and neck, the bullet exited his throat at a diminished speed. Specter estimated the exit velocity at 1,700 to 1,900 feet per second. The Anatomical Surrogate Technologies reenactment indicates it was probably much lower.

A bullet entered Governor Connally's back between the right armpit and shoulder blade, causing an entrance wound of eight to fifteen millimeters, with the long end parallel to the vertical axis of the Governor's body. We have already seen how Connally's back entry wound was neither large nor elliptical enough to have been caused by a yawing bullet. There are other considerations as well. If the 3.2-centimeter-long bullet had been in a full yaw, it would have hit more than just one rib (as demonstrated by the AST reenactment). When the bullet punched out ten centimeters of bone, it did not penetrate the surrounding muscle, which indicates that the bullet was traveling almost precisely along the path of Connally's fifth rib. (Please refer to my illustration "HSCA Connally Bullet Wound Placement" in the center of this book.)

There were no fibers from the Governor's clothes or bullet fragments in the thoracic wound, which led Drs. Gregory and Shaw to conclude that the wound was caused by an undeformed bullet. Because the bullet hit the rib at an angle, it is entirely possible that it shattered that bone without serious deformation to the bullet, whether or not it had already passed through another solid target to diminish its velocity. (Please refer to my illustration "Connally Chest Wound with Lung Location.")

The exit wound on Connally's chest was large (five centimeters, more than the entire length of Commission exhibit 399) and circular, indicating a fully yawed bullet taking tissue and bone with it upon exit. Inside his chest, the bullet had been deflected downward, as the angle of declivity in the wound channel increased from the original vertical trajectory of approximately twenty degrees to the twenty-seven degrees measured between the entrance and exit wounds.

Connally's right lung was punctured, but not by the bullet itself. The bottom lobe and pleura were torn by pieces of rib bone turned into secondary projectiles by the bullet. How did the bullet enter his back and pass through his chest without directly puncturing the lung? (Please refer to my illustration "Connally's Chest Wound Looking Straight Forward" to see how the bullet itself would have punctured Connalley's lung if he had been looking forward or turned to his right.)

While most sketches and reenactments have the bullet passing straight through Connally's thorax, this is clearly wrong. As Dr. Shaw testified, the bullet channeled along the fifth rib, following its declination. Yet the bullet had to follow the rib close enough to never strike the thin membrane covering the lung.

How close did the bullet have to hug the Governor's rib in order to pass through his chest without striking his lung? My illustration "Connally's Back to Chest Wound" shows what must have happened.

After exiting Connally's chest, the bullet then entered his right forearm, causing a jagged wound measuring two centimeters in its greatest diameter on the dorsal side just above the wrist.

By the time it entered Connally's forearm, the bullet was in a full yaw and traveling base-first. Dr. Charles Gregory removed several bits of mohair cloth "throughout the wound and especially in the superficial layers" close to the entrance wound in Connally's wrist. Several tiny lead fragments were also removed (one fragment was left in the wrist) and later matched to the base section of Commission exhibit 399.

The exit wound on the palm side of the forearm was smaller and more uniform. Dr. Gregory described it as a "small laceration, perhaps a centimeter in length." This is consistent with the bullet continuing base-first and exiting without taking much bone or tissue with it.

The entrance wound in Connally's thigh measured one centimeter and also deposited a tiny lead fragment that was observed but never recovered.

All this evidence points to a bullet entering Connally's back nose-first at a downward angle, making a 180-degree yaw upon exiting his chest, entering the dorsal side of the wrist base-first, and continuing through to lodge base-first in the thigh. The thigh wound was only a few centimeters deep, and the bullet could have easily become dislodged while Connally was in the limousine or being moved onto the stretcher. At Parkland Hospital, Connally's clothes were removed from him while he was still on the stretcher in trauma room 2. The bullet probably fell out of his clothing and remained on the stretcher when he was transferred to the operating table.

One argument made by critics is that there were too many bullet fragments in Connally's body for them all to have come from Commission exhibit 399. Dr. Pierre Finck and Robert Shaw, who examined Kennedy and Connally, respectively, but did not see both victims, both offered this opinion in their testimony to the Warren Commission. If the fragments in Connally, including those recovered by the Parkland Hospital surgeons and the few left in his body, weighed more than what Commission exhibit 399 lost from its intact state, then the bullet could not have caused all of his wounds.

Before it was fired, the bullet weighed an estimated 161 grains. (FBI ballistics experts found Mannlicher-Carcano bullets from the same lot of ammunition ranging in weight from 160.85 to 161.5 grains.) Recovered from the stretcher in Parkland Hospital, Commission exhibit 399 weighed 158.6 grains. That means some 2.4 grains were missing from the bullet. All of the fragments recovered from Connally's wrist were described by Dr. Gregory as being "flakes of metal." He estimated their weight in terms of micrograms and said that it would be "less than the weight of a postage stamp." One small fragment was left in Connally's thigh, and possibly even smaller fragments remained in his wrist. Still, it seems unlikely that these fragments would weigh any more than the minuscule fragments recovered from his body. One estimate of all the fragments either recovered from or left in Connally's body adds up to 1.5 grains. All of the fragments recovered from Connally were lead, the only part of the bullet where any portion was lost prior to testing. And they have been matched to Commission exhibit 399 by neutron activation analysis.

As improbable as it might seem when you first see a photo of this bullet and hear the wounds described, it is indeed possible that it could have inflicted all those wounds and ended up relatively undeformed with very little weight loss.

Yet, just because the single bullet could have inflicted those wounds doesn't mean that it did.

Eyewitness Evidence

When a murder is committed in a public place with literally hundreds of witnesses, there are going to be discrepancies among eyewitness statements, particularly considering the tragic nature of the event. The eyewitness record in the JFK assassination is vast and often contradictory. But that's no reason to ignore all the eyewitness evidence. An experienced homicide detective knows that witnesses are not always 100 percent reliable. Their eyes and memory play tricks on them. Sometimes they change their stories or remember things that the physical evidence proves to be impossible. Yet used judiciously, eyewitness testimony is an extremely important source of evidence. It must be examined in the context of other evidence, with an understanding of both the value and the limits of human observation.

Official statements were made by 178 eyewitnesses to the assassination. There were perhaps a dozen more who did not give statements but later spoke to journalists or authors. Obviously, we cannot examine each one of these reports in detail. So we should start at the center of the crime scene and work outward from there, focusing on the eyewitnesses who were closest to the events and paying the most attention.

Governor Connally is the single most important witness, because he was the only living victim. He was an intelligent and courageous man who, through the trauma of an assassination and his own wounding, was able to recall the shooting in precise detail. His testimony to the Warren Commission deserves to be quoted at length.

I heard this noise which I immediately took to be a rifle shot. I instinctively turned to my right because the sound appeared to come from over my right shoulder, so I turned to look back over my right shoulder, and I saw nothing unusual except just people in the crowd, but I did not catch the President in the corner of my eye, and I was interested, because once I heard the shot in my own mind I identified it as a rifle shot, and I immediately—the only thought that crossed my mind was that this is an assassination attempt. So I looked, failing to see him, I was turning to look back over my left shoulder into the backseat, but I never got that far back in my turn. I got about in the position I am now facing you, looking a little bit to the left of center, and then I felt like someone had hit me in the back.

Connally was not able to see a visible reaction from Kennedy because he could not see him over his right shoulder and was shot before he could look over his left. This means he could not have been too far to the left of the President, otherwise he would have been able to see him over his right shoulder. (Arlen Specter's later reenactment required Connally to be seated well to the left of Kennedy in order for him to receive in his right shoulder a bullet exiting the President's neck.)

Specter should have been aware of this testimony, since he was questioning the witness. He then asked Connally to give his best estimate of the time span between the sound of the first shot and the feeling that he was wounded.

A very, very brief span of time. Again my trend of thought just happened to be, I suppose along this line, I immediately thought that this—that I had been shot. I knew it when I just looked down and I was covered with blood, and the thought immediately passed through my mind that there were either two or three people involved or more in this or someone was shooting with an automatic rifle. These were just thoughts that went through my mind because of the rapidity of these two, of the first shot plus the blow that I took, and I knew I had been hit, and I immediately assumed, because of the amount of blood, and in fact, that it had obviously passed through my chest, that I had probably been fatally hit.

So I merely doubled up, and then turned to my right again and began to—I just sat there, and Mrs. Connally pulled me over to her lap. She was sitting, of course, on the jump seat, so I reclined

with my head in her lap, conscious all the time, and with my eyes
open.

If he wasn't certain whether or not Kennedy had been hit by the first bullet, Connally was sure that he himself had been hit by the second.

GOVERNOR CONNALLY: Well, in my judgment, it just couldn't conceivably have been the first one because I heard the sound of the
shot. In the first place, don't know anything about the velocity of
this particular bullet, but any rifle has a velocity that exceeds the
speed of sound, and when I heard the sound of that first shot, that
bullet had already reached where I was, or it had reached that far,
and after I heard that shot, I had the time to turn to my right, and
start to turn to my left before I felt anything. It is not conceivable
to me that I could have been hit by the first bullet, and then I felt
the blow from something which was obviously a bullet, which I
assumed was a bullet, and I never heard the second shot, didn't
hear it. I didn't hear but two shots. I think I heard the first shot
and the third shot.

MR. SPECTER: Do you have any idea as to why you did not hear the
second shot?

GOVERNOR CONNALLY: Well, first, again I assume the bullet was traveling faster than the sound. I was hit by the bullet prior to the
time the sound reached me, and I was in either a state of shock
or the impact was such that the sound didn't even register on me,
but I was never conscious of hearing the second shot at all.
Obviously, at least the major wound that I took in the shoulder
through the chest couldn't have been anything but the second
shot. Obviously, it couldn't have been the third, because when the
third shot was fired I was in a reclining position, and heard it,
saw it and the effects of it, rather—I didn't see it, I saw the
effects of it—so it obviously could not have been the third, and
couldn't have been the first, in my judgment.

When asked to describe the position in which he was sitting when hit by
the bullet, Connally stated that his right wrist was over his left leg, which

aligned him perfectly for a bullet coming from his right rear to inflict all his injuries. He himself believed that the bullet came from that direction, and his recollection is quite vivid and clear.

> I have all my life been familiar with the sound of a rifle shot, and the sound I heard I thought was a rifle shot, at the time I heard it I didn't think it was a firecracker or blowout or anything else. I thought it was a rifle shot. I have hunted enough to think that my perception with respect to directions is very, very good, and this shot I heard came from back over my right shoulder, which was in the direction of the School Book Depository, no question about it. I heard no other. The first and third shots came from there.

In her testimony, Nellie Connally described the President and her husband being hit by separate bullets.

> MRS. CONNALLY: I heard a noise, and not being an expert rifleman, I was not aware that it was a rifle. It was just a frightening noise, and it came from the right. I turned over my right shoulder and looked back, and saw the President as he had both hands at his neck.
>
> MR. SPECTER: And you are indicating with your own hands, two hands crossing over gripping your own neck?
>
> MRS. CONNALLY: Yes, and it seemed to me there was—he made no utterance, no cry. I saw no blood, no anything. It was just sort of nothing, the expression on his face, and he just sort of slumped down. Then very soon there was the second shot that hit John. As the first shot was hit, and I turned to look at the same time, I recall John saying, "Oh, no, no, no." Then there was a second shot, and it hit John, and as he recoiled to the right, just crumpled like a wounded animal to the right, he said, "My God, they are going to kill us all."

Here is how the Warren Report characterized the Connallys' testimony:

> [Governor Connally] never saw the President during the shooting sequence, and it is entirely possible that he heard the missed shot and

that both men were struck by the second bullet. Mrs. Connally testified that after the first shot she turned and saw the President's hand moving toward his throat, as seen in the films at frame 225. However, Mrs. Connally further stated that she thought her husband was hit immediately thereafter by the second bullet. If the same bullet struck both the President and the Governor, it is entirely possible that she saw the President's movements at the same time as she heard the second shot.

This is a distortion of Nellie Connally's testimony, which was clear and unequivocal that the President had already begun reacting to the first shot when the second shot hit her husband. While her testimony "does not preclude the possibility" that the first shot missed, it certainly argues against it. And John Connally's subsequent statements to the press indicate that while he wouldn't testify to it, he was convinced that the first bullet hit Kennedy and the second bullet hit him.

Three days after the assassination, John Connally told television reporters, "I turned to my left to look in the backseat; the President had slumped." In 1966, after viewing the Zapruder film once again, this time in the presence of his wife and doctors, Connally told *Life* magazine:

> "They talk about the 'one bullet' or 'two bullet theory,' but as far as I am concerned, there is no 'theory.' There is my absolute knowledge, and Nellie's too, that one bullet caused the President's first wound, and that an entirely separate shot struck me."
>
> "No one will convince me otherwise," Nellie said.
>
> "It is a certainly. I will never change my mind," Governor Connally said.*

Mrs. Connally's testimony is corroborated by the handwritten notes she compiled just days after the assassination. Thirty-three years after she wrote those notes, she found them while cleaning out an old file cabinet. She had not written the notes for publication, yet she eventually decided to write a

---

*Josiah Thompson, *Six Seconds in Dallas: A Micro-Study of the Kennedy Assassination* (New York: Berkeley Medallion, 1967), p. 85.

book titled *From Love Field.* Here is an excerpt concerning the shot sequence:

> [A] terrifying noise erupted behind us. Instinctively, I felt it was a gunshot.
>
> I looked back and saw the President's hands fly up to his throat. He made no sound, no cry—nothing. His expression hadn't changed—no grimace, no sign of pain. But the eyes—those eyes were full of surprise.
>
> At that instant I was shocked and confused. I had a horrifying feeling that the President not only had been shot, but could be dead.
>
> From the corner of my eye, I saw my husband, John, turn clockwise in his seat. But the car door prevented him from seeing clearly, so he twisted the other way, toward me. He had been in the war. He was a hunter. He knew the sound of gunshots.
>
> "No, no, no!" he cried out.
>
> Then—a second shot.
>
> My husband spun in his seat. He had been hit in the back by the second bullet.*

On the fortieth anniversary of the JFK assassination, Nellie Connally appeared on *The Larry King Show.* During the program she told the same story she had been telling for forty years. She remained convinced that President Kennedy was struck by the first bullet and her husband, now deceased, by the second. She also described how the Warren Commission argued with her about her recollections concerning the shot sequence.

The Connallys' testimony, and their later statements, are clear, vivid, consistent, and corroborative. Knowing that their recollections of the event differed in crucial respects from the Warren Commission's official hypothesis, they never revised or shaded their statements, believing them to be the truth. They also said that they agreed with the overall findings of the Warren Commission that Lee Harvey Oswald was the assassin and that he acted alone.

*Nellie Connally and Mickey Herskowitz, *From Love Field* (New York: Rugged Land, 2003), pp. 7–8.

Unfortunately for the historical record, Jacqueline Kennedy was not extensively questioned by the Warren Commission or any other investigation. Earl Warren felt that Mrs. Kennedy had suffered enough, and he decided, over the objections of other Commissioners and staffers, to allow her to give testimony in her home. Only Warren, J. Lee Rankin, and Bobby Kennedy were present. The questioning was brief (nine minutes long) and superficial—the entire transcript is a little more than 1,700 words. Descriptions that Mrs. Kennedy made of her husband's wounds were deleted from the record. Her testimony was taken on June 5, 1964, the last day of Commission hearings and more than five months after the event.

The two other witnesses in the presidential limousine were William Greer, the driver, and Roy Kellerman, head of the White House Secret Service detail. Greer reported hearing a shot that he at first thought was a motorcycle backfiring. "And then I heard it again. And I glanced over my shoulder. And I saw Governor Connally like he was starting to fall." Greer said he "tramped on the accelerator and at the same time Mr. Kellerman said to me, 'Get out of here fast.' "

When Kellerman heard a noise, he turned to his right to determine what it was. He saw the President with his hands up around his neck. Kellerman also said he heard the President saying, in his distinctive Boston accent, "My God, I am hit," although no other witnesses reported hearing this, and the damage to Kennedy's trachea probably would have made such an utterance impossible.

The presidential limousine was closely followed by the 1956 Cadillac limousine that contained Secret Service agents and two presidential aides. All of the Secret Service agents submitted signed statements shortly after the assassination.

In his statement, Sam Kinney recalled:

As we completed the left turn [onto Elm Street] and on a short distance there was a shot. At this time I glanced from the taillights of the President's car, that I use for gauging distances for driving. I saw the President lean toward the left and [he] appeared to have grabbed his chest with his right hand. There was a second of pause and then two more shots were heard.

George Hickey reported:

> I heard a loud report which sounded like a firecracker. It appeared to come from the right and rear and seemed to me to be at ground level. I stood up and looked to my right and rear in an attempt to identify it. Nothing caught my attention except people shouting and cheering. A disturbance in 679X [the follow-up car] caused me to look forward toward the President's car. Perhaps two to three seconds elapsed from the time I looked to the rear and then looked at the President. He was slumped forward and to his left, and was straightening up to an almost erect sitting position as I turned and looked. At that moment he was almost sitting erect I heard two reports which I thought were shots.

Once again the first shot is heard and a reaction is seen from the President after the first shot but before the second. After the last shot, Hickey picked up the AR-15 automatic rifle from the bottom of the car, cocked it, but did not fire. (One book, *Mortal Error* by Bonar Menninger and Howard Donahue, claims that Hickey fired Kennedy's fatal head shot by accident and the Secret Service conspired to cover it up. There is no evidence to support this theory other than the author's hypothetical bullet trajectory and a great deal of conjecture.)

Glen Bennett stated that as the motorcade traveled toward the freeway:

> I heard what sounded like a firecracker. I immediately looked from the right/crowd/physical area/and looked towards the President who was seated in the right rear seat of his limousine open convertible. At the moment I looked at the back of the President I heard another fire-cracker noise and saw the shot hit the President about four inches down from the right shoulder.

Emory Roberts: "12:30 the first of three shots fired, at which time I saw the President lean toward Mrs. Kennedy."

Paul Landis's report states:

> I heard what sounded like the report of a high-powered rifle from behind me, over my right shoulder. When I heard the sound there

was no question in my mind what it was. My first glance was at the President, as I was practically looking in his direction anyway. I saw him moving in a manner which I thought was to look in the direction of the sound. I did not realize that President Kennedy had been shot at this point.

John Ready and William McIntyre did not see any reaction from the presidential limousine during the first two shots.

Clint Hill's responsibility in the motorcade was to protect Jacqueline Kennedy. He rode on the running board on the left front side of the follow-up car.

I heard a noise similar to a firecracker. The sound came from my right rear and I immediately moved my head in that direction. In so doing, my eyes had to cross the Presidential automobile and I saw the President hunch forward and then slump to his left.

(In James Altgens's photo corresponding to Zapruder frame 255, reprinted in the center of this book, you can see Clint Hill looking directly at the President and about to step onto the street.)

Taken together, these are powerful statements from reliable witnesses. Only Bennett reported seeing the President hit by the second shot. All the other Secret Service agents saw the President move or slump to the left. They were trained professionals whose responsibility it was to protect the President. Their observations are detailed and generally corroborative. The moment they witnessed was exactly what they had been training for; even if they were unable to prevent the assassination, they were very well situated to observe it.

Riding in the follow-up car, presidential aide Kenneth O'Donnell testified: "He was leaning out waving. He may have just been withdrawing his hand. And the shot hit him and threw him to the left."

Presidential aide Dave Powers, sitting beside O'Donnell in the follow-up car, stated in an affidavit: "The first shot went off and it sounded to me as if it were a firecracker. I noticed then that the President moved quite far to his left after the shot from the extreme right hand side where he had been sitting. There was a second shot and Governor Connally disappeared from sight."

Several civilian eyewitnesses also testified to seeing President Kennedy slump to the left immediately after they heard the first shot.

Texas School Book Depository employee Harold Norman, watching from a fifth-floor window directly beneath the sniper's nest, told the Warren Commission: "I heard a shot, and then after I heard the shot, well, it seems as though the President, you know, slumped or something, and then another shot."

Fourteen-year-old Linda Willis: "When the first one hit, well, the President turned from waving to the people, and he grabbed his throat, and he kind of slumped forward, and then I couldn't tell where the second shot went."

Abraham Zapruder: "I heard the first shot and I saw the President lean over and grab himself like this (holding his left chest area)."

Zapruder's secretary, Marilyn Sitzman (from an interview with Josiah Thompson): "There was nothing unusual until the first sound, which I thought was a firecracker, mainly because of the reaction of President Kennedy. He put his hand up as if to guard his face and leaned toward the left, and the motorcade proceeded down the hill." *

The Warren Commission tended to discount, or even argue against, eyewitness testimony. Some of this skepticism was due to the fact that the stories of some witnesses did get better with each telling. Still, the Commission should have credited the statements of the people closest to the event and those who were trained and responsible professionals. Unfortunately, it gave greater weight to its own conclusions after viewing the Zapruder film than to the eyewitnesses who had lived through the event.

If Kennedy and Connally were hit by the same bullet, their reactions would have been nearly simultaneous, or at least close enough to be indistinguishable from each other in time. Yet they were not even close. The Warren Commission reconciled this gap in time between the two victims' visible reactions by hypothesizing that when Connally was wounded, "There was conceivably a delayed reaction between the time the bullet struck him and the time he realized that he was hit, despite the fact that the bullet struck a glancing blow to a rib and penetrated his wrist bone."

The Warren Commission speculated that Connally could have ignored his wounds for anywhere from one-half to two seconds. (The HSCA would

*Thompson, *Six Seconds in Dallas*, pp. 6–7.

later argue that Connally was shot at frame 190, which meant his reaction would have been delayed by nearly two and a half seconds.) This was argued despite Connally's clear and vivid testimony of feeling the shot hit him "as if someone doubled his fist and came up behind you and just with about a twelve-inch blow hit you right in the back right below the shoulder blade."

Connally was describing the entrance wound. This is a good indication that he felt it immediately. He did not describe his other wounds. In fact, he did not realize he had been shot in the wrist and leg until he woke up after surgery. He certainly didn't think he had a delayed reaction. He felt the shot as soon as it entered his back. The pain and shock was so intense that it blocked out all other sensation, even the other two wounds.

Dr. Robert Shaw was present and sworn in at Connally's testimony to the Warren Commission. He described the Governor's thoracic wound in these terms:

It was both a shocking and painful wound, and the effects of the wound, the immediate effects of the wound, were very dangerous as far as Governor Connally was concerned, because he had what we call a sucking wound of the chest. This would not allow him to breathe.

The only way Connally did succeed in breathing was to cover the wound with his arm. Dr. Shaw speculated that Connally would not have been able to maintain breathing for a half-hour with that type of wound.

Dr. Charles Gregory stated that "a necessary consequence of the shot through Connally's chest would be a compression of the chest wall and an involuntary opening of the epiglottis, followed by escaping air forcing open the mouth."* This reaction would have followed a fraction of a second after Connally was hit.

Connally's physical reactions are clearly visible by frame 238 (reprinted in the center of this book). His right shoulder buckling, cheeks puffing, and hair out of place are all involuntary responses. These are not reactions that can be delayed; they are evidence of being wounded. Dr. Shaw told the Warren Commission: "From the pictures, from the conversations with Governor Connally and Mrs. Connally, it seems that the first bullet hit the

*Thompson, *Six Seconds in Dallas*, p. 89.

President in the shoulder and perforated the neck, but this was not the bullet that Governor Connally feels hit him; and in the sequence of films I think it's hard to say that the first bullet hit both of them."

By comparison, Kennedy's back/neck wound went through soft tissue, possibly without striking any bones. He might not have noticed anything until he took a breath, at which point his injured trachea would have caused difficulty breathing. This might also explain why his hands were raised to his throat, as if he were choking.

The eyewitness evidence casts serious doubts on the single bullet theory. Yet how does it stand up when considered in the light of physical evidence?

CHAPTER 14

Two Trajectories

EYEWITNESS EVIDENCE is important, but not incontrovertible. By contrast, you cannot argue with physical evidence. It can be misinterpreted, mishandled, or ignored. Yet it will remain unchanged, even forty years after the crime.

By examining the ballistic and medical evidence, we have already seen how it is possible that Commission exhibit 399 inflicted Kennedy's nonfatal wounds and all of Connally's wounds. The eyewitness evidence, however, appears to contradict the single bullet theory. What happens when we examine the bullet's alleged trajectory?

A bullet traveling at approximately 2,000 feet per second will continue in a straight line until it hits something. After that, we don't know where the bullet will go. But the linear momentum of a missile—the general direction in which it is propelled—will remain unchanged, no matter how serious the deflection. It cannot begin traveling in a completely different direction unless it hits a solid object at a perpendicular and bounces off, with most of its energy expended.

The trajectory of a deflected bullet is impossible to determine with any precision. A small metal object traveling through the air at 2,000 feet per second can be defleted forty-five degrees upon hitting a twig, or it can travel straight through a man's body.

If we can't predict with much accuracy what a bullet will do once it hits a solid target, we can predict what it won't do. Certain trajectories are physically impossible. In considering the flight of the Magic Bullet, I will examine both the vertical and horizontal trajectories.

Vertical Trajectory

Governor Connally was seated in front of, slightly to the left of, and lower than President Kennedy. Could a bullet exiting Kennedy's throat hit Connally and continue on to cause all the Governor's wounds?

Here are three photographs taken from different perspectives just prior to the assassination, which give us a better understanding of President Kennedy's and Governor Connally's positions in the limousine.

Three perspectives on the presidential limousine. *Courtesy of National Archives.*

Courtesy of National Archives.

AP/WideWorld Photos.

The interior of the presidential limousine, showing the positions of the rear and jump seats.
Courtesy of National Archives.

Above is a photo of the limousine interior showing the relative positions of the rear and jump seats.

On the opposite page is a more detailed sketch, based on the schematic provided to the HSCA, showing the exact measurements of the interior of the presidential limousine.

The Warren Report described the President's first entry wound as located "in the vicinity of the lower neck." (This wording was changed from "upper back" by Gerald Ford during a revision of the text.) Without access to the autopsy photographs or X-rays, and relying solely on the autopsy doctors' recollections, the Warren Commission had a medical artist draw an illustration showing the approximate locations of the President's back/throat wound.

Using the X-rays and autopsy photographs as reference, the HSCA

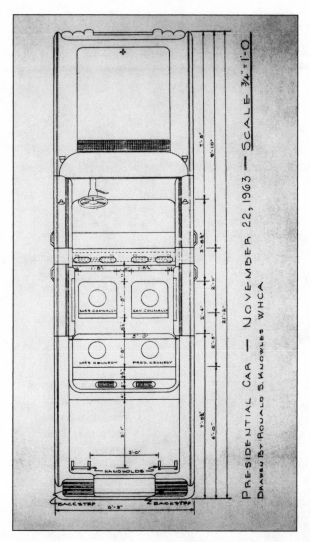

The HSCA presidential limousine schematic.
Courtesy of National Archives

forensic panel determined that this wound was lower than originally estimated by the Warren Commission.

The Warren Commission had placed the back wound higher on
Kennedy's body than was actually the case. This might have been an innocent mistake, because the Commissioners did not have complete information. Yet it does make the single bullet theory more likely, since the higher
the entry wound on Kennedy's back, the greater the downward angle toward
the exit wound on his throat.

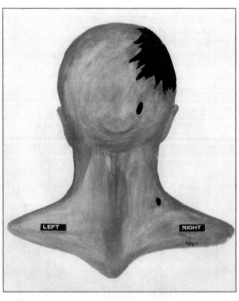

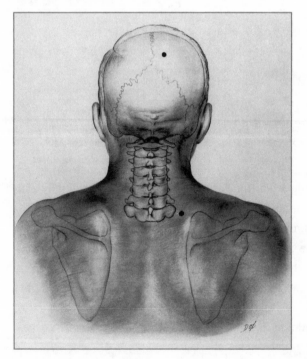

(Above left) The Warren
Commission artist's
rendition of President
Kennedy's back and
throat wounds. *Courtesy of
National Archives.*

(Above right) Warren
Commission artist's
rendition of Kennedy's
entrance wounds.
Courtesy of National Archives.

The HSCA artist's rendition
of President Kennedy's
entrance wound locations.
Courtesy of National Archives.

The vertical angle from the sniper's nest to the presidential limousine measures in downward angles from twenty-four degrees in frame 185 to nineteen degrees in frame 231. The angle of the bullet to target decreases as the target moves away from the sniper, who is stationary.

This means that the bullet striking Kennedy's back would have entered at an angle of declivity ranging from nineteen to twenty-four degrees. It would have continued to travel in that direction until it was deflected by some solid object or lost its gyroscopic stability and began yawing. Contradicting the Warren Commission's estimated wound channel, the HSCA forensic panel, working with all the available evidence, concluded that the bullet traveled across Kennedy's body in a slightly upward direction, if he were perfectly erect. According to the panel, the wound channel through Kennedy's upper body looked something like it does in my illustration "HSCA Diagram of JFK Head Position and Possible Trajectory Angles" in the center of this book, which demonstrates the possible angles of his posture when the wound occurred.

The upward trajectory could be explained in a couple of different ways. After entering the President's back inches below the neck line, the bullet might have been deflected up, either through nicking a bone or by simply yawing through the soft tissue. Kennedy's X-rays show a deformation of the first thoracic vertebrae that could have been caused either by direct contact with the bullet or by the shock waves of the bullet passing through adjacent tissue.

Even if the bullet was not deflected inside Kennedy's neck, it could have taken this upward direction because of his posture at the moment of impact. If he had been hunched over, a bullet traveling at a downward angle could have passed through his body from a lower point of entry to a higher point of exit. Yet, if the President had been hunched over enough to have a descending bullet rise through his body, we would have seen his posture change. In the Zapruder film and all the other photographs from the motorcade, Kennedy is sitting straight up. He wore a corset and an Ace bandage tied in harness fashion around his lower back and thighs to give him lower back support. This is why Kennedy is often seen standing very erect, even rigid.

Another possible explanation for the upward trajectory between the entrance and exit wounds is that the bullet was yawing upwards. This could have occurred as traveling through fourteen centimeters of soft tissue affected the gyroscopic stability of the bullet and caused it to deviate upwards.

If Kennedy's first wound occurred at frame 210, the vertical angle from the sniper's nest would have been 21.3 degrees. Whether by deflection, body position, or yaw, the bullet began moving upwards through the soft tissue of Kennedy's back and throat before exiting. How did it then begin moving downwards to enter just to the left of Connally's right armpit at a downward angle?

The bullet traveled through Connally's chest at a downward trajectory of 27 degrees, which, as we have seen in a previous chapter, was the result of its being deflected along the wound channel. Yet the bullet also had to enter at a downward angle, and this is simply not possible if it had already caused Kennedy's back/throat wound. After adjusting for differences in the height of the two men and their seats, we know that Kennedy was one and a half to three inches above Connally (depending on whether we use the Warren Commission or HSCA measurements). For the bullet to have entered several inches lower on Connally's body than it exited Kennedy's, it would have to have been traveling at a severe downward angle.

The medical evidence doesn't show this. In fact, the slight upward trajectory through Kennedy's neck requires him to have been significantly hunched over in order for the bullet to have exited his throat at the downward angle necessary to cause Connally's entrance wound.

The Warren Commission, concluding that the single bullet was fired somewhere between frames 210 and 224, argued that Kennedy could have assumed this position while Zapruder's view of the limousine was obscured by the Stemmons Freeway sign. That's a convenient explanation, but it's still highly improbable that the President hunched over in such a manner only to recover within a small fraction of a second—after being hit by a bullet.

If the bullet exited Kennedy's throat while he was in a hunched position, it would have been very difficult for the bullet then to enter the right side of Connally's back just beneath the shoulder blade. More likely, if the President had been in such a position when he received his first wound, the bullet would have exited his throat and landed somewhere in his lap.

The HSCA avoided this problem, and created an even more serious one, by concluding that both Kennedy and Connally were hit at frame 190 (based on the acoustics evidence). Here Kennedy is seated erect, and in no time during the sequence between frame 190 and frame 207 does he hunch forward.

The vertical trajectory renders the single bullet theory highly problematic. Yet it is not the only trajectory we must consider.

Horizontal Trajectory

The horizontal trajectory is the direction a bullet moves from side to side. Although very few investigations into the JFK assassination have focused on the horizontal trajectory, it is one of the most important clues in this case.

The horizontal trajectory of bullets fired from the Texas School Book Depository at the presidential limousine at three separate locations corresponding with Zapruder frames 185 to 190, 231 to 235, and 313 have a gradually less acute angle as the limousine travels down Elm Street. My schematic of Dealey Plaza in the center of this book illustrates these three horizontal trajectories.

When Arlen Specter attempted to demonstrate the trajectory of the single bullet in the railroad warehouse following his May 24, 1964, reenactment, he drew a straight line from the exit wound in Kennedy's throat to the entrance wound in Connally's back without considering the direction in which the bullet was traveling and where it would have gone once inside Connally. (Please refer to my illustration "Arlen Specter Demonstrates 'Single Bullet' Trajectory after Reenactment.")

According to Specter's trajectory, the bullet entering Connally's back would have continued traveling left to right, wounding the Governor in the shoulder. Single-bullet scenarios always require that Connally be turned to his right at the moment he was wounded—contrary to his sworn testimony—in order to have the bullet strike him between the armpit and the shoulder blade. Yet if Connally had been turned in that direction, the bullet would not have been able to cause the wounds he suffered.

Connally was turning to his left when he was shot. This is corroborated not only by his testimony but also by the medical evidence. If he had been turning to his right, a bullet traveling from left to right would have entered his lung, not hugged the fifth rib as it did. If he had been turning to his right and the bullet was traveling from right to left, as we see in Specter's scenario, it would have continued in that direction through his shoulder and upper arm. Either way, the horizontal trajectory demonstrates that Connally was not hit when in the position necessary for the single bullet theory to be possible.

The bullet that struck Kennedy in the upper back was fired from his right

President Kennedy's necktie knot would have deflected any bullet exiting toward the left. *Courtesy of Bettmann/Corbis.*

rear. It entered his back four to five centimeters to the right of his midline and exited at the midline, or a half-centimeter to the left. Just prior to exiting Kennedy's throat, the bullet passed between the strap muscles on the right side of the trachea, tearing the trachea and causing damage to the muscles. This might have sent the bullet even farther to the left. Although the wound channel was never precisely determined by the autopsy doctors, by drawing a straight line from the entrance wound to the exit wound, we see a clear movement from right to left, as described in my illustration "JFK Back/Neck Wound (HSCA)" in the center of this book.

This leftward horizontal trajectory is corroborated by the tears in Kennedy's shirt. The hole in the back of his shirt corresponding to the entrance wound is located five and three-quarters inches below the top of the collar and one and seven-eighths inches to the right of the midline. Holes in the front of the shirt corresponding to the exit wound are found just below the top button and just below the top buttonhole. When the top button of the shirt is fastened, these two holes line up, indicating that they were caused by the same object.

There is also a small nick on the left side of Kennedy's necktie knot. The necktie was tied in an uneven yet tight four-in-hand knot. The material was silk and the tie was thin, as was the fashion in 1963. The photo on the opposite page shows the appearance and position of President Kennedy's tie just prior to the assassination.

Examining the necktie, FBI ballistics expert Robert Frazier could not determine whether the nick was caused by a bullet. However, he did state that "it was caused by a projectile of some type which exited from the shirt at this point." No metallic traces were found in the necktie nick. (There were traces of blood, which could have been deposited at any time from any of Kennedy's wounds.) Yet the nick lines up with the two holes just beneath the top button and buttonhole. And the position of the nick on the left side of the necktie knot indicates that the bullet was moving from right to left and was quite possibly deflected even farther to the left by grazing the necktie knot.

How does a bullet traveling from right to left through the President's body exit his throat and hit the Governor on the far right side of the back, just beneath the shoulder blade? Even more troubling, how does that bullet then travel through Connally's back at a horizontal trajectory moving from the right of his right shoulder blade and exiting beneath his right nipple?

It can't.

Dr. Cyril Wecht pointed this out to the HSCA in his dissent from the forensic medical panel's conclusion supporting the single bullet theory. At right is a sketch that Wecht introduced as evidence illustrating the impossibility of this horizontal trajectory in the single bullet theory. Even if he got the measurement of the horizontal angle wrong,

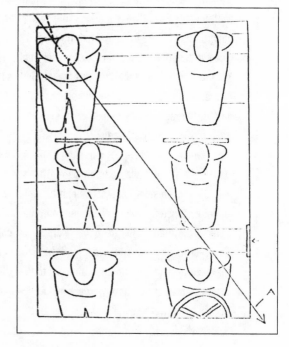

This is how Dr. Cyril Wecht saw the horizontal trajectory.

Courtesy of National Archives.

WAS COMMISSION EXHIBIT 399 PLANTED?

It's easy enough to talk about planting evidence, until you realize the implications of these charges. A defense attorney only has to raise questions, yet a homicide detective must answer them.

I don't believe the Magic Bullet could have been planted, for the following reasons:

1. If someone planted evidence implicating Lee Harvey Oswald, why would that person do it in such a way as to risk that it wouldn't be found? Without any assurance that the evidence would be found, the person discovering the evidence would have to be involved in the conspiracy. (And there is no evidence of this. Besides, if Tomlinson was part of the conspiracy, why would he pass the stretcher once and wait to discover the evidence the second time he saw it?)

2. While the stretcher was accessible and in a public place, who knew it was Connally's? There was another stretcher right beside the one where the bullet was discovered, and there has been much speculation as to whom that stretcher belonged.

3. If conspirators wanted to frame Oswald, why use an almost undamaged bullet? At that point in the case, no one except the Parkland Hospital doctors had any idea what the wounds to JFK and Connally were like (and no conspirator would have anticipated, or possibly even known, that Connally was wounded). Surely a fragment with matchable ballistics marks would be a safer plant than a near-perfect bullet. And if a bullet were to be planted, wouldn't it be placed on Kennedy's stretcher?

4. The planting of the bullet on the stretcher would also require co-conspirators inside trauma room 1 and at the autopsy at Bethesda Naval Hospital (the hospital requested by Jackie Kennedy while en route back to Washington on Air Force One) in order to retrieve any bullets or fragments in Kennedy's body that did not come from the Mannlicher-Carcano.

5. Tests would later prove not only that Commission exhibit 399 came from Oswald's gun but that the bullet was fired from the same rifle as all the other fragments found in the presidential limousine. If the bullet was a plant, so was the rest of the bullet evidence (including the bullet from the Walker shooting).

6. Fibers recovered from the bullet were microscopically matched to fibers from Governor Connally's suit, and lead fragments recovered from his wrist were matched by neutron activation analysis to the bullet. The conspirators would have to have known that the Governor would be wounded in the wrist and have had access to his wardrobe prior to the shooting.

Dr. Wecht is the only person I have ever heard even *mention* the horizontal trajectory.

Wecht's colleagues on the medical panel tried to claim that because the President is not visible on the Zapruder film between frames 210 and 224, a change in Kennedy's and Connally's relative alignment could have occurred during that sequence. (This argument ignores the HSCA's own findings that the single bullet was fired at frame 190, where both men are visible on the film. Apparently it was made prior to the presentation of the acoustics evidence and the Committee's subsequent change in its hypothesis about the shot sequence.)

If the two men changed their positions behind the Stemmons Freeway sign, according to Wecht:

> Connally would have had to have moved a foot or more to his left and then moved back, and/or the President would have had to have almost leaned out of the car and then to have come back to his position. And I am not being the least bit facetious. That is what would have had to have occurred in that nine-tenths of a second interval if we are to assume that this bullet went through the two men in the fashion attributed to it in the single bullet theory.

I examine the horizontal trajectory further in two illustrations—"Warren Commission Seating Positions" and "Horizontal Angles of Bullet"—in the center of this book.

Itek Corporation, a company specializing in photographic reproduction and enhancement, performed a stereophotogrammetric analysis, basically rendering the Zapruder film into 3-D. Itek found that Connally was sitting 10.2 to 20.3 centimeters to the left of a line extending forward from Kennedy.

Even with Connally placed at the most extreme left position possible, the bullet would have hit him in the left shoulder and continued moving right to left, through his body, well away from any of his actual wounds.

No matter where you place Kennedy and Connally, it just doesn't work.

The horizontal trajectory evidence is the most powerful argument against the single bullet theory. Everything else—the relatively undamaged nature of the bullet, the vertical trajectory, the timing of the shot—might be problematic, even highly improbable, but all are possible. The horizontal trajectory is not possible under any conditions.

Dallas assistant district attorney Bill Alexander said, "The single bullet theory is like the immaculate conception. You either believe it or not."

Like many controversies in the JFK assassination, the single bullet theory is supported by those who believe in it and discredited by those who don't. Yet this is not a question we can leave unanswered. And it is not a matter of opinion.

The single bullet theory does not work. This is a fact based on evidence. Commission exhibit 399 still has to be accounted for and explained.

CHAPTER 15

Rethinking the Shot Sequence

BOTH SIDES on the JFK assassination controversy agree about one thing: the case against Lee Harvey Oswald as the lone gunman hinges on whether or not the single bullet theory is true.

"To say they were hit by separate bullets is synonymous with saying that there were two assassins," says Norman Redlich, Warren Commission assistant counsel.

"Without the single bullet theory, there cannot be one assassin, whether it is Oswald or anybody else," according to Dr. Cyril Wecht.

This has become conventional wisdom among almost everyone who has investigated the JFK assassination. It is why the single bullet theory is ridiculed so mercilessly by critics and why the Warren Commission and its defenders try so hard to prove it beyond any possible doubt. It is an article of faith, accepted without argument.

And it is wrong.

The single bullet theory is not supported by the evidence, yet all the evidence points to Oswald as the lone gunman. Is it possible to reconcile these two apparently opposed conclusions?

Yes. They could be reconciled if there were only three shots and each one hit a human target.

Nearly everyone who has investigated this case has made three mistaken assumptions:

1. That Kennedy was shot at or just prior to frames 223 to 224, based on his observable reactions on the Zapruder film.
2. That a clear shot was obscured by the oak tree at the southeast corner of Elm Street from frame 166 to frame 207 inclusive.
3. That at least one shot missed the limousine and all its occupants.

These assumptions have prevented both government investigators and their critics from arriving at a full understanding of the shot sequence and therefore made it impossible for anyone to solve the case beyond a reasonable doubt. They have made the single bullet theory a necessity for those who believe Lee Harvey Oswald was the lone gunman and provided critics with what appears to be evidence of a conspiracy.

When the Zapruder film was viewed by Arlen Specter and other Warren Commission investigators on January 27, 1964, they saw a problem that had not previously existed. The FBI and Secret Service investigations had already concluded that three shots were fired, the first causing Kennedy's nonfatal wounds, the second causing all of Connally's wounds, and the third causing Kennedy's head wound. Looking closely at the Zapruder film (which had also been seen by the FBI and Secret Service), Specter thought that Kennedy's visible reaction was too close in time to Connally's for them to have been caused by a different bullet fired from the C2766 Mannlicher-Carcano.

The Secret Service hadn't worked out the shot sequence according to Zapruder frames or the time it took to reload, aim, and fire the murder weapon. Yet Specter realized that if Kennedy could not have been shot before frame 207, and Connally was shot between frames 231 and 237, there wasn't enough time for two shots. Kennedy showed no reaction to a gunshot wound until he emerged from behind the Stemmons Freeway sign at frame 223. The earliest he could have been hit, according to this analysis, was frame 210, as he went behind the sign. There still wasn't enough time for the assassin to reload, aim, and fire the murder weapon before Connally was obviously wounded.

If two shots had been fired that close together in time, there had to be a second shooter, whether or not there was any ballistics evidence coming from another weapon.

The solution to this problem was the single bullet theory, with the supporting hypothesis that Connally had a delayed reaction to his wounds. The belief that Connally had a delayed reaction was supported only by the fact that the single bullet theory made it necessary in order to explain why he showed no signs of being wounded prior to at least frame 231. And the idea that Kennedy would immediately show a visible reaction to his back/throat wound comes from what I believe is an excessive reliance on the Zapruder film by Arlen Specter and other government investigators (including the HSCA) who wanted every question answered by the film, regardless of what the other evidence said.

In his testimony following the reenactment, Robert Frazier warned the Warren Commission about watching the film too closely for the victims' reactions to their wounds:

> I do not know the reaction time which would exist from the time a bullet struck until someone made a move. It may be a half second, it may be a full second. It may be a tenth of a second. It depends upon the intensity of the pain, and actually what happened. And therefore, in looking at the film you can't say a bullet struck right here because he started to move his hands here. It may have been a full second, a half second behind that spot.

This is especially relevant concerning Kennedy's nonfatal wound, since he was obscured from Zapruder's view by the Stemmons Freeway sign from frame 207 to frame 223, and no one can say with certainty when he began visibly reacting.

It's helpful to step back and recognize how much time we're talking about here. Sixteen Zapruder frames (the period Kennedy was obscured by the sign) is less than one second.

Take a normal breath. That was about thirty Zapruder frames. These are the time increments under consideration in this case. It is possible that Kennedy was shot one second, or two or three or five, before he showed a reaction visible on the Zapruder film. As valuable as the film is, we need to examine other evidence in order to come up with a more complete picture of how the assassination occurred.

All the evidence shows three shots being fired from the Texas School Book Depository. There are three separate wound paths in the two victims. That would seem to indicate three shots and three hits. The Warren Commission decided, however, that one bullet fired at the motorcade missed the limousine and its occupants entirely. This conclusion was arrived at prior to the decision that the single bullet theory was valid, and it was used to both support that theory and make it necessary in the first place. Arlen Specter would eventually complete the circular argument by claiming that the single bullet theory was valid because one bullet missed, and one bullet missed because both Kennedy and Connally were hit by the same bullet.

One of the major reasons why Specter came up with the single bullet theory in the first place was to account for the fact that evidence from only two bullets was recovered from the victims and the limousine. There was evidence of only two bullets. Three shots had been fired. One fragmented bullet accounted for Kennedy's fatal head wound. Therefore, Commission exhibit 399 had to have caused every other wound. Two years after the Warren Report was issued, Specter told *Life* magazine:

> The fact that neither any bullet or fragments, nor any bullet marks, were recovered from the limousine which were not connected to Kennedy's head wound was the single most compelling reason why I concluded the bullet hit both men.*

On the fortieth anniversary of the assassination, Specter defended his single bullet theory at Cyril Wecht's forensic sciences and law symposium called "Solving the Great American Murder Mystery: A National Symposium on the 40th Anniversary of the JFK Assassination" with the following statement: "That bullet had to go somewhere. There was no mark inside the limousine. It exited from the president at a very high velocity and the governor was right in front of him."

In his book *Passion for Truth,* Specter writes:

Life magazine (November 25, 1966).

It all boiled down to one key fact: When the bullet exited the President's neck, the limousine was in such a position that the bullet had to strike the car's interior or someone in it. Our exhaustive examination of the limousine had shown that no bullet had struck the car's interior.*

Testifying before the Warren Commission, FBI agent Robert Frazier made the same argument, with qualifications:

> I cannot say that three bullets did not strike in the automobile from my examination, but it appears . . . due to the reconstruction at Dallas . . . that if the one bullet did strike the President, then it landed in the automobile, and if it landed in the automobile, and we found no evidence of it having hit the car itself, then I say it is possible that it struck the Governor.

In other words, since there was no indication that the bullet exiting Kennedy's throat struck anywhere else inside the limousine, it must have struck Connally. And since three shots had been fired, one of them must have missed the limousine and its occupants entirely.

The missing bullet theory has never really been questioned, not even by critics who argue against the most inconsequential of the Warren Commission's findings. Critics want a shot to miss because that makes another shooter more probable. And it forces those who believe in Lee Harvey Oswald's guilt to support the creaky single bullet hypothesis.

What evidence is there of a missing shot?

James Tague was standing on Commerce Street just east of the triple underpass watching the motorcade when he was superficially wounded by a projectile. Tague and deputy sheriff Eddy R. Walthers located a section of the curb on Main Street that contained a nick that might have been caused by a bullet or fragment. FBI investigators removed the section of curbing on August 5, 1964, and tested it for metallic traces. They found traces of lead and antimony but no copper. "This mark," J. Edgar Hoover stated in a letter

---

*Arlen Specter, with Charles Robbins, *Passion for Truth: From Finding JFK's Single Bullet to Questioning Anita Hill to Impeaching Clinton* (New York: William Morrow, 2000), p. 110.

accompanying the test results, "could not have been made by the first impact of a high velocity rifle bullet." The copper jacket of an undamaged bullet would have left traces if it had struck the curb first.

Although many people on both sides of the controversy have used the Tague injury to prove that a bullet missed the limousine entirely, the FBI evidence shows that it is much more likely that Tague was hit by a piece of concrete chipped off the curb by a lead fragment exiting President Kennedy's head.

There were other reports of a possible missing bullet or fragment. Royce G. Skelton, watching the motorcade from the railroad bridge, reported seeing a shot "hit in the left front of the President's car on the cement." Dallas police officer J. W. Foster testified that he saw a shot hit the grass near a manhole cover in the vicinity of the triple underpass. Other witnesses described seeing sparks, projectiles, or ricochets. However, no bullets, fragments, or marks were found in searches of the areas described by these witnesses, except for the Tague curb.

In the end the Warren Commission concluded that a shot missed, although the Commissioners could not decide which one.

> From the initial findings that (a) one shot passed through the President's neck and then most probably through the Governor's body, (b) a subsequent shot penetrated the President's head, (c) no other shot struck any part of the automobile, and (d) three shots were fired, it follows that one shot probably missed the car and its occupants. The evidence is inconclusive as to whether it was the first, second, or third shot which missed.

According to the Warren Commission, the first shot could have missed because the assassin fired sometime between frames 166 and 207 and the bullet was deflected by the foliage, causing it to miss the limousine and its occupants entirely. The second shot could have missed because there was enough time between the presumed first hit at frame 210 and the undeniable head shot at frame 313 for the assassin to have fired another shot (approximately two and a half seconds), although this contradicts all the eyewitnesses who saw the second shot hit Governor Connally and Connally himself, who felt it without hearing the second rifle report. The third shot could have missed, the Report hypothesized, because that was the farthest and most difficult shot. Also, some eyewitnesses reported seeing a bullet or fragment hitting nearby, which could have been the third shot.

The diminishing conviction with which it considered the possibility of each shot missing indicates that while the Warren Commission did not take an unqualified position as to which shot missed, it believed it was the first.

> If the first shot missed, the assassin perhaps missed in an effort to fire a hurried shot before the President passed under the oak tree, or possibly he fired as the President passed under the tree and the tree obstructed his view. The bullet might have struck a portion of the tree and been completely deflected.

Let's consider this. If the assassin was aiming from the sixth-floor, southeast window of the Texas School Book Depository, he could have begun tracking his target even before the limousine made the turn from Houston onto Elm. Here the assassin had a clear shot but did not take it—probably because the pipes along the east side of the window were in his way. Also, the shooter had already set up the boxes for a shot down Elm Street, where he knew the President's limo would continue. After the limousine rounded the corner, he probably didn't have a clear shot until frame 161, unless he leaned far out the window and possibly exposed himself to witnesses.

Contrary to the Warren Commission's speculation, the first shot had the highest probability of being the most accurate, particularly if the gunman was more accustomed to dry-firing than shooting live ammunition, as Oswald reportedly was. He was relaxed and not anticipating any recoil. It wouldn't be surprising that the second shot was the least accurate, as he was reacting to the recoil and quite possibly did not know whether he hit the target with the first bullet. Indeed, forty years later, we're still not certain what the second shot did.

Let's keep in mind that one shot did miss. Governor Connally was not the target, and he was hit by the second shot. (Oswald apparently did not know that Connally had been wounded, as he expressed surprise upon learning this during his interrogation.) This is entirely consistent with a hurried second shot after firing through the foliage around frame 186.

The Warren Commission was convinced, however, that one shot missed the limousine and its occupants entirely—even if it couldn't decide which

Houston Street from the sniper's nest. *Courtesy of National Archives.*

one it was. To prove this, the authors of the Report (Arlen Specter wrote the first draft of that chapter, and it was edited by other staffers) selected testimony that appeared to corroborate the hypothesis and misrepresented testimony that contradicted it. The Report quotes the statement of Secret Service agent Glen A. Bennett, seated in the right rear seat of the follow-up car.

> I looked at the back of the President. I heard another firecracker noise and saw that shot hit the President about four inches down from the right shoulder. A second shot followed immediately and hit the right rear high of the President's head.

These pipes might have kept the assassin from shooting onto Houston Street. *Courtesy of National Archives.*

After quoting Bennett's statement, the Report offers this evaluation: "Substantial weight must be given to Bennett's observations." Then it goes on to describe how Bennett had written notes on the flight back to Washington shortly after the assassination. What the Report does not do, however, is quote from Bennett's notes directly.

The President's auto moved down a slight grade and the crowd was very sparse. At this point I heard a noise that immediately reminded me of a firecracker. Immediately upon hearing the supposed firecracker, I looked at the Boss's car. At this exact time I saw the shot that hit the Boss about 4 inches down from the right shoulder. A second shot followed immediately and hit the right rear of the President's head.

Which shot did Bennett see hit the President? It's not clear from his notes, although his later report indicates he believed it was the second shot. The Warren Report quotes Bennett's statement while ignoring or arguing against those of other eyewitnesses (Nellie Connally, Clint Hill, Sam Kinney, George Hickey, Dave Powers, Ken O'Donnell, Harold Norman, Linda Willis, Abraham Zapruder, and Marilyn Sitzman) who indicated that the first shot hit President Kennedy. To confuse the issue even further, the Report goes on to state: "It is possible, of course, that Bennett did not observe the hole in the President's back, which might have been there immediately after the first noise."

Elm Street from the sniper's nest. *Courtesy of National Archives.*

Governor Connally believed that the first bullet hit Kennedy, yet he was careful not to testify to something he had not observed firsthand. We have already seen how the Warren Commission chose to interpret his observations:

> Governor Connally's testimony supports the view that the first shot missed, because he stated that he heard a shot, turned slightly to his right, and, as he started to turn back toward his left, was struck by a second bullet. He never saw the President during the shooting sequence, and it is entirely possible that he heard the missed shot and that both men were struck by the second bullet.

After making what appears to be an argument for the first shot missing, the Report then backs off, saying: "If the first shot did not miss there must be an explanation for Governor Connally's recollection that he was not hit by it."

As confusing as the section on the missing shot can be, it seems clear that the Warren Commission leaned toward the first shot having missed, because of the oak tree at the corner of Elm Street: "It is doubtful that even the most proficient marksman could have hit him through the oak tree."

During their reenactment, performed well before the single bullet theory had ever been proposed, Secret Service investigators concluded that the oak tree obscured the target from frames 166 to 207 inclusive. This conclusion has been accepted as evidentiary fact by both sides of the JFK controversy, despite the photo from Arlen Specter's reenactment that shows that the foliage did not completely obscure the target at that time. (This is even more apparent in the film footage shot by Shaneyfelt during the reenactment.) Although the target is not completely unobstructed around Zapruder frame 186, it is entirely possible that the assassin fired during this sequence and that the bullet made its way through the thin oak leaves and branches to hit the President. It is also possible that the President was more visible than the reenactment photos indicate. If Kennedy was seated a few inches to his left, if the limousine hugged the left side of the lane, if a breeze kicked up, or if the shooter was in a slightly different position from the one Frazier and Shaneyfelt took in the sniper's nest—the target could have been much more visible.

Remember the testimony of Harold Norman, watching the motorcade from directly below the sniper's nest. "I heard a shot, and then after I heard the shot, well, it seems as though the President, you know, slumped or something, and then another shot." If Norman could see the President, then the shooter could see him as well. Norman heard the first shot—it was so close that he felt it—and gave this statement without knowledge of the single bullet theory or the other witnesses who reported seeing the President slump or move to his left after the first shot was fired.

On at least two occasions, Specter has stated that Kennedy could have been wounded by a shot fired around frame 186 and Connally wounded by a second shot. During his HSCA testimony and a 1966 interview with *CBS News,* Specter admitted that the target was visible through a break in the foliage around this time. Aside from the reenactment photo, which shows the target partially visible, there was no mention of this in the Warren

Report, and even when he acknowledges the possibility of an earlier shot opportunity, Specter continues to defend the single bullet theory as the most reasonable explanation.

Even if a shot was possible around frame 186, the Report stated, "it is unlikely that the assassin would deliberately have shot at him with a view obstructed by the oak tree when he was about to have a clear opportunity."

But the shooter had no idea that he would be able to get off three shots. He wasn't even sure he would have a second shot, and he could have fired within this brief window of opportunity. Besides, why would the Warren Commission first argue that a shot was probably deflected by foliage and then state that it was unlikely that the shooter fired at the target until he had a clear shot?

It is much more likely that three shots were fired and that all three hit someone, proving both the single bullet theory and the conspiracy theorists wrong.

For the following reasons, I believe the first shot was fired around frame 186 and hit President Kennedy:

1. The trajectory evidence renders the single bullet theory impossible.
2. There is evidence of only three shots fired.
3. The head shot at frame 313 leaves us with two shots that must account for two separate wound tracks in the two men.
4. There is no evidence proving that one bullet completely missed the limousine and all its occupants.
5. Several witnesses observed the President being hit by the first shot.
6. The oak tree did not completely obscure the target.
7. The Zapruder film shows a lag in observable reaction times between the two victims, and it is much more likely that Kennedy, not Connally, had a delayed observable reaction.

In debates about the shot sequence, Arlen Specter and other supporters of the single bullet theory would ask: If Kennedy and Connally were struck by separate shots, where did that bullet go? That question would often end the argument because no one ever had a good answer. Until now.

CHAPTER 16

Evidence Ignored

IN A CASE where even the most tangential facts are recorded, testified to, explained, and questioned in brain-numbing detail, I find it surprising that one of the most important pieces of evidence in the JFK assassination has gone almost entirely unnoticed for forty years. The Warren Commission made several references to it without coming to any conclusions or even deciding if it was in fact evidence. Hardly any critics have examined this clue despite the fact that it raises serious questions about the single bullet theory.

I am talking about the dent in the strip above the windshield in the presidential limousine. This dent was first observed in the parking lot of Parkland Hospital. While the ultimately futile efforts to resuscitate the President were being made in trauma room 1, AP photographer James Altgens took a photo, reprinted on the following page.

The dent was later noted by FBI investigators during their search of the limousine in the White House garage that began fourteen hours after the assassination. During this search FBI agents were looking for evidence of any bullets that had either remained in or struck the limousine. (Secret Service agents had already performed a cursory search for "personal effects

Altgens's photo of the presidential limousine at Parkland Hospital. *Courtesy of the Sixth Floor Museum at Dealey Plaza. Tom Dillard Collection, the* Dallas Morning News. *All rights reserved.*

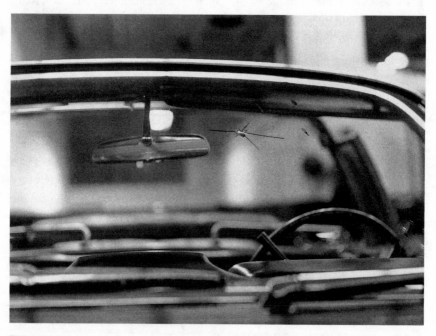

The cracked windshield of the presidential limousine. *Courtesy of National Archives.*

and other items.") FBI agents Robert Frazier, Charles Killion, and Cort Cunningham spent two and a half hours searching the vehicle. They closely examined all the visible surfaces, including the metal and upholstery, and checked the carpet for bullet holes or furrows, although they did not remove the carpet where it was glued to the floor.

The windshield was later removed, and small lead traces were recovered from inside the crack. Both the presence of these lead traces and the direction and nature of the crack indicated that the windshield had been struck by a projectile traveling from the inside rear of the limousine. The lead scrapings were compared to the lead found in the base of Commission exhibit 399 and determined to be similar but not matched.

We can determine when the windshield was cracked by examining two photos taken by the same photographer. Viewing once again James Altgens's photograph taken around frame 255, we see that the windshield is intact.

Just after the third shot, Altgens took another photograph. The crack in the windshield is now visible. Both of these photos are reprinted in the center of this book.

The time difference between these two photographs is about four seconds. It appears that the crack in the windshield was caused by a fragment exiting the President's skull as a result of the third shot.

Physical evidence corroborates this finding, since any bullet fragment exiting the President's skull would have been traveling at a severely reduced velocity after expending most of its energy along the wound channel. The more a bullet fragments, and the smaller those fragments are, the more energy the fragments lose within the target, because the drag force of smaller fragments is much greater than that of larger fragments or intact bullets. In addition, the estimated trajectory from Kennedy's exit wound to the windshield works. In the Zapruder film, we see small fragments flying above and beyond Kennedy's skull, toward the front of the limousine.

James Altgens followed the motorcade to Parkland Hospital, where he took additional photographs of the presidential limousine before Secret Service agents placed the bubble-top on the vehicle. When the limousine was taken back to Washington and searched in the White House garage, a photograph of the dent in the windshield trim was taken by FBI agent Robert Frazier.

As you can see, the dent is slightly off-center to the right on the edge of the windshield frame just above the passenger sun visor. The dent has a cen-

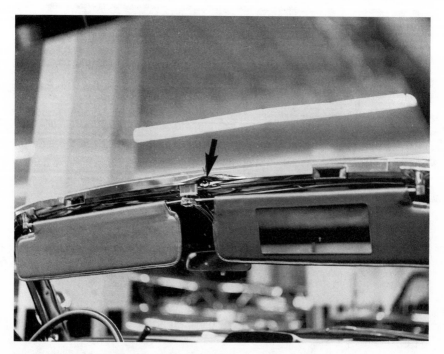

The dent in the windshield trim. *Courtesy of National Archives.*

ter point of impact where the deepest penetration is observed. All the remaining damage seems to expand from that point of impact, which is round and convex. The dent appears to have been from the impact of a projectile, and the force exerted on the metal seems to have been slightly from the right, moving somewhat to the left and up. It is elongated on the right, as if the pressure was initially greater on that side or the force was moving across the surface of the metal from right to left. It appears to have been caused by something striking the trim and creating a round, uniform crater.

If the dent in the windshield trim was caused by a bullet, when did it occur?

Frazier described the dent in his Warren Commission testimony as having "been caused by some projectile which struck the chrome on the inside surface." Asked by Allen Dulles whether the dent could have been caused by a bullet fragment, Frazier responded in the affirmative, stating that he believed the dent could have been caused by either of the two large fragments found in the front seat and later matched to the head shot. Frazier went on to say that he did not believe it could have been caused by "a bullet which was traveling at its full velocity from a rifle, but merely from a fragment traveling at a fairly high velocity."

Arlen Specter then posed two hypothetical questions to the witness. If a bullet had gone through President Kennedy's neck, causing the wounds described in the autopsy protocol, what would have happened if that bullet exited his throat and went on to hit the windshield? Frazier said it would have shattered the windshield.

What if the same bullet hit the trim?

"It would have torn a hole in the chrome," Frazier testified, and "penetrated the framing both inside and outside of the car." In advancing this opinion, Frazier noted that he had not tested the metal in the car and was merely assuming that a bullet traveling at a speed of 1,772 to 1,779 feet per second (the speed they estimated the bullet traveled after passing through Kennedy's upper body) would have caused much more damage.

The estimated exit velocity of 1,772 to 1,779 feet per second seems not only more precise than possible but also way too fast. After having traveled about 150 feet, the bullet would already have lost some 200 feet per second from its original muzzle velocity of 2,296 feet per second. Then it traversed fourteen centimeters of soft tissue in President Kennedy's upper body. If it was traveling at a speed significantly lower than 1,700 feet per second, the bullet would not have had enough velocity to cause all of Connally's wounds.

That estimate is based on tests performed at the Aberdeen Proving Grounds, where 6.5-millimeter Mannlicher-Carcano bullets were fired into material simulating human tissue and their speed measured upon exit from the material. During these tests the bullets were undeflected and did not go into a significant yaw. Yet we have seen in the Anatomical Surrogate Technologies reenactment that a bullet passing through fourteen centimeters of simulated human tissue travels at a velocity insufficient to replicate all of Connally's wounds. There is no way of estimating the velocity of the bullet once it exited Kennedy's throat, but I doubt it was 1,770 feet per second.

Why did Frazier and Specter dismiss the possibility that the dent in the windshield trim was caused by a bullet exiting Kennedy's throat?

First, let's clear up an important misperception. The windshield trim is not made of chrome. Chrome is a coating, not a solid piece of metal. The windshield trim on the 1961 Lincoln is stainless steel. The stainless trim is a polished metal without plating. Had this trim been chrome-plated steel, upon impact the plating would have flaked off and exposed the bare steel underneath.

Although the stainless steel trim is certainly stronger than windshield safety glass, Frazier seemed to have been under the impression that similar bullet fragments would have caused more damage to the trim than to the windshield. He overestimated the damage that an almost intact bullet traveling at a diminished speed would have caused to the stainless steel trim. Frazier and Specter had both repeatedly assumed that any bullet striking Kennedy would have, upon exit, gone on to either strike someone else in the limousine or cause visible damage to the limousine itself. This assumption was one of the pillars of the single bullet theory. During the reenactment, when Frazier looked through a four-power scope at the target, he concluded that any shot hitting Kennedy would probably have remained in the limousine. Using Frazier's testimony, both before and after the reenactment, Specter concluded that the dent in the windshield trim could only have been caused by a bullet fragment exiting Kennedy's head, and not an almost undeformed bullet exiting from his throat.

On page 77 of the Warren Report, we read the following:

Although there is some uncertainty whether the dent in the chrome on the windshield was present prior to the assassination, Frazier testified that the dent "had been caused by some projectile which struck the chrome on the inside surface." If it was caused by a shot during the assassination, Frazier stated that it would not have been caused by a bullet traveling at full velocity, but rather by a fragment traveling "at a fairly high velocity." It could have been caused by either fragment found in the front seat of the limousine.

On page 105:

The minute examination by the FBI inspection team, conducted in Washington between 14–16 hours after the assassination, revealed no damage indicating that a bullet struck any part of the interior of the Presidential limousine, with the exception of the cracking of the windshield and the dent on the windshield chrome. Neither of these points of damage to the car could have been caused by the bullet that exited the President's neck at a velocity of 1,772 to 1,779 feet per second.

If one of the fragments that left the President's head caused the crack in the windshield, then we can assume that fragment was traveling at a velocity low enough not to penetrate the windshield. Yet, according to the Warren Commission, a fragment traveling at the same approximate speed caused a circular crater on the stainless steel windshield trim exactly on the bend of the metal where it was the strongest, for it had to support the clamps of the convertible bubble-top.

The Warren Commission never determined whether the dent was caused by a projectile during the assassination or had existed prior to November 22, 1963. A memo dated January 6, 1964, from Secret Service director James Rowley to J. Lee Rankin, general counsel to the Warren Commission, offered another explanation for the dent.

Special Agent Gies, who was responsible for the care and maintenance of this vehicle, believes that this damage was on the car prior to November 22nd, 1963, and it is his recollection that this damage was in New York at the Empire Garage (Lincoln-Mercury dealer) on November 1961. Gies thinks the damage was done while he and employees of the garage were removing the header on the leatherette top. . . . If this was the case, no effort was made to repair the dent prior to the assassination.

Paul Michel, service director of the Empire Garage, was present and assisted with the November 1, 1961, repairs. Although Michel did not remember any damage occurring at that time, he stated that it was possible that some damage did occur, since a crank had broken off near the top of the windshield.

During their testimony to the Warren Commission, Secret Service agents William Greer and Roy Kellerman both stated that they had not observed the dent in the windshield trim prior to the assassination. These two men were in the front seat of the limousine on a regular basis. Knowing a little about the way civil servants are required to keep records concerning public vehicles, I'm surprised that if this damage had occurred more than two years prior, nobody noticed it except agent Gies. Even stranger, why would Gies not fill out a report citing the damage?

Referring to Frazier's photograph in his memo cited earlier, Rowley contributed this opinion:

> It may be significant to mention here that this photograph accentuates the damage. This indentation is so slight that it could pass unnoticed in ordinary viewing of the area, especially since the sun visors, being in a horizontal position most of the time, would frequently cut out the view of this portion of the frame.

Yet the Altgens photo was taken from approximately ten feet behind the limousine. And the dent is clearly observable in a high-quality print of the photo.

Why didn't the Warren Commission determine whether the dent was there prior to the assassination? Specter assumed that it was caused by a bullet fragment. Rowley's memo claims that the dent had a more innocent explanation. The HSCA never cleared up this question. And none of the books or articles by independent researchers I have read can provide an answer.

Although there are several photographs of the windshield in the National Archives digital image collection of Warren Commission exhibits, there are none of the windshield trim. I wrote to the Archives asking if the windshield trim was in its possession. I was told that the only evidence associated with the windshield trim in the Archives was Commission exhibit 349, the photo taken by Frazier during the search of the limousine at the White House garage. In most cases, the Commission exhibit number designates the piece of evidence itself. Commission exhibit 349 is a photograph of an item of evidence that should have been preserved but wasn't.

So what happened to the windshield trim?

At 10:00 A.M. on the morning of November 23, F. Vaughn Ferguson, an employee of the Ford Motor Company, came to the White House garage at the request of the Secret Service to view the limousine, which was covered with canvas and under guard. Ferguson was asked to examine the windshield and make arrangements to have it replaced. The next day Ferguson returned to the White House garage to find the limousine no longer guarded. The

Secret Service had attempted to clean the leather upholstery, but bloodstains remained on the upholstery buttons. Ferguson took a knife and removed caked blood from around the buttons. There was also a large bloodstain on the floor covering that Ferguson did not attempt to remove.

On November 25, Ferguson called Arlington Glass to have someone come to the garage and replace the windshield. The Arlington Glass employees told Ferguson and Morgan Gies, the Secret Service agent in charge of the limousine, that if they were to remove the windshield, it would cause additional damage to the glass. Gies told them to go ahead. They put their feet against the inside of the windshield and pushed it out from the frame. On doing so, they created larger cracks below the original damage to the glass. The windshield was preserved as evidence, and metallic fragments were taken from the inside of the original crack. These fragments were tested by the FBI on March 20, 1964, and determined to be lead. The minute quantity of lead recovered from the crack in the windshield made further testing, such as neutron activation analysis, impossible.

The same day the windshield was removed, Ferguson continued cleaning and performing minor repairs on the limousine. When he was finished, Gies pointed out the dent in the windshield trim and asked why he hadn't repaired it. Ferguson replied that it was his experience that "trying to remove a dent of that size [would] lead only to additional marks that further marred the trim," according to an intracompany memo he wrote on December 18, 1963. Gies had expected Ferguson to "repair" damage with potential evidentiary value. At the time, the limousine was under the control of the Secret Service, while the FBI was in charge of the recovery and preservation of evidence. The FBI took the windshield glass but did not do anything about the dent in the trim other than photograph it.

Meanwhile, the new President needed a new limousine. After conferring with experts from within and outside the government, the White House decided to rebuild the original limousine rather than commission an entirely new vehicle, which would take too long. On December 12, the limousine was delivered to the Hess & Eisenhart Company in Cincinnati, which had made the original modifications to the limousine. The Warren Commission officially released the limousine as evidence on December 20, and work on "Project D-2," or "Quick Fix," as it came to be called, began shortly thereafter.

Hess & Eisenhart installed a permanent, nonremovable top; bulletproof glass; titanium body armor; a steel plate in the rear floor to protect against bombs; bullet-resistant tires; an explosion-proof gas tank; a supplemental air-conditioning unit for the passenger compartment; and a new high-compression engine. The original windshield trim was replaced with stronger materials to support the bulletproof glass and permanent roof.

And so an important piece of evidence in the assassination of the President of the United States ended up as scrap metal.

The Rowley memo was written on January 6, 1964, after work on Quick Fix had begun; by that point, the windshield trim was probably already lost. Did Gies claim that the damage to the trim had occurred prior to the assassination in order to downplay the loss of this evidence? Is that why the Warren Commission never determined exactly what caused the dent in the windshield strip and whether it had any connection to the assassination? Did Specter and Frazier wiggle their way around this evidence because they knew it had not been preserved?

It seems clear to me that once they realized that this evidence had been destroyed, however inadvertently, the Secret Service, the FBI, and the Warren Commission ignored the damage to the windshield trim and downplayed its evidentiary value whenever they could not avoid mentioning it. Unfortunately, we often see this in high-profile cases, when investigators are more willing to ignore lost evidence than admit that they should have preserved it.

Although early investigators in the JFK assassination case might not have realized the importance of the dent in the windshield trim, they certainly considered it evidence. When the limousine was first searched after the assassination, neither Frazier nor any of the other agents had seen the Zapruder film. They were not aware of future questions concerning the sequence and timing of the shots. They didn't know how many shots had been fired by how many shooters. If they knew a suspect was in custody, they had no idea that Oswald would be murdered and that a presidential commission would be established to gather and analyze evidence in the case.

Frazier clearly saw the dent and recognized it as probably being the result of a projectile. He photographed the windshield trim in order to preserve his initial observation. But that was the end of the line for this particular piece of evidence. It should have been removed from the limousine and tested for blood and bullet fragments. The size and shape of the dent should

Cracked windshield with visible blood spatter. *Courtesy of National Archives.*

have been compared to a 6.5-millimeter Mannlicher-Carcano bullet. And the trajectory from the dent should have been measured backwards to the President's exit wounds to see if the dent could have been caused by a bullet or fragment and possibly to determine from which shot it came.

Instead, all that remains of this evidence is a handful of photographs. Let's take a closer look at one of them, reprinted above.

Here we can clearly see blood spatter on the inside of the windshield. The pattern of the blood spatter indicates that the blood splashed against the windshield coming from the right rear. We can assume that these bloodstains came from the President's head wound.

There is also visible damage to the back of the rearview mirror, probably from the bullet fragment bouncing off the windshield. This means that the missile would have remained in the limousine and was probably one of the fragments recovered from the President's head wound.

What about the dent in the windshield trim? If the fragments exiting Kennedy's head were too small and traveling at too low a velocity to cause the dent, it could have been made by a bullet exiting the President's throat and traveling in vertical trajectory slightly upward and a horizontal trajectory from right to left. That appears to be a much more probable cause of the dent than either a fragment from the head shot or some undocumented mishap in a New York City garage that went unobserved for more than two years.

To completely understand the evidentiary value of the dented windshield, we must return to JFK's autopsy. Dr. James Humes identified the back wound as an entry and probed it with his little finger. Humes felt what he thought was the end of the wound channel, and since he couldn't find an exit wound, he concluded that the bullet must have fallen out of the back muscles during cardiac massage at Parkland Hospital.

Had he known that the bullet entering Kennedy's back had exited his throat just below the Adam's apple, Humes certainly would have determined that the wound channel ran from the entrance wound to the exit wound. He then would have realized that the bullet must have deviated from its initial downward trajectory sometime after entering the soft tissue in Kennedy's back. Although it would have been helpful if the autopsy doctors had dissected the neck tissue and determined the precise wound channel, we can still conclude that the bullet moved upwards through the President's neck area, either deflected by the first thoracic vertebrae or yawing as it passed through the soft tissue. This is the vertical trajectory inside the President's body. The horizontal trajectory went from right to left, possibly deviating even further to the left as the bullet passed through the strap muscles on the right side of the trachea and exited, nicking the left of the necktie knot.

Robert Frazier was asked by Warren Commissioner John McCloy whether it was possible that the first shot went through Kennedy's neck and exited without hitting Connally, who was struck by the second shot. "If [a bullet] had deflection in the President's body, it could have," he replied, "and [if] he happened to be in a certain position in the car which would affect the angle, the bullet may have exited from the automobile."

All the evidence shows that the first shot came from the southeast-corner, sixth-floor window of the Texas School Book Depository. This was approximately sixty feet above the presidential limousine. Let's take another look at the HSCA sketch showing various possible angles of Kennedy's head and upper body when he was shot in the back (which I described in the illustration "HSCA Diagram of JFK Head Position"). Despite the variation of vertical trajectory implied by the HSCA, assuming that Kennedy was shot around frame 186, where he is visibly erect on the Zapruder film, there was a much narrower range of possibility.

The angle from the sixth-floor southeast-corner window of the Texas School Book Depository to the presidential limousine was twenty-four degrees. So a bullet fired from the sniper's nest at Zapruder frame 186 would have entered President Kennedy's back at a twenty-four-degree declivity and traveled at least some distance at that angle. When we add a bullet entering from a twenty-four-degree angle to the HSCA sketch, we see a clear change of trajectory as the bullet passes through Kennedy's back and neck. (Please refer to my illustration "Bullet Probably Entered.")

Clearly, the bullet had to deviate at some point inside the President's upper body. The downward trajectory was consistent for at least the length of Humes's little finger, and then it deflected to a slight upward angle. Even if we aren't sure exactly why, we can be certain that it did, because the bullet exited Kennedy's throat and left evidence of its path on his shirt collar and tie.

When we connect up the known points of intersection from Kennedy's entrance and exit wounds, taking into account both the upward angle and the slightly right-to-left trajectory, we can see how the bullet that exited Kennedy's throat could have struck the windshield trim and then exited the vehicle. (Please refer to my illustrations "Seat and Body Positions at 'Z' 185–190" and "Warren Commission Seating Positions.")

In his testimony following the reenactment, Robert Frazier was asked by Arlen Specter whether a bullet exiting President Kennedy's throat could have missed the interior of the limousine and all of its occupants. Frazier said that if you looked through a telescopic sight at a limousine traveling west on Elm Street, as he did during the reenactment, you would see that a bullet would have to hit either the vehicle, or at least one of its occupants "if it had no deflection in its path."

Yet we have seen that the bullet passing through Kennedy's neck was deflected, slightly up and to the left. And we see the round dent in the chrome strip above the rearview mirror, which both Specter and Frazier were aware of, having referred to it on several occasions.

Specter was aware of all this evidence. Why didn't he come to this same conclusion?

I believe that Specter wanted a shot to miss because he didn't want to have an unrecovered bullet responsible for any wounds. A missing bullet could have come from another rifle. He wanted to account for every piece of evidence and wrap the case up as tightly as possible. The windshield trim had been lost before Arlen Specter began working on the case. Although its disappearance wasn't his fault, it was his responsibility, and he clearly wished to avoid focusing on this unrecovered evidence. A missing shot also resolved the problems created by the mistaken assumption that Kennedy could not have been shot before frame 207. The Zapruder film showed that Connally was definitely shot by frame 237. And thirty frames wasn't enough time for Oswald to have made two shots with the Mannlicher-Carcano. Enter the single bullet theory.

The Warren Commission was established in order to quell suspicions of a conspiracy. It did not want to introduce evidence that might raise more questions than it answered. This concern is evident when you read the transcripts of the Warren Commission's executive sessions. A great deal of time was taken up by discussions of whether certain investigative paths should even be followed, for the Commissioners were well aware that all their evidence would become public record. Following the Warren Commission's institutional logic, Arlen Specter proposed a theory that he was never able to satisfactorily prove, because it was contradicted by evidence he had to ignore or gloss over. For Specter, a flawed theory was preferable to a missing bullet and lost evidence.

It is a rare murder case where every single piece of evidence is recovered. As a working assistant district attorney, Specter should have understood this. A murder case is like a jigsaw puzzle: even if some pieces are missing, you can still see the picture. Unfortunately, Specter tried to present a case without any holes whatsoever. In doing so, he cast a shadow of doubt over the Warren Commission's findings that lasts until today.

Still, there is plenty of evidence to reconstruct the crime.

CHAPTER 17

The Assassination of
John F. Kennedy

7:15 A.M. Linnie Mae Randle observes Lee Harvey Oswald carrying a long package wrapped in brown paper. He places the package in the rear seat of Buell Wesley Frazier's car and waits for Frazier to come out to the carport. When Frazier arrives, he notices the package and asks Oswald what it contains. Oswald tells him curtain rods.

7:30 A.M. Frazier and Oswald arrive at a parking lot near the Texas School Book Depository. Frazier remains in his car with the motor running for several minutes to recharge his battery. Oswald leaves in a hurry, carrying his package toward the loading dock entrance of the Depository.

Oswald spends the morning on the sixth floor, arranging boxes so that the southeast-corner window is obscured from view. He builds a small stack of boxes in front of the window to use as a gun rest. These boxes are lighter than the textbook boxes. Although he carries his clipboard around with him, he makes no notations that morning.

11:40 A.M. Oswald is observed by Bonnie Ray Williams on the sixth floor, near the east windows.

11:45 A.M. Oswald is observed by Charles Givens on the sixth floor.

12:00 to 12:15 P.M. Williams returns to the sixth floor to eat his lunch.

Oswald waits nearby in the sniper's nest beside him, hidden by a stack of boxes.

When Williams is finished, he goes down to the fifth floor to watch the motorcade with Howard Norman and James Jarman.

Oswald has already reassembled his Mannlicher-Carcano and loaded four bullets into the clip. He has a few minutes to wait for the motorcade.

12:15 P.M. Arnold Rowland sees a man in a window near the top of the Texas School Book Depository. He is a white male with a slender build and dark hair, dressed in a light-colored shirt. He stands in parade rest position several feet back from the window and is holding a rifle. Rowland asks his wife if she would like to see a Secret Service agent. When she looks up at the window, the man is no longer visible. Rowland considers notifying the police but decides the man must be a Secret Service agent.

Carolyn Walther also looks up at the Texas School Book Depository. She sees a man wearing a white shirt, with blond or light brown hair. He is holding a rifle with the barrel pointed down. The rifle has a short barrel and seems large around the stock.

12:23 P.M. Howard Brennan sees a man standing in the southeast-corner, sixth-floor window of the Texas School Book Depository. He observes the man come and go "a couple times."

12:29 P.M. The lead car of the presidential motorcade turns onto Main Street from Houston Street.

From the sniper's nest, the presidential limousine comes into view, traveling down Houston Street toward the Texas School Book Depository.

This is the moment Lee Harvey Oswald has been waiting for all his life. His body remembers his Marine Corps training. BRASS—Breath, Relax, Aim, Slack, Squeeze. The art of shooting accurately. Take a breath . . . let out half of it . . . relax the muscles in your shoulders, settle into the rifle . . . aim at the target . . . take up the slack in the trigger . . . squeeze the trigger so gently that every round fired is something of a surprise.

Oswald is ready, but does not fire. The limousine is traveling toward him, and it is difficult to track. He knows he will get a better shot once the limousine turns and the target is moving away from him. He gets into position, kneeling in front of the stack of boxes and aiming the rifle down Elm Street.

The limousine makes the 120-degree turn onto Elm Street.

In the lead car, Secret Service agent Forrest Sorrels radios to Secret Service agents already at the Trade Mart: "We'll be there in five minutes."

12:30 P.M. Nellie Connally turns back to President Kennedy and says, "Mr. President, you can't say that Dallas doesn't love you."

"That is very obvious," Kennedy replies.

Amos Euins sees "a pipe thing sticking out" of the southeast-corner, sixth-floor window of the Texas School Book Depository.

Lee Harvey Oswald sees the target through a break in the foliage. He fires.

The bullet enters Kennedy's upper back, passing through the soft tissue and exiting from his throat just below the Adam's apple. He feels a shock but does not immediately realize he has been wounded. The bullet exits Kennedy's throat, yawing upwards and traveling from right to left. It passes between John and Nellie Connally and between William Greer and Roy Kellerman, hitting the windshield strip above the rearview mirror. The bullet deflects off the strip and hurtles over the limousine, bouncing off the street and landing harmlessly somewhere beyond.

Pigeons scatter from the roof of the Texas School Book Depository building.

John Connally recognizes the noise as a rifle shot and immediately thinks this is an assassination attempt. He starts to turn to his right to see if the President has been injured. He says, "Oh, no, no, no."

Nellie Connally turns to her right and sees the President slumping. His arms raise toward his throat.

Jackie Kennedy turns toward her husband. He has a "quizzical look" on his face.

From the follow-up car, Secret Service agents Sam Kinney, George Hickey, and Clint Hill, along with presidential aides Ken O'Donnell and Dave Powers, all hear the rifle shot and see the President wounded.

From a window directly below the sniper's nest, Harold Norman hears the first shot and sees the President slump.

Several other witnesses see the President slump or move to the left immediately after the sound of the first shot.

James Worrell looks up toward the Texas School Book Depository building and sees six inches of a rifle barrel sticking out of a high window. The rifle has a long stock, and only a few inches of the metal barrel are visible.

Mrs. Earle Cabell sees a "projection" from the southeast-corner, sixth-floor window of the Texas School Book Depository.

Seeing small fragments flying around inside the President's limousine, spectator Jack Franzen assumes that someone has tossed a firecracker inside the vehicle.

Harold Norman hears the bolt of the rifle pull back and the empty shell eject, bouncing off the plywood floor above him.

James Jarman says, "I believe someone is shooting at the President." Norman replies, "I believe it came from up above us."

President Kennedy has been wounded for approximately one second before he tries to take another breath. The wound to his trachea and the bruising of his right pleura cause him pain and difficulty in respiration.

After hearing the first shot and thinking it was a firecracker thrown from the Texas School Book Depository, Howard Brennan looks back up at the southeast-corner, sixth-floor window. He sees the man he previously observed in the window. Now that man is aiming a rifle.

Amos Euins looks back up at the window and sees "the pipe thing." This time he sees a man behind it.

Not knowing if he hit the target, and uncertain whether he will get another shot, Oswald quickly reloads and takes aim.

Oswald fires, missing high and to the right. The bullet enters Connally's right back, between the armpit and the shoulder blade. Connally feels "as if someone doubled his fist and came up behind you and just with about a twelve-inch blow hit you right in the back right below the shoulder blade." When he tries to take his next breath, he feels the intense pain of a sucking chest wound and fractured rib.

Nellie Connally turns to her husband. She sees him "crumpled like a wounded animal."

Governor Connally screams, "My God, they're going to kill us all!"

Mrs. Connally reaches over to pull him onto her lap.

Thinking that he missed once again, Oswald reloads the rifle and takes aim. This is his last chance. He takes a deep breath, remembering once again his Marine Corps training. Breathe. Relax. Aim. Slack. Squeeze.

Howard Brennan sees the man standing up and resting against the left windowsill, with gun shouldered to his right shoulder and taking aim, then firing his last shot.

Amos Euins looks back up at the window and sees the man shoot again.

The bullet strikes Kennedy in the back of the head. At least three large bullet fragments exit the right parietal region of the skull. One of these fragments strikes the windshield, landing in the front seat of the limousine. Another fragment also comes to rest in the front seat. A third fragment ricochets off the street, continuing on to strike a section of curbing that wounds James Tague in the face.

Blood and brain tissue flies out from Kennedy's skull to the right front. Nellie and John Connally feel the spatter like buckshot falling over them. The cloud of blood and tissue hangs in the air long enough to be deposited on the limousine trunk lid, and motor officers drive into it. Jackie Kennedy climbs onto the rear trunk of the limousine to retrieve a piece of her husband's brain.

"Get out of here fast," Roy Kellerman says.

William Greer tramps on the accelerator.

Clint Hill almost falls off the back of the limousine as it accelerates. He gets one foot on the rear running board and climbs onto the hood. Having retrieved the piece of brain, Jackie is already turning back toward the rear seat. Clint Hill climbs into the rear seat and covers both the First Lady and the President as the limousine races to Parkland Hospital.

Dallas Times-Herald photographer Bob Jackson shouts, "Look up in the window! There's the rifle!"

Newsreel cameraman Malcolm O. Couch, seated in the press car with Jackson, looks up and sees "about a foot of a rifle being—the barrel brought into the window."

At the southeast-corner, sixth-floor window of the Texas School Book Depository, Oswald stands up, the rifle still in his hands.

Howard Brennan sees the man draw the gun back from the window and pause for another second as though to assure himself that he hit his mark. Then he disappears from Brennan's view.

Chaos erupts throughout Dealey Plaza.

Oswald walks quickly over to the northwest corner of the sixth floor. He hides his rifle near where he left his clipboard earlier that day. He walks downstairs to the second-floor lunchroom and goes to the Coke machine. Outwardly, Oswald appears calm. Perhaps he doesn't believe what just happened. Hearing the sirens and the shouts from outside, Oswald tastes power for the first time in his life. This gives him a surge of confidence that allows him to remain calm when a police officer runs into the lunchroom, pointing a gun at him.

Police officer Marrion Baker is searching for the assassin, along with Texas School Book Depository supervisor Roy Truly. Baker sees a young man standing in front of the Coke machine. He asks Truly, "Does this man work here?" Truly says he does.

Baker and Truly continue upstairs.

Exiting the Depository, Oswald runs into a man with short hair wearing a suit. The man shows him a press pass, which he takes for Secret Service identification. He asks Oswald for the location of the nearest phone. Oswald points toward a pay phone just inside the building. The man runs toward it. Oswald exits onto Dealey Plaza and sees what he has created. People are screaming. Some are lying on the ground. Men cover their wives and children. A police officer runs up the grassy knoll with several witnesses following him. They are looking for the assassin.

Oswald walks east on Elm Street, away from Dealey Plaza. He reaches into his pocket to see if he has change for the bus. He smiles to himself, enjoying a secret that he can't share with anyone right now but that will soon become common knowledge. Lee Harvey Oswald is no longer an ordinary man. Now he is part of history.

CHAPTER 18

The Trajectory of Error

"The tragic, tragic thing is that a relatively simple case was horribly botched from the very beginning, and then the errors were compounded at almost every other step along the way. Here is a historic event that will be discussed and written about for the next century, and gnawing doubts will remain in many minds, no matter what is done or said to dispel them."

—Dr. Milton H. Helpern, New York City medical examiner*

FROM THE BOTCHED AUTOPSY to the single bullet theory, errors were made throughout the investigations of the JFK assassination. As serious as some of these mistakes were, they did not obscure the truth in this case. That was accomplished by everyone who made this case much more complicated than it needed to be.

A detective might not be a very educated man, but he knows how people kill each other. He has seen violent death. He has some understanding of the criminal mind. He uses common sense. And perhaps most important of all, he has judgment. He can weigh evidence and decide what is important and what is not. He can think for himself. He can make decisions. This is how murders are solved every day in the United States. Most of these cases have less evidence than the Dallas police had against Lee Harvey Oswald before his arraignment.

Despite all this evidence, three out of four Americans believe there must have been a conspiracy.

There was a conspiracy in this case. In fact, there were several. There

---

*Marshall Houts, *Where Death Delights* (New York: Coward-McCann, 1967), p. 55.

was no conspiracy to kill President Kennedy. Instead, there were conspiracies to protect the living.

We see it time and time again in high-profile cases and political scandals. People engage in conspiracies to cover up facts unrelated to the original crime and therefore create suspicion that they themselves are guilty of the crime.

The following conspiracies occurred following the JFK assassination:

1. *A conspiracy to prove what happened to be the truth.* On December 9, 1963, assistant attorney general Nicholas Katzenbach urged Earl Warren to release immediately a statement that would establish beyond a reasonable doubt that Oswald was the assassin and there was no evidence of a conspiracy. Similar pressures from President Lyndon Johnson, FBI director J. Edgar Hoover, the Warren Commissioners, and other government officials are also documented. Luckily, they had the right suspect. Their desire to charge Oswald does not prove that any of them had a role in the assassination or conspired to cover it up.

2. *A conspiracy to cover up embarrassing mistakes unrelated to Oswald's guilt or innocence.* The FBI and the CIA were guilty of withholding, destroying, and lying about evidence—including CIA plans to assassinate Fidel Castro and FBI contacts with Oswald. This does not prove that either agency had any role in the assassination or conspired to cover it up.

3. *A conspiracy of professional jealousy.* According to William Sullivan, former assistant director of the FBI, his boss, J. Edgar Hoover, "did not want the Warren Commission to conduct an exhaustive investigation for fear that it would discover important and relevant facts that we in the FBI had not discovered in our investigation, therefore, it would be greatly embarrassing to him and damaging to his career and the FBI as a whole." This does not mean that J. Edgar Hoover had any role in the assassination or conspired to cover it up.

4. *A conspiracy to hide the fact that President Kennedy had Addison's disease and was regularly taking steroids and other drugs, including amphetamines and procaine.* Robert Kennedy exerted pressure on the autopsy doctors not to fully examine his brother's body. He himself got rid of the brain and other physical evidence. As a result, the medical record is incomplete. This does not prove that Robert Kennedy had any role in the assassination or conspired to cover it up.

5. *A conspiracy of "good taste."* Jackie Kennedy was the closest witness to the victim. Her deposition at her home nearly six months after the event contained no useful information. Earl Warren had decided to spare the President's widow the further trauma of being asked to provide extensive testimony. He also refused to allow anyone to view the autopsy X-rays and photographs. Years later, Robert Blakey released some of the autopsy photographs, after they were cropped. These decisions were all made in the name of "good taste." They do not prove that Earl Warren or Robert Blakey had any role in the assassination or conspired to cover it up.

6. *A conspiracy to fudge evidence in support of the single bullet theory.* Over the years investigators have cheated the locations and measurements of the wounds, the physical positioning of the victims, the dimensions of the limousine, the bullet trajectories, and other important evidence in order to make their reenactments of the single bullet theory work. This does not prove that they had any role in the assassination or conspired to cover it up.

7. *A conspiracy by committee.* Government committees are conspiratorial by nature. They are secretive, suspicious, and often fearful of the truth being revealed. This does not mean that the Warren Commission, the Clark Panel, the Rockefeller Commission, the Church Commission, the House Select Committee on Assassinations, or the Assassinations Records Review Board had any role in the assassination or conspired to cover it up.

8. *A conspiracy to bury lost evidence.* Whether they were working together or were simply covering their own respective posteriors, Arlen Specter, James Rowley, Morgan Gies, Robert Frazier, and others attempted to diminish the evidentiary value of the dented windshield trim to conceal the fact that it was never recovered. This does not mean that Arlen Specter, James Rowley, Morgan Gies, or Robert Frazier had any role in the assassination or conspired to cover it up.

9. *A conspiracy of ambition.* The single bullet theory was the sole original investigative hypothesis generated by the Warren Commission. Arlen Specter called the single bullet theory the Commission's "most dramatic contribution" and claimed that he was more responsible for it than anyone else. At the time, Specter was an assistant district attorney in Philadelphia. Today he is the senior U.S. senator from Pennsylvania and chairman of the Judiciary Committee.

10. *A conspiracy to prove a conspiracy.* Forty years of assassination literature have given us countless arguments, with varying degrees of responsibility to the facts, that Oswald was either innocent or part of a larger conspiracy. Sometimes critics cherry-pick statements by witnesses, distorting their testimony. Sometimes they misrepresent evidence by not presenting it in its totality. Sometimes they ignore stronger evidence that contradicts their claims. Once a claim is made in one book, it echoes through other works, until it begins to resonate as fact. Only after devoting a great deal of time and study to the case is a reader able to know what is true and what isn't.

All of these conspiracies were undertaken for different reasons yet had the same result—to make it more difficult to solve the JFK assassination beyond a reasonable doubt.

Both critics and defenders of the Warren Commission argue that if only we had more information, we would be able to put this case to rest. Of all the difficulties we face in examining the JFK assassination, one thing we do not have is a lack of information. On the contrary, there is far too much.

As the investigations multiplied, they created more information, which generated a web of coincidence through which conspiracies began to seem at first possible, then probable. The solution was always seen as thwarted by a lack of information. If only the government had released more documents; if only this possibility had been explored further; if only greater scientific expertise could be brought to bear upon the evidence.

One assumption that has plagued almost every investigator is the idea that more advanced technology might somehow solve the case to everybody's satisfaction. Of course, technology has a role in solving homicides. It would be stupid not to take advantage of high-tech tools like DNA analysis and computers. Yet technology should only be used to enhance, not replace, the traditional tools of homicide detection. Both the Warren Commission and the HSCA hoped that technology would answer all their questions and give them objective proof. Instead of considering the Zapruder film for what it was—an extremely detailed eyewitness record of one perspective on the assassination—the Warren Commission saw it as the only reliable piece of evidence, and it based several important conclusions on watching the Zapruder film absent other evidence. Instead of viewing the

Dictabelt with skepticism, the HSCA allowed it to trump all the accumulated evidence that showed Lee Harvey Oswald had acted alone.

After coming to conclusions based on a single piece of evidence, which they gave the value of scientific truth, the Warren Commission and the HSCA both tried to shoehorn the rest of the case to fit their hypotheses. The Zapruder film and the Dictabelt were evidence that lifted the responsibility of judgment from the investigators. They no longer had to think and instead let technology do their thinking for them.

No matter what kind of experts present it, evidence should always be judged in the context of other evidence. No machine can do this. And a human who relies too heavily on machines to do his thinking and his decisionmaking will come up with the kind of hopelessly flawed conclusions that we have seen in the governmental investigations.

The Zapruder film is no different than the video recording of a liquor-store robbery turned homicide. It gave investigators a very rich picture of the timing and certain events of the assassination, yet the physical evidence paints a more detailed and absolute picture of the crime. With the Zapruder film, we see how technology can make the investigator's job more precise, even more complicated, but not any easier.

Information is a human creation and therefore infinite. Although information can help us understand events, at a certain point it begins to obscure them. That point was reached very early on during the JFK investigation, probably before the Warren Report was even issued. Reading Epstein's book *Inquest,* we see how the Warren Commission staffers were inundated with information and had no governing perspective on how to handle it. This was not merely an administrative problem but an imaginative one. Not a single person on the Warren Commission was an experienced homicide investigator, the kind of person who would step back from the mound of documents and ask the essential questions. Who killed John F. Kennedy? How did it happen?

We never have all the facts, and waiting for them only results in paralysis. Every day we act on what information we have, incomplete and imperfect as it is, because we must reach conclusions and move on.

The homicide detective understands this. He knows he will never know everything. He hopes he will have the information necessary and sufficient to close a case. If an experienced homicide team had been in charge of the

JFK investigation, it would have come to a fairly quick conclusion that Lee Harvey Oswald was the assassin and that he acted alone.

Then, of course, the story would have been over. And we didn't want that.

The day Jack Ruby shot Lee Harvey Oswald, newscaster Howard K. Smith said: "We don't know if Oswald really committed the crime, and perhaps we will never know."

His words were prophetic. Today, with more than 450 books on the subject and even more articles, with websites dedicated to the most esoteric aspects of the assassination and the various conspiracy theories, we seem to know even less about the killing of John F. Kennedy than we did shortly after it happened.

One of the difficulties is simply the provenance of information. The official investigations, particularly the Warren Commission, were viewed with skepticism almost from the beginning. While skepticism is a healthy reaction to the findings of blue-ribbon government panels, many critics strayed far into the fever dreams of paranoia, claiming that almost every significant piece of evidence was either planted or altered and envisioning conspiracy scenarios that included literally hundreds of accomplices.

During his testimony to the HSCA, former Warren Commission assistant counsel David Slawson was asked if he felt that this new investigation would have a better chance of getting to the truth of the Kennedy assassination.

"No," Slawson replied. "I think the historical moment has passed. For good or bad, history is not going to get much more than we have right here."

Today we are living in an age of instant history, recorded live in a hall of mirrors. The JFK assassination was the first high-profile murder case in the television age. In it we saw all the frenzy and excess and confusion present thirty years later in the O. J. Simpson case. We heard, for the first time, catchphrases like "rush to judgment" and claims of planted evidence. We saw grainy, out-of-focus photographs claiming to show evidence of another suspect. Thankfully, the Simpson case has gone away. The JFK assassination remains with us.

Just prior to the assassination, CBS and NBC had lengthened their nightly broadcasts from fifteen to thirty minutes. This larger news hole certainly added to the feeding frenzy over the assassination. Once Oswald was dead and the Warren Report issued, the story should have been finished. But the media did not want to let go, because their audience was insatiable. When various researchers, some responsible, others not, began questioning the Warren Commission's findings and creating what is now an immeasurable bibliography of critical literature, the media gave them airtime and column inches. Soon, only the more outrageous claims would claim our jaded attention.

Confronted with too much information regarding a highly charged public controversy, people believe what they want to believe. In the JFK assassination, they can select facts that confirm their prejudices. I have heard people who have never even fired a gun tell me that Oswald wasn't a good enough marksman to have made those shots and that the Mannlicher-Carcano was an inaccurate, unreliable weapon. I have heard people say that there must have been a conspiracy, even if they're not sure why they believe this. Now you can find expert witnesses who will "prove" almost anything concerning the evidence in the JFK assassination. The single bullet theory is possible, or not. The acoustics evidence is valid, or not. Lee Harvey Oswald was guilty, or not.

The controversy over the assassination has become an argument rather than a search for the truth, with each side growing more and more stubborn as time goes on. The debate continues, going nowhere and achieving nothing but the further entrenchment of each side in their respective positions.

If you make a mistake in the beginning and don't correct it, the trajectory of that error grows as time passes, taking you further and further from the truth. It's time to correct the errors and misconceptions concerning this case.

All the evidence shows that Lee Harvey Oswald fired three shots with his Mannlicher-Carcano from the southeast-corner, sixth-floor window of the Texas School Book Depository, killing President John F. Kennedy and wounding Governor John B. Connally. All the evidence shows that Oswald acted alone. There is no evidence of a second gunman, or of any conspiracy involving Oswald or anyone else.

These are the facts.

Ever since John F. Kennedy was assassinated, his death has remained unresolved. We have grieved, yet we cannot move on. A cloud hangs over his murder and our nation because we refuse to accept what is so clearly the truth—that his assassination was a simple act of murder, committed by a man who left evidence proving his guilt. It is time we lay John F. Kennedy, and his assassination, to rest. The case is solved.

AP/WideWorld Photos.

Bibliography

GOVERNMENT REPORTS

President's Commission on the Assassination of President Kennedy (Warren Commission), *Report* (Washington, D.C.: U.S. Government Printing Office, 1964; reprint, New York: Barnes & Noble Books, 2003).

President's Commission on the Assassination of President Kennedy (Warren Commission), *Hearings and Exhibits,* vols. 1–26 (Washington, D.C.: U.S. Government Printing Office, 1964).

House Select Committee to Study the Assassination of President Kennedy, *Final Report* and *Hearings* (Washington, D.C.: U.S. Government Printing Office, 1979).

BOOKS

Adler, Bill. *The Weight of the Evidence: The Warren Report and Its Critics.* New York: Meredith, 1968.

Anson, Robert Sam. *"They've Killed the President!": The Search for the Murderers of John F. Kennedy.* New York: Bantam, 1975.

Baden, Michael. *Unnatural Death: Confessions of a Medical Examiner.* New York: Random House, 1989.

Belin, David W. *November 22, 1963: You Are the Jury.* New York: Quadrangle/New York Times Books, 1973.

———. *Final Disclosure: The Full Truth About the Assassintaion of President Kennedy.* New York: Scribner's, 1988.

Bishop, Jim. *The Day Kennedy Was Shot.* New York: Random House, 1968.

Blakey, G. Robert, and Billings, Richard N. *The Plot to Kill the President.* New York: Times Books, 1981.

Bloomgarden, Henry S. *The Gun: A "Biography" of the Gun That Killed John F. Kennedy.* New York: Grossman Publishers, 1975.

Brener, Milton E. *The Garrison Case: A Study in the Abuse of Power.* New York: Clarkson N. Potter, 1969.

Brown, Walt. *The People v. Lee Harvey Oswald.* New York: Carroll & Graf, 1992.

———. *Treachery in Dallas.* New York: Carroll & Graf, 1995.

Buchanan, Thomas G. *Who Killed Kennedy?* New York: G. P. Putnam's Sons, 1964.

Callahan, Bob. *Who Shot JFK? A Guide to the Major Conspiracy Theories.* New York: Fireside, 1993.

Canal, John. *Silencing the Lone Assassin: The Murders of JFK and Lee Harvey Oswald.* St. Paul, Minn.: Paragon House, 2000.

Connally, Nellie, and Mickey Herskowitz. *From Love Field: Our final Hours with President John F. Kennedy.* New York: Rugged Land, 2003.

Crenshaw, Dr. Charles A., with Jens Hansen and Gary Shaw. *JFK: Conspiracy of Silence.* New York: Signet, 1992.

Curry, Jesse. *JFK Assassination File.* Dallas: American Poster and Printing, 1969.

Davidson, Jean. *Oswald's Game.* New York: W. W. Norton, 1983.

Davis, John H. *Mafia Kingfish: Carlos Marcello and the Assassination of John F. Kennedy.* New York: McGraw-Hill, 1988.

Di Maio, Vincent J. M. *Gunshot Wounds: Practical Aspects of Firearms, Ballistics, and Forensic Techniques.* Boca Raton, Fla.: CRC Press, 1999.

Epstein, Edward Jay. *Inquest: The Warren Commission and the Establishment of Truth.* New York: Viking Press, 1966.

———. *Counterplot.* New York: Viking Press, 1969.

———. *Legend: The Secret World of Lee Harvey Oswald.* New York: Reader's Digest Press/McGraw-Hill, 1978.

———. *The Assassination Chronicles: Inquest, Counterplot, and Legend.* New York: Carroll & Graf, 1992 (includes the previous three titles).

Fetzer, James H., ed. *Assassination Science: Experts Speak Out on the Death of JFK.* Chicago: Catfeet Press, 1998.

———. ed. *The Great Zapruder Film Hoax: Deceit and Deception in the Death of JFK.* Chicago: Catfeet Press, 2003.

Fonzi, Gaeton. *The Last Investigation.* New York: Thunder's Mouth Press, 1993.

Ford, Gerald R., with John Stiles. *Portrait of the Assassin.* New York: Simon & Schuster, 1965.

Galanor, Stewart. *Cover-Up.* New York: Kestrel, 1998.

Garrison, Jim. *A Heritage of Stone.* New York: G. P. Putnam's Sons, 1970.

———. *On the Trail of the Assassins: My Investigation and Prosecution of the Murder of President Kennedy.* New York: Sheridan Square Press, 1988.

Gentry, Curt. *J. Edgar Hoover: The Man and the Secrets.* New York: W. W. Norton, 1991.

Groden, Robert. *The Killing of a President: The Complete Photographic Record of the JFK Assassination.* New York: Viking Studio Books, 1993.

Hepburn, James. *Farewell America.* Vaduz, Liechtenstein: Frontiers, 1968.

Hinckle, Warren, and William W.Turner. *The Fish Is Red: The Story of the Secret War Against Castro*. New York: Harper & Row, 1981.

———. *Deadly Secrets: The CIA-Mafia War Against Castor and the Assassination of J.F.K.* New York: Thunder's Mouth Press, 1992.

Holland, Max. *The Kennedy Assassination Tapes*. New York: Knopf, 2004.

Hosty, James P., Jr., with Thomas C. Hosty. *Assignment: Oswald*. New York: Arcade Publications, 1996.

Houts, Marshall. *Where Death Delights*. New York: Coward-McCann, 1967.

Hurt, Henry. *Reasonable Doubt: An Investigation into the Assassination of John F. Kennedy*. New York: Holt, Rinehart & Winston, 1985.

Joesten, Joachim. *Oswald: Assassin or Fall Guy?* New York: Marzani and Munsell, 1964.

Kantor, Seth. *Who Was Jack Ruby?* New York: Everest House, 1978.

Kirkwood, James. *American Grotesque: An Account of the Clay Shaw–Jim Garrison Affair in the City of New Orleans*. New York: Simon & Schuster, 1970.

Lambert, Patricia. *False Witness: The Real Story of Jim Garrison's Investigation and Oliver Stone's Film* JFK. New York: M. Evans and Co., 1999.

Lane, Mark. *Rush to Judgment: A Critique of the Warren Commission's Inquiry into the Murders of President John F. Kennedy, Officer J. D. Tippit, and Lee Harvey Oswald*. New York: Holt, Rinehart & Winston, 1966; reprint, New York: Thunder's Mouth Press, 1992.

———. *A Citizen's Dissent: Mark Lane Replies to the Defenders of the Warren Report*. New York: Holt, Rinehart & Winston, 1968.

———. *Plausible Denial*. New York: Thunder's Mouth Press, 1991.

Lattimer, Dr. John K. *Kennedy and Lincoln: Medical and Ballistic Comparisons of Their Assassinations*. New York: Harcourt, Brace, Jovanovich, 1980.

Lewis, Richard Warren. *The Scavengers and Critics of the Warren Report: The Endless Paradox*. New York: Delacorte Press, 1967.

Lifton, David. *Best Evidence: Disguise and Deception in the Assassination of John F. Kennedy*. New York: Macmillan, 1980; reprint, New York: Carroll & Graf, 1988.

Livingstone, Harrison E. *Killing the Truth; Deceit and Deception in the JFK Case*. New York: Carroll & Graf, 1993.

———. *Killing Kennedy: And the Hoax of the Century*. New York: Carroll & Graf, 1995.

Livingstone, Harrison Edward and Robert J. Groden. *High Treason*. Baltimore: Conservatory Press, 1989; reprint, New York: Berkeley, 1990; reprint, New York: Carroll and Graf, 1998.

Mailer, Norman. *Oswald's Tale: An American Mystery*. New York: Random House, 1995.

Mallon, Thomas. *Mrs. Paine's Garage and the Murder of John F. Kennedy*. New York: Pantheon Books, 2002.

Manchester, William. *The Death of a President*. New York: HarperCollins, 1967.

Marrs, Jim. *Crossfire: The Plot That Killed Kennedy*. New York: Carroll & Graf, 1989.

Martin, Ralph G. *A Hero for Our Time: An Intimate Story of the Kennedy Years*. New York: Macmillan, 1983.

McDonald, Hugh C., as told to Geoffrey Bocca. *Appointment in Dallas*. New York: Zebra, 1975.

McMillan, Priscilla Johnson. *Marina and Lee*. New York: Harper & Row, 1977.

Meagher, Sylvia. *Accessories After the Fact: The Warren Commission, the Authorities, and the Report.* New York: Bobbs-Merrill, 1967.

Menninger, Bonar, and Howard Donahue. *Mortal Error: The Shot That Killed JFK.* New York: St. Martin's Press, 1992.

Moore, Jim. *Conspiracy of One: The Definitive Book on the Kennedy Assassination.* Fort Worth, Tex.: Summit Group, 1990.

Myers, Dale K. *With Malice: Lee Harvey Oswald and the Murder of Officer J. D. Tippit.* Milford, Mich.: Oak Cliff Press, 1998.

Nechiporenko, Oleg M., and Todd P. Bludeau. *Passport to Assassination: The Never-Before-Told Story of Lee Harvey Oswald by the KGB Colonel Who Knew Him.* New York: Birch Lane Press, 1993.

Newman, Albert. *The Assassination of John F. Kennedy: The Reasons Why.* New York: Clarkson N. Potter, 1970.

Newman, John. *Oswald and the CIA.* New York: Carroll & Graf, 1995.

North, Mark. *Act of Treason: The Role of J. Edgar Hoover in the Assassination of President Kennedy.* New York: Carroll & Graf, 1991.

Oglesby, Carl. *The JFK Assassination: The Facts and the Theories.* New York: Signet, 1992.

Popkin, Richard H. *The Second Oswald.* New York: Avon Books, 1966.

Posner, Gerald. *Case Closed: Lee Harvey Oswald and the Assassination of JFK.* New York: Random House, 1993.

Prouty, L. Fletcher. *JFK: The CIA, Vietnam, and the Plot to Assassinate John. F. Kennedy.* New York: Birch Lane, 1992.

Reeves, Thomas C. *A Question of Character: A Life of John F. Kennedy.* New York: Free Press, 1991.

Russo, Gus. *Live by the Sword: The Secret War Against Castro and the Death of JFK.* Baltimore: Bancroft Press, 1998.

Sauvage, Léo. *The Oswald Affair: An Examination of the Contradictions and Omissions of the Warren Report.* Cleveland: World Publishing, 1966.

Savage, Gary. *JFK: First Day Evidence.* Monroe, L.: Shoppe Press, 1993.

Scheim, David. *Contract on America: The Mafia Murder of President Kennedy.* New York: Shapolsky Books, 1988.

Scott, Peter Dale. *Deep Politics and the Death of JFK.* Berkeley: University of California Press, 1993.

Specter, Arlen, with Charles Robbins. *Passion for Truth: From Finding JFK's Single Bullet to Questioning Anita Hill to Impeaching Clinton.* New York: William Morrow, 2000.

Stafford, Jean. *A Mother in History.* New York: Farrar, Straus & Giroux, 1966.

Stone, Oliver, and Zachary Sklar, with notes by Jane Rusconi. *JFK: The Book of the Film.* New York: Applause, 1992.

Summers, Anthony. *Conspiracy.* New York: McGraw-Hill, 1980.

Thompson, Josiah. *Six Seconds in Dallas: A Micro-Study of the Kennedy Assassination.* New York: Bernard Geis Associates, 1967; reprinted and revised, New York: Berkeley Medallion, 1975.

Trask, Richard B. *Pictures of the Pain: Photography and the Assassination of President Kennedy.* Danvers, Mass.: Yeoman Press, 1994.

Trost, Cathy, and Susan Bennett. *President Kennedy Has Been Shot: Experience the Moment-to-Moment Account of the Four Days That Changed America*. Naperville, Ill.: Sourcebooks, 2003.

Twyman, Noel. *Bloody Treason: The Assassiation of John F. Kennedy*. Rancho Santa Fe, Calif.: Laurel, 1997.

Weisberg, Harold. *Whitewash I-IV*. Self-published, 1965–74.

———. *Never Again!* New York: Carroll & Graf, 1993.

Yazijian, Harvey, and Sid Blumenthal. *Government by Gunplay: Assassination Conspiracy Theories from Dallas to Today*. New York: New American Library, 1976.

Zirbel, Craig I. *The Texas Connection: The Assassination of President John F. Kennedy*. Scottsdale, Ariz.: Texas Connection Co., 1991.

Appendix: Participants in Official Investigations of the JFK Assassination

PRESENT AT THE BETHESDA NAVAL HOSPITAL AUTOPSY

Commander James J. Humes, Bethesda's senior pathologist

Commander J. Thornton Boswell, Bethesda's chief of pathology

Lieutenant Colonel Pierre A. Finck, chief of Bethesda's military environmental pathology division and chief of the wounds ballistics pathology branch at Walter Reed Medical Center

Admiral Calvin B. Galloway, commanding officer of Bethesda

Rear Admiral George C. Burkley, White House physician to President Kennedy

Captain James H. Stover Jr., commanding officer of the Naval Medical School

John Thomas Stringer Jr., medical photographer

Commander James H. Ebersole, Bethesda's assistant chief radiologist

Floyd Albert Riebe, medical photographer

Jan Gail Rudnicki, laboratory assistant, assisting Dr. Boswell

Paul K. O'Connor, laboratory technologist

Jerrol F. Custer, X-ray technician

James Curtis Jenkins, laboratory technologist

Edward F. Reed, X-ray technician

James E. Metzler, hospital corpsman, third-class

Captain David Osborne, chief of surgery

Brigadier General Godfrey McHugh, Air Force aide to President Kennedy

Lieutenant Commander Gregory H. Cross, resident in surgery

General Philip C. Wehle, commanding officer of the U.S. Military District, Washington, D.C.

Chester H. Boyers, chief petty officer in charge of Bethesda's pathology division

Dr. George Bakeman, U.S. Navy

Secret Service agents Roy Kellerman, William Greer, and John J. O'Leary

Richard A Lipsey, personal aide to General Wehle

Samuel Bird, lieutenant stationed at the ceremonial duties office, Fort Myers, Virginia,
Third Infantry Division

FBI agents James W. Sibert and Francis X. O'Neill

THE WARREN COMMISSION

Commissioners
Chief Justice Earl Warren, chairman
Senator Richard B. Russell
Senator John Sherman Cooper
Representative Hale Boggs
Representative Gerald R. Ford
Mr. Allen W. Dulles
Mr. John J. McCloy

General Counsel
J. Lee Rankin

Assistant Counsel
Francis W. H. Adams
Joseph A. Ball
David W. Belin
William T. Coleman Jr.
Melvin Aron Eisenberg
Burt W. Griffin
Leon D. Hubert Jr.
Albert E. Jenner Jr.
Wesley J. Liebeler
Norman Redlich
W. David Slawson
Arlen Specter
Samuel A. Stern
Howard P. Willens

Staff Members
Phillip Barson
Edward A. Conroy
John Hart Ely
Alfred Goldberg
Murray J. Laulicht
Arthur Marmor

Richard M. Mosk
John J. O'Brien
Stuart Pollak
Alfredda Scobey
Charles N. Shaffer Jr.
Lloyd L. Weinreb

CLARK PANEL

Dr. William Carnes, professor of pathology, University of Utah, Salt Lake City; member of Medical Examiner's Commission, State of Utah
Dr. Russell Fisher, professor of forensic pathology, University of Maryland; chief medical examiner, State of Maryland
Dr. Russell Morgan, professor of radiology, Johns Hopkins University
Dr. Alan Mortiz, professor of pathology, Case Western Reserve University

ROCKEFELLER COMMISSION

Commissioners
Nelson Rockefeller, vice president of the United States
John Connor, CEO, Allied Chemical
Douglas Dillon, former secretary of the Treasury; managing director, Dillon Read
Erwin Griswold, former solicitor general
Lane Kirkland, secretary-treasurer, AFL-CIO
Lyman Lemnitzer, former NATO commander
Ronald Reagan, governor of California
Dr. Edgar Shannon, president, University of Virginia

Executive Director
David Belin, former assistant counsel to the Warren Commission

HOUSE SELECT COMMITTEE ON ASSASSINATIONS

Louis Stokes, Ohio, chairman
Richard Preyer, North Carolina
Walter Fauntroy, District of Columbia
Yvonne Brathwaite Burke, California
Christopher Dodd, Connecticut
Harold Ford, Tennessee
Floyd Fithian, Pennsylvania
Samuel Devine, Ohio
Stewart McKinney, Connecticut
Charles Thone, Nebraska
Harold Sawyer, Michigan
Robert Blakey, chief counsel and director

HSCA MEDICAL FORENSIC PANEL

Michael M. Baden, M.D., chairman of the panel; chief medical examiner, New York City, New York

John I. Coe, M.D., chief medical examiner, Hennepin County, Minnesota

Joseph H. Davis, M.D., chief medical examiner, Dade County, Florida

George S. Loquvam, M.D., director, Institute of Forensic Sciences, Oakland, California

Charles S. Petty, M.D., chief medical examiner, Dallas County, Texas

Earl F. Rose, M.D., LL.B., professor of pathology, University of Iowa, Iowa City

Werner V. Spitz, M.D., medical examiner, Detroit, Michigan

Cyril H. Wecht, M.D., J.D., coroner, Allegheny County, Pennsylvania

James T. Weston, M.D., chief medical investigator, School of Medicine, University of New Mexico, Albuquerque

ASSASSINATION RECORDS REVIEW BOARD

John Tunheim, U. S. District Court judge

Henry Graff, professor emeritus, Columbia University

Kermit Hall, dean of the College of Arts and Sciences, dean of the College of Humanities, and professor of history and law, Ohio State University

William Joyce, associate university librarian for rare books and special collections, Princeton University

Anna Kasten Nelson, historian in residence and professor of foreign relations, American University

Index